God or Christ?

God or Christ?

The Excesses of Christocentricity

JEAN MILET

CROSSROAD · NEW YORK

1981
The Crossroad Publishing Company
575 Lexington Avenue, New York NY 10022

Printed in the United States of America

LIBRARY OF CONGRESS CATALOGING IN PUBLICATION DATA

Milet, Jean.
God or Christ?

Translation of: Dieu ou le Christ?
Includes bibliographical references and index.
1. Theology, Catholic—History. 2. Sociology, Christian (Catholic) I. Title.
BX1751.2.M5213 306'.6 81-5566
ISBN 0-8245-0104-7 AACR2

Contents

Prelude

Despite its title, this is not a theological work, nor, despite the usual concerns of its author, is it a philosophical study (it is not even a study in the philosophy of history). It is a study in *social psychology*.

It examines a social phenomenon, and does so in accordance with the procedures of social psychology. Over the last few decades, the Catholic church has in fact undergone an important development. For almost twenty centuries its structures, i.e. its intellectual, emotional and practical expressions, have been organized around two poles: worship of God and worship of Christ. A remarkable equilibrium was established between these poles, to such a degree that one could talk of a religious bipolarity peculiar to Christianity, and in a particular way peculiar to Catholicism. An observer does not need to be trained in social psychology to be able to note that this judicious equilibrium tends to become unbalanced from the seventeenth century onwards, when the christological pole becomes predominant. This disturbance of equilibrium was accentuated in the eighteenth century and then in the nineteenth, to such a degree that in large sectors of twentieth-century Catholic religious life it is possible to discern a complete predominance of the christological pole, to the detriment of the pole which forms the organizing principle for belief in God. This disturbance in equilibrium has had notable consequences. So much so, that sometimes a sociologist will find it difficult to recognize in certain expressions of the Catholic church today manifestations of the faith which inspired the early church.

I shall pursue this study as a sociologist – more precisely, as a psychologist and sociologist; in other words, I shall try to discover the facts, establish relationships, identify guidelines and show logical connections. Finally, I shall indicate the likely consequences. In a single phrase, I shall be concerned with 'social logic'. I shall not make any value judgments, but leave readers to evaluate the situation for themselves.

What I have written may show believers certain hidden orientations in their church, and consequently may prick their consciences and even prod them into action, if they judge the time to be ripe. For those outside the church it may prove to be a case study showing how a social entity can modify its deepest structures and what consequences may result (following what are now the well-known norms of social logic).

Look at the evidence which follows, and judge it as you will.

I

Christianity, a Religion with Two Polarities

1. The problem

In this study I shall be more particularly concerned with the situation in Roman Catholicism. However, it goes without saying that I regard this as just one of the expressions of Christianity. So this first analysis will be more fundamentally concerned with Christianity.

I think it can be said that Christianity as a whole is a religion with two polarities. By that I mean that all the elements of the religious life which inspire it are ordered around *two poles of attraction*: belief in God and belief in Christ. All forms of behaviour, beliefs, ritual practices, individual and collective virtues, hopes for the future, and so on – in short, all its structures – grow up around these two poles, and end by forming a twofold network of reactions which, by their weaving and interweaving, make up the fabric of Christian religious life.

The development of these different structures obeys laws with which social psychology is now familiar.[1] It is possible to identify them and then study them at leisure, to discover the lines of force which determine the rhythms of life and over the long run direct forms of behaviour. The inner religious life of Catholicism arises from the interplay of these structures.

In this connection, it is easy to see that in the particular case of Catholicism (and here it differs from the majority of other monotheistic religions, in particular Judaism and Islam), we have a religion of a bipolar type. The believer is invited to pattern his faith – and consequently to order his life – on belief in God and belief in Christ: this bipolarity subsequently produces a very close-knit and very complex interplay of psychological and social structures. Of course, here I am thinking of the Catholic church as a religious society, and not as the ideological sub-stratum of certain social concentrations (such as history provides, for example, in Ireland, French-speaking Canada or Croatia). In fact, every member of the spiritual community which is described as 'Christianity' – and this is particularly true of Catholicism – must begin, first of all, by putting his trust in a supreme being, thought to be endowed with personality (conceived of, by analogy, in human terms), regarded as being good and the source of infinite charity, and presented as the absolute goal of all contemplation and all action. So much so, that all Christians must understand themselves in relation to him and regard him as their sovereign judge (it is not history which judges the Christian, but God). In addition, the Christian must also put his trust, a total trust (which can even be carried as far as martyrdom), in a historical figure who lived in Palestine (in the Near East), under the emperor Tiberius, and who is presented as having been sent by God to help men to regain, in rediscovered innocence, a friendship with God which can assure them of eternal happiness in contemplation of the divine perfection. (The man in question gave his life to acquire this power.) It is very clear as a result of this brief description that in their psychological and social attitudes Christians feel drawn towards two poles: towards God, as their ultimate end; and towards Christ, as the means of reaching it. The vital force of the religious life at the heart of Christianity, and of Catholicism in particular, resides in the tension between these two poles. To put it quite simply, from the start: to reduce, attenuate or alter in one way or another – and here I am still using the language of social psychology – the attraction exercised by one or other of these two poles is to alter the very essence of Christianity and to rob it of its nature. In sociological terms, it is to substitute another religion for it.

Now – and here we come to the object of this study – it so happens that above all over the last century, one can observe a curious development within Catholicism. One of the two poles seems increasingly to be getting the better of the other, and this development tends to produce a real imbalance within this church, which is evidenced by the inner tensions which threaten its very existence as an institution. In fact it is a matter of common knowledge that since the beginning of this century Roman Catholicism – at least in its most flourishing manifestations – has tended increasingly to favour belief in Christ over belief in God. For many people, now, to be a Christian is first and foremost to 'believe in Christ', to 'live in conformity to Christ', and to spread Christianity is to 'proclaim Jesus Christ'. Belief in God is virtually hidden: there are those who go so far as to think and say that it is belief in Jesus Christ which will lead to belief in God, the latter coming as a kind of bonus. Others, finally, push things so far – within Catholicism, which they still claim to profess, presenting themselves as its interpreters – that they have come to talk of a 'Christianity without God'. There is no longer need to put one's trust in a God; belief in the historic Christ should be enough and should suffice for all needs: to satisfy the spirit, to gratify man's desires and to ensure his spiritual and moral salvation.

This is the situation with which the observer is confronted. What is to be made of it? What does this evolution signify? Are we present at the birth of a new church, which will take the place of the one that has gone before, shaped in the same sociological mould but now with a completely different content? Anyone with the slightest interest in the internal transformations which the Catholic church has undergone, above all over the last fifty years, whether as a member of the church or as an observer of the evolution of cultures and civilizations, will be perplexed. What is going on? How should one react?

I propose to study the problem here from a strictly sociological perspective. Let me explain. One could certainly make a study in depth of the fundamental significance of this evolution, i.e. at a philosophical and theological level. It could be asked, for example, whether the fact that belief in God seems to be diminishing in comparison with belief in Christ might not mean that human thought can no longer accept this idea of God, and that being unable to console itself for the loss of its God ('God is dead' . . .), it desperately clutches at belief in his 'prophet' with the hope that this belief will make it possible to save what are referred to as the 'values' peculiar to Christianity. One could also put the problem the other way round and ask whether – with the help of historical study – knowledge of Christ has not progressed to the point when one is led to recognize in him the intellectual and moral values of a philosopher, a 'master thinker' who leads us directly to God. All these questions could in fact be raised – and, basically, should be raised. But think of the magnitude of the task! This would be a matter to occupy a whole generation of seekers (or some exceptional genius, of the stature of an Augustine, Thomas Aquinas or Pascal – and where are we to find someone like that?). The task is boundless. That is clear. And that is why in this book I have set myself a much more modest goal: I want to help the reader to begin to become aware of the issues involved. Before assessing the degree of credibility of the developments which are now suggested to us, we may perhaps find it useful to look at the phenomenon that can be found in the church, and above all to assess its magnitude. There will then be a number of points to establish (always in the spirit of a study in social psychology): it is simply a matter of discovering the facts, which here, in the circumstances, are beliefs and practices.

The questions, then, that I shall ask will be: Is it really a determining feature of Roman Catholicism that it should be a bipolar religion, living from a twofold belief – in each case of equal intensity – belief in God and belief in Christ? Down the centuries, has there not rather been a certain predominance in favour of belief in God? Are we not witnessing a change of direction which began in the seventeenth century, a reversal which step by step was to lead to a restructuring of Roman Catholicism around belief in Christ? How far will this change of direction go, and what will be its consequences? What is the present position? What situation has been produced within Roman Catholicism? How can we define it in sociological terms? These are the main questions which arise (and the most perceptive of them conceal a great many others). These are the questions which I want to consider – as objectively as possible. However, I shall begin by establishing a fact. What are the structural bases of the particular belief which can be found in Catholicism?

(a) The first polarity – belief in God

Do I have to recall the obvious? Christianity – and *a fortiori* Roman Catholicism – takes its origin from Jewish faith (as Pope Pius XI recalled in particularly difficult circumstances, 'spiritually, we are Semites'). This faith is embodied in the mystical experience of Abraham, the father of the Semitic line: he believed in the existence of a God, personal and spiritual, Lord of men and worlds, as a result of a revelation which he is said to have received at Ur, in Chaldaea, almost forty centuries ago (thirty-seven, to be exact). Later, this faith would be put to the test by reason, when it came up against the cultural expansion of the Greeks, that amazing small nation, about twenty-five or twenty-six centuries ago. This belief in God then came to acquire added plausibility. By reason alone, brilliant thinkers also arrived at the conclusion – with Plato, then Aristotle and some others – that man must recognize the existence of a supreme being, spiritual (but perhaps not personal . . .), Lord of men and worlds. After the coming of Christ, the conjunction of these two currents of thought was to give birth to a kind of intensified belief in the existence of a God, spiritual and personal; and this belief attained full growth in the fourth and fifth centuries of our era (Augustine, for example, is one of the best representatives of it). These are the historical facts, presented in their barest form. However, as a basis for my analysis and to give my essay in social psychology the foundation it needs, we must take up the outline again and go into it in more detail, stressing above all the social-psychological attitude[2] which the rise of this belief in a God, at the same time both transcendent and personal, with its twofold origin, brings about in the thoughts and the hearts of those who accept it.

(b) The God of Abraham

The conditions under which this God reveals himself govern all the subsequent development of the faith which is put in him. As far as the facts indicate, what we have in the first place is a kind of 'rift' which is produced in a person's inner horizon. This man who had hitherto lived in the shadows 'has seen a great light'. A presence has been revealed to him beyond all possible imaginings, transcending anything that human thought could conceive: the presence, outside him, of a reality which dominates him in every way, the existence of which he could not even suspect, that of a Being in the supreme sense, the only one who can say 'I am' in the full meaning of the phrase. In historical and sociological terms, it is here that we have an absolute point of departure:[3] if we look at the texts which report this revelation, we shall see that anyone who might venture to suppose that Abraham could have drawn his faith from any other source than this revelation (earlier influences, whether Sumerian or otherwise, or quite simply the historical maturity which the human mind could be thought to have attained by that time) would have understood nothing of the originality of the venture of Abraham's belief in this God, transcendent and personal, as confirmed by the sociological study of the facts. This is something that we can establish: there is an 'absolute point of departure'. Here is something that we think we can observe – as always, from the strictly sociological perspective which we have adopted. Abraham has no ancestor in his belief in God. This is the beginning of a great sociological adventure (which has lasted down to our own time).

Having noted this fact, let us consider the forms which this faith goes on to take, and the way in which it begins to spread and to be handed down. What Abraham discovers is the presence of a superior reality, ruling, yet invisible (in contrast to the other superior powers worshipped up to that time, in particular among the Sumerians). Furthermore, this reality has a special characteristic: it does not leave witnesses indifferent to itself: it demands a response from the conscience. 'He believed, and his faith was reckoned as righteousness.' It calls for the dedication of every resource of heart and will: 'Go. Leave for Canaan.'[4] Furthermore, the event is to be the starting point for an immense human adventure, of a biogenetic kind, if it can be said, 'You will be the father of a great posterity; you will be the father of all believers.' This is not a point of information, pure and simple (analogous to the discovery of Pythagoras' theorem or the Archimedean principle). It is a setting in motion, a movement of spirits, hearts and wills, a real 'mobilization' of humanity. A social current is created which is bound to have considerable repercussions: it will leave its mark on the surface of the earth, and across history.

The movement is carried on by Abraham's successors (in fact his descendants). It is given new impetus in the person of Moses, some six centuries later. The mysterious reality which set Abraham on his way, followed by all his posterity, reveals his identity a little more: he is the being possessed with the fullness of existence: 'I am he who is'. He claims submission and adoration. 'You will worship the Lord your God'; and on Mount Sinai he hands on his instructions, his 'commandments'. From all the evidence, this God reveals himself through 'personal' features. He is not blind destiny, nor is he a magical force. He is a person, 'I am', though it is understood that his capacities are infinitely superior to the recognized capacities of human personality as they are known. All the same, it is important to know that the God of Abraham, Isaac and Jacob, the God of Moses, is a God endowed with 'personality'. That will be very important indeed at a later stage. It will be possible for 'inter-personal' relations to be established between God and *his* people, and the existence of these interpersonal relations will be of the utmost interest to the observer considering them from the perspective of social psychology.

In this connection we can already isolate certain features. To sum the matter up in a phrase, the God of the Bible in fact establishes 'privileged' relations with his people (something which, it seems, will not be found elsewhere in any other religion, whether Assyrian, Babylonian, Greek, Roman or Eastern). This God calls for worship in personal terms, worship which is of a particular kind. It brings into play a number of psychological and socio-psychological drives. It is offered with a certain amount of fear: there is reverence for a force which on every occasion is no less dominating, even if it claims to be benevolent ('Who dares to lift up his voice against me?', the divine voice will say to the holy man Job as he rails against the misfortune that has been inflicted on him). It is offered with respect, respect for the greatness (above all, the greatness of the work of creation) and the magnificence with which the deity surrounds himself: the angels, the superior beings (viz. the stars), the great forces of the universe serve as elements to give him resplendent glory. Finally, confronted with this divine majesty, it is appropriate to give way to extravagant shouts of praise: before this august presence the 'believer' can usually do no more than realize his 'nothingness', though he must also feel himself overcome by the mystic 'surges' of total reverence and total deference.

This is the feeling which will overcome Elijah and his disciples on Mount Carmel; it is the feeling which, taken to the point of paroxysm and turned into a devouring passion, will overcome the spirits of all the representatives of Jewish prophecy for almost half a millennium, from Isaiah, Jeremiah, Ezekiel and Daniel to Amos, Malachi and Zechariah. Here is a spiritual movement which is nurtured on the intensive contemplation of this thrice-holy God, praised on the harp by David, entreated by those carried off to Babylon amid blood and tears, and worshipped by all the pious Jews dispersed to the four corners of the Greek, Roman or Eastern world. The *Shekinah*, the 'glory of God' which shines before the path of the children of Israel after the episode of the burning bush on Mount Horeb, remains the beacon which guides the march of the believing people across the places of its exile and across the time of its incomparable history.[5]

All these elements are combined to produce the structural polarization of the whole of the life of the believing people around this belief in God. This God will 'draw all things to him', thoughts, feelings, actions and even creations (there will be no Jewish culture outside divine worship). Nothing must depart from him: every movement, every decision, every tactic adopted apart from him is said to be sacrilegious or idolatrous. There is literally a 'polarization'.[6]

(c) The God of Greek wisdom

At the same time – and as far as we can see, without any link being established between the two cultural currents – Greek thought for its part came to discover the existence and the presence of a supreme being, also transcending the world (something which Asia never came to discover), Lord of worlds and of men. This was the discovery which in fact Aristotle eventually made, after the long centuries of groping towards it. Of course, here we have more a supreme thought ('A thought which thinks itself') than a sovereign existence. The God of Aristotle will not say, 'I am.'[7] Furthermore, he will not be thought to be personal, nor will he call for personal relations with human beings. So there is a notable difference between the God of the Bible and the God of Aristotle. The God of the Greeks is alien to mankind: the Greeks do not have an equivalent to the Book of Job (Oedipus struggles without hope of reprieve against a blind destiny) or to the Psalms. Furthermore, Aristotle's God hardly exercises any influence on the life of the Greek cities: he does not bring into being a 'believing people'. He remains the object of the refined contemplation of an intellectual élite, within certain clearly defined circles and over a quite limited period.

Despite this, however, the God of Aristotle nevertheless came to exercise a perceptible influence on the social development of Christianity, above all from the third and fourth centuries onwards, and this influence served to reinforce the belief in God inherited from the Jewish tradition. It came into play when the first Christian thinkers made contact with this Greek wisdom. Had the latter proved to be irremediably atheistic, these Christians would have been faced intellectually with a crisis of conscience: they would have to have made a choice between their faith and culture. However, that did not prove to be the case, and the Christian thinkers of the early centuries could even in a certain sense feel strengthened in their faith, at least according to appearances. This reaction to the 'happy encounter' with Greek wisdom can already be seen with St Paul (it is echoed in his speech on the Acropolis, and the Epistle to the Romans accepts it implicitly). He does not come to reveal the existence of God to these educated people; they know of God's existence, at least in a confused way ('You, Athenians, are the most religious of men').[8] The 'happy encounter' will be welcomed above all by the church fathers of following centuries: St Athanasius, Gregory of Nyssa, Cyril of Alexandria and above all St Augustine. True, the God inherited from Greek tradition did not coincide exactly with the God of the Bible (above all if the philosophers encountered happened to be Neo-Platonists), but the consequences, from the perspective of social psychology, were the same. The God of Greek wisdom would also 'draw all things to him', if one agreed to recognize his presence and his greatness. The same 'attraction upwards' could be felt. So much so, that the polarization around the transcendent God which had already been clearly realized in the Jewish tradition could not but be reinforced by an encounter with the God of Greek wisdom. This polarization would even lead to excess, known, as we shall see, under the name of Gnosticism.

To stress the main point, if we put ourselves back to the eve of the Christian era, we can see that the most lively of religious currents, that of Abrahamic faith, blended with the more subtle speculations of Greek thought, could logically (i.e. not only by intellectual logic, but also by social logic) lead only to the formation of a strongly unified religion, entirely devoted to the worship of a sole, omnipotent God, Lord of men and worlds, to whom human beings owed respect, honour and glory. Thus at the beginning of the Christian era conditions were established for the appearance of a 'monotheistic' religion, to offer men the same goal to work for, gather them together within the same structures and organize them round the same pole: belief in the one God.

(d) The second polarity – belief in Christ

At this point we have to note that an entirely new fact threw into confusion the basic elements of the problem (I shall consider this fact, objectively, in accordance with the method that I have adopted, that of social psychology, which means that I shall not raise apologetic or even theological questions). The new fact was this. The very people who up to that point had felt drawn by the attractions of a single spiritual 'pole', as religious and moral men, now found themselves called (as we see from reading the astonishing texts at that time circulating in the same religious centres of the Mediterranean world, i.e. the gospels and similar works) to place themselves wholly, with their thoughts, their lives and their activities, around a second spiritual 'pole': belief in Jesus Christ. The attraction of this second pole proved to be extremely strong: it might be said to be equal to the first. We can see how men and women died in faith for this second belief with as much ardour as their spiritual ancestors died for the first. People came to die for Christ at the time of the persecutions of Decius or Diocletian with the same faith as that with which they died in Babylon for God, at the time of the deportation to Babylon and the persecutions of Nebuchadnezzar. What had happened? Had one pole of faith been substituted for another? Were they both complementary, thus giving rise to a degree of 'bipolarity'? It is important to clarify the facts. Still reacting as a sociologist, I shall try to assess the structural significance of the new faith which was put forward, and its relationship to the first faith. What were the 'sayings' of this Jesus of Nazareth? Precisely what did he do? What was his personal position in relation to the former faith, ordered around the only pole hitherto accepted, belief in one God? Precisely what did he claim for himself and his mission?

As is generally known, Jesus did not just present himself as a new prophet, coming after a great many others to revive belief in God. He presented himself as the very manifestation of God, as God himself 'come among man'. He calls himself 'divine person' (on the same occasion, we learn that there are three persons in God and that Jesus himself is the second, united substantially to the first, the Father, and to the third, the Holy Spirit). According to the first witnesses to his message, he is 'God born of God, light born of Light, true God born of true God'. The statements made in this connection (which I shall analyse in due course) are quite unequivocal: the man Jesus, descended from a Nazareth family, must be regarded as a God, the equal of the God of Abraham, Isaac and Jacob, and, as Greek and Latin commentators will say later, equal to the God of Aristotle and the neo-Platonic tradition: he will be called the Logos incarnate, the Word incarnate.

This statement is important: it confounds human understanding. Before measuring its impact on human awareness, let us consider certain declarations which confirm these facts. Jesus endorses the 'messianic' declaration of his disciple Peter. 'You are the Christ, the Son of the living God,' says Peter. Jesus replies: 'You are blessed, Simon son of Jonah, because this revelation has not come to you through flesh and blood, but from my Father who is in heaven' (Matt. 16.17). He claims personally, and fully, attributes which are appropriate only for God: 'I am the way, the truth and the life' (cf. John 4.12; or again 5.26; 14.6). He requires faith in his person equal to that which hitherto had been placed in God himself: 'He who believes in me, rivers of living water will flow from his breast' (John 7.38). He adopts attitudes which could only be taken by God, as sovereign Lord of men and consciences: 'Go, your sins are pardoned' (Matthew 9.2; or Luke 5.20). He claims to be Lord of morality and the Law: of his own accord he modifies the rules relating to divine worship; thus he claims to be 'Lord of the sabbath' (cf. Matt. 12.8; Mark 2.28). Finally, he goes so far as to attribute to himself the formula by which God himself is designated on Mount Horeb: 'Before Abraham was, I am'; and, 'He who sees me, sees the Father' (John 14.9). This is the belief which was accepted by his first disciples and which would be lived out by the first generations of those who were soon to be called 'Christians'. Thus the faith which Jesus now called for from his followers was equal to that which people had in God.[9] We can guess the tension which would arise in the hearts of each one of them.

The actions of Jesus point in the same direction, and tend to demand the same faith as his sayings. We have his disillusioned comment, 'If you do not believe in my words, at least believe in my actions.' Now the gospel narratives attribute to him a way of acting which also argues in favour of his authentic divinity. There is no need to recall all the details; a few instances should be enough. We are told how he commands nature and calms the elements. He brings health to the ill. He announces the future.

He reveals the secrets of men's consciences. Finally, he triumphs over death itself by a glorious resurrection. According to what we learn from the witnesses of the time, all these actions were spontaneously interpreted as expressions of an authentic 'theophany' – doubted for a long time, but finally accepted by righteous souls. Here is an expression of the very power of God.[10] To claim that he was God, to say that if the temple were destroyed he could rebuild it in three days . . . very, very much less would be called for to justify the accusation of sacrilege, laying claim to divine titles and functions, which would lead to the death penalty at the hands of a Jewish tribunal, with the consent of the Roman authorities. These are the facts, the quite surprising facts, which were spread around at that time by the stories about Jesus. We can see that this was quite enough to introduce confusion into the monotheistic (I almost said 'monolithic') faith of the witnesses of the time.

However, the new faith spread. The immediate witnesses, the apostles, and then intimate disciples or ancient adversaries, won over by a flash of illumination, like St Paul on the Damascus road, set about not only spreading this new faith, but trying to make it known and understood. This gave rise to the gospel texts, and reflective texts often exchanged in the form of letters, and then the first doctrinal formulations (like the Apostles' Creed). St John is perhaps one of those who go furthest in trying to elucidate the disturbing mystery concerning the content of the new faith. In this respect, the Prologue of his Gospel is one of the most astonishing texts. He does not hesitate to declare formally that the one 'whom he has seen, whom he has touched with his hands', with whom he has spoken, is a deity equal to the God of Abraham (and, he suggests, the God of Greek wisdom). 'In the beginning was the Word, and the Word was with God, and the Word was God . . .; and this Word was made flesh and dwelt among us.' St Paul had already used the same language, and had proposed the same analysis, in his famous letters, above all in his letters to the Romans, the Ephesians, and so on, as in his contribution to the Letter to the Hebrews ('He is the splendour of the glory of the Father', Heb. 1.3).

The doctrinal development to follow will only aim to confirm the content of the new faith which has been introduced in precise texts, which make use of technical terms. In brief, it is a question of trying to clarify two points: Is Jesus God himself, manifesting himself among men? And if so, what relationship is one led to establish between this Jesus-God and the transcendent God of Abraham on the one hand and of Greek wisdom on the other?

As we know, this task proved to be extremely difficult. It called for several centuries of reflection and discussion, which was often violent. Before we study the psychological and social tensions which were to emerge – as was inevitable – among the believers who by then were calling themselves 'Christians',[11] as a reminder let us retrace certain stages which will also serve as points of reference.

Let us begin with the great points in the discussions, or to put it another way, with what will later be called the 'major heresies'. The best known, and without doubt the most characteristic, is clearly that of Arius, at the beginning of the fourth century. Like many others (and doubtless with the majority of believers at this time), Arius could not bring himself to accept that this Jesus could be called 'God born of God, true God born of true God': he had too much feeling for the oneness of God, for his unalterable transcendence, to go so far as this 'mental confusion' which could lead to seeing God in Christ. He was certainly willing to allow that Jesus was inhabited by a kind of 'divine personality', but it was understood that this divine personality was not God himself but one of his 'creations'. In this case, the 'polarization' of the faith around the oneness of the divine being would not be altered. There would be a predominant belief, belief in God, and a belief subordinate to the first, the content of which was still to be defined, belief in Christ. However, as is well-known, this theory was contested at the Council of Nicaea (325) and then the Council of Constantinople (381).

A different attitude was adopted by Nestorius, another great thinker of the fifth century. He, too, was unable to bring himself to accept this 'mental confusion' which consisted in identifying Jesus purely and simply with God. He contented himself with considering Jesus to be a privileged 'messenger' of God, a kind of super-prophet, who will have had exceptional relations with the deity. He, too, maintained a single pole for faith: there is only one belief which counts, belief in God; belief in Christ is no more than an aid to that. Nestorius, too, had to be challenged in turn, at the Council of Ephesus (431).

A third name emerges from this period (the fifth century), in the debate on the mystery surrounding the personality of Jesus, that of Eutyches. He, too, could not accept that belief in Christ was equivalent to belief in God. He proposed a solution which was the opposite of what had gone before. There is no other reality in Christ than the manifestation of the divinity; it is the humanity of Jesus which is unreal; it is no more than an appearance. Christ is only an 'apparition' of God among men, an apparition like that which took place at the oak of Mamre, a kind of theophany in anthropomorphic garb. This was clearly one way of avoiding the difficulty. It, too, did not gain acceptance: it was rejected at the Council of Chalcedon (451).[12] Those in authority in the growing church (which was now four centuries old, and had spread all round the Mediterranean at every social level) maintained, against all opposition, the difficult affirmation: God is God, but Jesus also is God. The real difficulty lay above all in the vocabulary to be used. Given the terms available at the time, how was it possible to express the inexpressible mystery that formed the content of the new faith, which could hold together in a single fervour belief in God and belief in Christ?[13] No more than a dozen terms were available to play with, and their semantic content was often uncertain. We need only recall the most famous of them: *hypostasis* (approximately equivalent to our term 'person'); *ousia* (both being and substance); *physis* (meaning both 'nature' and 'universe'); *homos* (identical); *homoios* (like); and so on. Another difficulty in using these terms was the development of the Greek language at this decadent period of Hellenism. Be that as it may, agreement was eventually reached on a precise text at the time of the Council of Chalcedon (451). From that point on, this text would be regarded as the official statement of the belief of the Catholic church on the difficult problem of the identity of Jesus and the way of conceiving his relationship with God. Because of the discussion to follow, I think it worthwhile quoting the text at some length.

The declaration of the Council of Chalcedon was as follows:

> Following the holy fathers, we all unanimously teach that our Lord Jesus Christ is to us one and the same Son, the self-same perfect in Godhead, the self-same perfect in manhood; truly God and truly man; the self-same of a rational soul and body; consubstantial with the Father according to the Godhead, the self-same consubstantial with us according to the manhood; like us in all things, sin apart (Heb. 4.15); before the ages begotten of the Father as to the Godhead, but in the last days, the self-same, for us and for our salvation of Mary the Virgin *theotokos* as to the manhood.
>
> One and the same Christ, Son, Lord, only-begotten; acknowledged in two natures unconfusedly, unchangeably, indivisibly, inseparably; the difference of the natures being in no way removed because of the union, but rather the property of each nature being preserved, and (both) concurring into one *prosopon* and one *hypostasis*; not as though he were parted or

divided into two *prosopa*, but one and the self-same Son and Only-begotten God, Word, Lord, Jesus Christ; even as from the beginning the prophets have taught concerning him and as the Lord Jesus Christ himself has taught us, and as the symbol of the fathers has handed down to us.

So we may note that simultaneously and with equal force these lines affirm that Jesus is one divine person (the Word), and that at the same time he is a human being, like us in all things (sin apart). The positions here are clearly defined, though of course at the same time the content of the mystery (i.e. the mystery of the incarnation) remains complete. This declaration continued to be the basis of the official doctrine of the church on the matter. In principle, no one has the right to depart from it, without in so doing departing from the church. As confirmation, we can note that all the great thinkers of the Catholic church, its theologians and the fathers of its various Councils, appropriate the content of this declaration. For example, this happens with St Thomas Aquinas, who faithfully takes up the same themes in his theology of the incarnation. He writes in his *Summa Theologica*: 'The Christ is the Word of God, the eternal and inner word of the Father, who in union with the Father breathes and inbreathes the spirit of the divine love' (*STh* I, q.43, art.7, and IIIa, q.7, art.8, see also his *Commentary on St John*, 6.45, no.944).

The fathers of the Council of Trent take up the same positions, and the modern councils follow them. For Vatican I the actions of Christ in particular – especially in the miracles and the prophecies – convey his own divinity: see the constitution *De Fide*, DS nos.3009, 3033, 3034. For Vatican II, see *The Constitution on the Sacred Liturgy*, no.5; *The Constitution on the Church*, no.7 and *The Constitution on the Church in the Modern World*, no.22. All these documents refer, implicitly or explicitly, to the declarations of Chalcedon.

So we must conclude here that from the earliest period, and like his successors in later times, the Christian finds himself confronted with the necessity of adopting from now on what one might call a 'double faith', which he has to maintain with equal intensity: his faith in God and his faith in Christ. However, despite the difficulties which may arise, the production of a declaration is always possible: it is simply a matter of choosing the formulae carefully. Real life is a different matter. The Christian of the first ages immediately began to feel that from that point on he had to orient his faith in two different directions. Thus in his thought, his action, his personal and social behaviour, he found himself living in a perpetual state of 'tension'. It is this inner tension that I now want to analyse: it contains the germ of all the later difficulties peculiar to Catholicism. It is important to discover them from the moment they arise.

2. The intellectual tension between belief in God and belief in Christ

It did not prove easy for the first Christians to live out this double faith, faith in God and faith in Christ. Each individual did so to some degree in his own way. Here we can distinguish between the Jewish Christians, i.e. those Christians who came from Judaism, and those whom we may call, somewhat sweepingly, Hellenistic Christians, in the sense that even if they were not Greeks, and came from very varied areas ('Parthians, Medes, Elamites . . . people of Egypt, from Cyrenaica, Rome and Crete . . .') they had directly or indirectly (often through the Romans) inherited Greek wisdom. In both cases the adoption of this new faith would prove painful and difficult.

Let us imagine the difficulty posed to a pious Jew. He was accustomed to putting all his trust in this God, feared, venerated and adored, who had so far spoken in the thunderclaps of the theophanies on Horeb and Sinai. This was a God whose name one did not even dare pronounce, whose face could not be seen without dying, a God who made men's hearts tremble and whose glory, the *Shekinah,* only appeared from time to time in the smoke of the Holy of Holies, in the temple at Jerusalem. This was the God who must now be believed to have manifested himself in the form of a weak child at Bethlehem, and then at Nazareth; the God who toiled on the roads of Judaea and Galilee, coming up against the incredulity and even the hostility of audiences greedy for instant sensations; he was the one who – as the height of improbability – was to be recognized under the disfigured features of the man put to death on Golgotha. Certainly, people talked of his hypothetical ultimate victory over death by an unexpected resurrection; but there had been very few witnesses of it, and here disagreement seemed to be combined with improbability. For a pious Jew, an assiduous temple worshipper, a scrupulous observer of the law, to be able to put his faith in such a new 'representation' of the deity required more than a change of mind: it called for a kind of 'delirious' abandonment of all the norms to which mind and heart had hitherto been subjected. One could even say that a mental effort of such magnitude was an unparalleled demand on a human being. We can understand how the great majority of

Jews, although witnesses of these facts, refused – with dignity, and even in the name of the most sacred principles – to accept this mental change (I almost said, this 'transmutation'). They were being asked to trample underfoot their most sacred convictions, to transform 'sacrilege' into a mystery of faith. So we can understand the reactions of Saul of Tarsus (before the Damascus road) and many others: indignation in the face of blasphemy. At all events, those who were won over by a mysterious force and followed Christ, along with their closest contacts, suffered the worst of inner torments.

It will have been almost the same with those who, at whatever distance, were followers of Greek wisdom: readers of Plato and Aristotle, well versed in the texts of Virgil and perhaps Cicero and Lucretius, those familiar with the Stoics, or at least those who respected the prudential rules of ancient wisdom, heirs of the old Eastern and Near Eastern cultures, all zealous propagandists for the *Pax Romana*. All these could not but be utterly shocked that they were being offered as the ultimate goal of their thought and action the figure and the teachings of an obscure Jew of Galilee, whose adventures had been headline news at the time of Tiberius, and whose supporters wanted them to believe that he was 'God born of God, true God born of true God', come among men to give them access, by his sacrifice, to an endless happiness: if not in this world, at least in another. For them the shock must have been equally terrible.[14] True, one could not cry blasphemy here; the idea was more grotesque, indeed 'folly'. Without doubt, for their part the apostles of the new faith took precautions. It seems that they brought people to this new faith in two stages, at least if we can trust the evidence that the apostle Paul gives about his method, for example when he arrives in Athens. He begins by evoking among his audience the sense of belief in God, a God conceived of in very general terms as a dominant force ruling the world: 'O Athenians, you who are the most religious of men: I have come to reveal to you the unknown God whom you seek.' It is only subsequently that he goes on to teach them that this unknown God, transcending the world, became visible in the form of a Jew in Palestine. We can imagine that it was here that all the difficulties began. 'We will hear you another time,' exclaimed his audience, put off by so much improbability. The tactics will certainly have been the same with the Romans and all the non-Jewish people, that is to say, those who had not yet been aroused to belief in one God, personal and invisible. In any case, we can gauge the difficulties which must have arisen in converting the most lucid minds of the time. For a Stoic, it was necessary first to show that the deity could be personal, and not blind and anonymous; for an Epicurean, that chance could find a superior law to dominate it and a superior thought to illuminate it; for the Platonist or neo-Platonist, that the divine could be espoused without forfeiting the human condition and that bodies could be saved as much as souls; for the Aristotelian (if there were still, or indeed had ever been, such) that the personal and free God who was to be spoken of could have relations with mankind, let alone relations of love, and that these relations could go so far as an incarnation. In all these cases the task of the apostle of Christ will have been overwhelming, inasmuch as there will constantly have been dangers of confusion: Greeks and Latins thought that in Christ they could recognize a new Hermes, and others an Apollo. Syncretisms – Gnosticism, which I shall talk of later – threatened on every side.

For Jews or non-Jews alike, there were difficulties everywhere. For Jews, in the last resort it was a matter of adding to their faith in God – which there was no question of attenuating – a faith in Christ, which needed to be of equal intensity. It was of the Jews above all, right from the start, that this 'bipolarity' of faith, which I have already shown to be a characteristic of Christianity, was required. As for non-Jews, above all the future Hellenistic Christians, they would be required to accede simultaneously to belief in God and belief in Christ: here Christians did not come up so much against doctrinal resistance as against incomprehension and dangers of mental confusion.

It is the problem of arriving at this bipolarity, so characteristic of Christian faith, that I now want to try to analyse, this time considering not just categories of people, but the different reactions of the human make-up: intelligence; emotions and the spiritual life; the will and practical action.

(a) Intellectual difficulties

To accept simultaneously – and without subordination of any kind – both belief in God and belief in Christ could not happen without causing intellectual difficulties to the believers of the first centuries. History shows this clearly enough. To begin with, we can imagine the tension from a simple reading of the gospels. Certainly, belief in the transcendent God is always there, but we can detect a second belief which subtly comes to compete with the first, by presenting different themes and calling for different practices. First of all, we can see that a new picture of God is being drawn. Among those who put their faith in Jesus Christ, the omnipotent God, Yahweh, the demanding Lord of men and worlds, who filled the souls of pious Jews with fear and terror, had to be replaced with the representation of a 'paternal' God, kind and merciful. These two images manifestly overlap in the minds of the first converts. Are they compatible? Pushing things to extremes, we might suspect that certain people asked, 'Must we change our God?' Simple people must have asked this question, but also Jewish thinkers, brought up on Alexandrian culture, whom these lyrical interpretations could not but disquieten. And above all, precisely who was this Jesus? The gospel is full of questions. Is he a new prophet, Elijah returned among men? Is he the awaited Messiah – but in that case where is his triumph? Is he a 'divine' being, a kind of living theophany, who claims for himself adoration and submission? All these questions burst out at the same time – it is easy to see how – in the spirit of the first witnesses to the gospels (or the audiences of the first apostles). Men's minds, even those of the most convinced, were torn apart. Towards which pole were they to turn: that of Abrahamic faith (among many of them reinforced by Greek wisdom) or that of the Christian faith? In short, who was to be worshipped, God in his temple or Christ in his gospels? Which way was faith to go? Hesitations could be felt everywhere. We can find them both in the very attitudes of the evangelists and the apostles, and in that of the 'wise and learned' men.

(b) Qualified bipolarity of the apostles

All the apostles and first disciples of Jesus certainly remained essentially committed to the faith, received from Abraham, in a transcendent God, but from now on they had to make room in their minds for a faith of equal (or almost equal) intensity in Jesus of Nazareth, saviour of men. And they had to struggle to live out this bipolarity, despite all the intellectual, psychological and emotional difficulties that it could bring with it. However, it is strange to note that they lived it out with notable qualifications, depending on their temperament and perhaps on their culture. I shall summarize this analysis, limiting it to three cases: that of St Peter, who was primarily responsible for the growing church; that of St Paul, the first theoretician of the new religious life; and that of St John, privileged recipient of the doctrine and its ultimate guarantor. They live out the bipolarity of their faith in three different ways. All three have the same faith in God, but they do not share the same faith in Christ. It seems that they do not all assign the same 'metaphysical situation' to Christ in relation to God and hence in relation to the believer. For St Peter, one arrives at God 'by' Christ; for St Paul, 'with' Christ; for St John, 'in' Christ. Let me go into these different points of view in more detail.

For St Peter, one arrives at God 'by' Christ. Of the three spiritual founders of the Christian church, he is the one who remains most completely faithful to the demands of the God of Abraham. One could almost say that for him, faith has only one pole: an inclination towards God. Strong though it is, faith in Christ (and Peter was the one who said, 'You are the Christ, the Son of the Living God') nevertheless does not go as far as to constitute a 'pole' with as much attraction as the first.[15] Jesus is the object of Peter's faith, not on his own account but in his capacity as 'mediator'. That is very evident from the way in which Peter always and above all presents himself as one who holds the faith of Abraham. What we know of him from elsewhere confirms this: here is a man from an insignificant people who 'speaks of God after the fashion of his ancestors, the Hebrews: his terminology is that of the synagogue'.[16] All his 'theological' thought is ordered around faith in the God of Abraham, all powerful, Lord of men and worlds. The very mission of Christ is understood only as an expression of the will of this God. 'It is the God of the patriarchs and the prophets who decides on the election of men to Christian grace, who sends his Son, glorifies him, bestows the Spirit on him; in short, it is the same God who is at the source of all the phases of the redemption of the world.'[17] Nevertheless, the Christ – this Jesus whom Peter had known well, with whom he had talked so often on the roads of Judaea and Galilee – is not a 'substitute' for God; he is the 'mediator'. 'The glorious heavenly heritage of the sons of Abraham will be bestowed on all those whom the Father has engendered by the Christ in the Spirit.'[18] Furthermore, Peter is so faithful to the spirit of belief in the God of Abraham that he only uses the new formula, 'the Father', which Jesus uses to designate God, on very few occasions (he seems to mistrust this 'innovation'). He uses it only five times, while he talks hundreds of times of the 'God of Abraham, Isaac and Jacob'.[19] For him, God remains this supreme being whom one must first fear and only then love.[20] God is primarily the Holy One *par excellence* (Lev. 11.44). It is this holiness, inaccessible as it is, which Christians must try to approach, resorting to the mediation of Jesus. Finally, in St Peter everything is related to God as to a unique (or at the least, predominant) 'pole'. Had he had to preach to the Athenians and to the Romans, Peter would have presented himself in the first place as the apostle of God, and only in the second place as the apostle of Jesus Christ. He would have come first to proclaim God.

For St Paul, one comes to God 'with' Christ. Paul shares with Peter the same belief in God: he is a 'Jew, son of a Jew': he recognizes only one God, the God of Abraham, Isaac and Jacob. But now he has encountered Jesus Christ. This raises a spiritual problem for him from now on. He has encountered Jesus Christ in a special way, which we must not forget: not historically, but mystically. He never knew Jesus Christ. For him, Jesus Christ is a 'voice' which he heard one day on the Damascus road, coming from heaven ('I am Jesus whom you are persecuting'). For him, Jesus is someone whom, one might say, he has heard through another burning bush. Here is a second call from heaven, after that of Horeb. So it would have been easy for him to make his belief in Christ a belief closer to belief in God than that of St Peter. The mystical Christ, the only one whom he had known, comes to play the part of a second pole in his own religious life. That helps us to understand the accents in his letters, in particular those to the Ephesians and Colossians, to the Corinthians and even to the Romans.[21] For Paul, as he sees it, Christ does not present himself in historical guise (since, to make the point again, Paul had never seen Christ), but mystically: Christ is not a visitor to the scenes of Judaea and Galilee; he is a visitor to the soul. That explains why Paul, more than Peter, is prone to make Christ the object of a particular faith which tends increasingly to become equal to the faith which he puts in God, and then to form in his make-up as it were another pole of his religious life. God and Christ become the double object of his faith. That is what makes me say that, for him, one must certainly come to God, but 'with' Christ. It is by being united to Christ that one may hope to be united with God. This theme returns constantly all through his letters. 'I have only one desire, to be with Christ'; 'For me, to live is Christ.'

For St John, one arrives at God 'in' Christ. While it goes without saying that St John shares the Jewish belief in the God of Abraham, all the same he is one of the apostles or disciples who refers to it least often. His thought is concentrated essentially on the person of Christ. The major *datum* of his faith is the fact that 'the Word was made flesh and dwelt among us'; it is the fact that we have been able to 'touch the Word of life'. The whole of John's life is dominated by his encounter with Jesus: for him, everything comes from Jesus: faith, hope and love. So moving in its consonance, the Fourth Gospel is entirely conceived of as a meditation on the person of Christ. It is the same with the letters. As for the text of the Apocalypse, while it is dominated by references to an omnipotent God, sovereign Lord of men and peoples, for the elect, salvation is only gained 'in' Christ. The elect must bear on their bodies 'the sign of the Lamb', to show that they are incorporated into his mystical body.[22]

These are three noticeably different interpretations showing how belief in Christ can be shaped as a complement to belief in God. They will subsequently determine three modes of living out the Christian faith. In terms of social psychology, the alert observer can in fact detect three currents in the church: the Petrine current, essentially based on faith, faith in God and the pattern of submission to his will; the Pauline current, based on hope, hope placed in salvation by Christ, and the development of the apostolate; and the Johannine current, based on love, on the love that Christians must practise among themselves.[23]

However, our concern is not there. What interests us is an outline of the reactions of the first Christians towards the new faith presented to them, faith in Christ, which had to be added to (or superimposed on, or substituted for . . . who can say?) the faith which they already had in God. Since it is well known that a human being's 'capacity for faith' is limited, and that the faith which he has in a new object can only be transferred from that which he has given to an old object, we are forced to ask ourselves what must have gone on in people's minds at the beginning of the Christian era. Before going further, however, let us dwell on a reaction which consisted in resolving the problem of the practice of a twofold faith by a subterfuge, which managed to absorb the one in the other. We are going to look at the Gnostics.

(c) The Greeks: Gnosticism

These Greek or, in the Hellenistic period, Graeco-Latin wise men to whom faith in Christ was presented were in fact tempted to safeguard their faith that the universe could be explained by a single principle (supreme thought, or the aeon as the supreme unifier of all things), by trying to integrate the new faith in Christ as well as possible into their existing intellectual structures. Taking the exaltation of knowledge (*gnosis*) as far as it could go, they were called Gnostics. They excelled in all the syncretisms. Their number is legion. Here we can do no more than indicate certain trends as they relate to the problem with which we are concerned. As Harnack pointed out, they all aimed at an 'acute Hellenization of Christianity'.[24] Because some of them were nevertheless of Jewish origin, we can see how in the first place this syncretism took a 'Jewish-Hellenistic-Christian form'. Among this group we may single out the Ebionites, the Elkasaites and the mysterious community to whom we owe the Pseudo-Clementine romance.

These groups of 'Judaizing Christians' (we would do better to call them 'Christianizing Jews') above all remained faithful to the Law of Moses. Their religious life revolved around a single pole, that of belief in the God of Abraham. Their completely new faith in Jesus Christ was confined to a 'pious reverence': they shared a whole series of different sentiments about it, moving from adoration for a myth to the respect due to a hero, through spiritual communion with the intercessor and imitation of the holiness of the elect one. These forms of Jewish-Christian Gnosticism never accept a really full faith (analogous to that in God) in the person of Christ: their faith remains determinedly concentrated on one pole.

We find the same thing with Gnosticism of purely Greek inspiration. The majority of these types of Gnosticism derive from intellectual circles in Alexandria and are steeped in Neo-Platonism. They often claim kinship with the Hellenistic Judaism of Philo. Despite the dozens of variants, they all have in common the adoption of a very exalted conception of the divine transcendence. They, too, are fundamentally opposed to any kind of idea of an incarnation of the divinity. Even if they incorporate the person of Christ into their doctrine, they do so in a mystical or symbolic way. The Christ is assimilated to some aeon, to some 'superior spirit' coming to associate itself with other spirits (pure or impure). These sects suffered different fates (some of them survived for several centuries and even, after various mutations, down to our modern world). However, none of them exercised any notable influence on the current of religious thought which, deriving from the faith of the twelve apostles, gave birth to the Christianity that we know. The little group of founders, gathered around Peter, fired by the apostolic ardour of Paul, James and Matthew, maintained in mutual love by the fervour of John and his disciples, continued to develop and prosper, despite intense persecutions. However, the profound paradox of the twofold faith to be lived, faith in God and faith in Christ, continued to make itself felt, indeed more than ever. It was not always easy to discern the challenge that it posed, and it was this very paradox – through weakness, but much more often through clumsiness – that produced the heresies which tore apart the first group of believers.

(d) The fight against the heresies

I have already called attention to the blossoming of these heresies on a doctrinal level. Here we find them again at the practical level of everyday religious life. The representatives of the different approaches to what was later to be called christology in fact underwent a real crisis of conscience.[25] How was it possible to live out one's faith in God and faith in Christ at the same time? For supporters of Arianism (in the fourth and fifth centuries), faith in God exercised an exclusive attraction. Their faith in Christ could only be notoriously subordinated to that (though with variants, depending on the patterns of thought). Everything depended on the link which they established, within the Trinity, between the person of the Word (second person) who was to become incarnate in the Christ, and the person of the Father. Some of these disciples of Arius (the 'homoiousians') saw only a relationship of substantial similarity between them; others (the 'homoians') only a relationship of similarity. Yet others ('the anhomoians') did not see any similarity between them at all. They lived out the mystery of Christ in different ways, depending on the variants thus introduced, according him a divine character with curious 'gradations'. However, all felt it essential that there should be one pole for faith, entirely concentrated on the pre-eminence of faith in God. They put Christ somewhere between God and the first creatures (the angels). As is well known, this attitude, this faith, was contested above all by Athanasius, and the doctrines inspired by Arius were condemned at the Council of Nicaea. It was declared there that the word was 'consubstantial with the Father' (the theory of total *homoousia* won the day): the Word is of the same 'substance' as the Father (and not just of the same nature . . .). So it is right to accord him – in his incarnate form, namely, as the Christ – the same faith (in content and intensity) as the Father. After a number of struggles in which St Basil, St Gregory of Nyssa, St Gregory of Nazianzen and St Hilary of Poitiers were involved, in the fifth and sixth centuries this approach succeeded in winning the day. It did so to such a degree that what I have called a 'bipolar' faith, which came from the apostles and the first generations of Christians, maintained itself despite its inherent difficulties. The Christian had to continue to share the 'spiritual energies' of his faith, in equal portions, between his faith in God and his faith in Christ.

For their part, the disciples of Nestorius, whose major viewpoints I have already indicated, endeavoured to cope with the difficulty in their spiritual life arising from bipolarity by in some way dividing their belief in Christ into two stages: thinking that there were two natures in Christ without links between them (and a hypothetical unity of person), they could use what one might call an 'alternating' faith. At one time they worshipped the divinity hidden in Christ (under the form of a mystical appearance); at another they revered the merits of the man Jesus. These subtleties were rejected at the Council of Ephesus (431). It was wrong to look for ways out: worship had to be addressed, in equal and similar ways, to Christ the God and Christ the man (the two making one only in the person of the incarnate Word). It was impossible to escape bipolarity: every time the church authorities felt that some distortion had arisen in the equilibrium to be maintained between the two faiths, they reacted, no matter what tensions this might produce.

The same thing happened with the third form of heresy that I mentioned (I am speaking here only of the most important ones; a great many others appeared): Eutychianism, or Monophysitism (in the fifth century). The followers of Eutyches (who can still be found as, for example, the Copts in Egypt and Ethiopia), felt more at ease if their faith did not have to be split in two. This faith was directed essentially to God; they hardly had any need to direct it to Christ, since for them the figure of Christ was 'unreal': it was a kind of apparition of God (in short, a 'fantasy').[26] Thus the problem was simplified, and psychological social attitudes were easier: monophysite belief (as the word itself indicates: there is 'monism' of the divine nature) essentially has one pole. However, after a number of reversals (for example at the 'Robber Synod of Ephesus' in 449), this attitude was in turn to be condemned with rigorous firmness at the Council of Chalcedon (451). We have seen how rigorously the text of the Council maintains the christological thesis of the one person in two natures. So those responsible for Christian faith did not want to leave any loophole: in all circumstances, no matter what inner tensions, whether psychological or social, might put the believer to the test, the twofold faith (to stress the point once again, equal in content and equal in intensity) was to be maintained in God, thrice holy, and in Christ himself.

The believing soul must turn towards God and towards Christ with the same movement of thought and love. Anyone who diminishes, to whatever small degree, the intensity of his belief in favour of one or other of these 'poles', to the detriment of the other, is declared a 'heretic' and rejected from the community. It is vitally important to 'hold both ends of the chain' with equal force. This becomes one of the rules of the game. There was no salvation outside this rigorous bipolarity. That was the 'golden rule'.

Our analyses must essentially be directed towards the practical sphere, since the whole of this study develops within the field of social psychology. The question which arises, then, is how the growing Christian community will take concrete steps to maintain with equal fidelity both its belief in God (in the God of Abraham, Isaac and Jacob . . .) and its faith in Jesus Christ (God incarnate among men). We can expect considerable tension between these two poles of attraction in the realms of religious affectivity (in other words, piety), spiritual and moral (and perhaps intellectual) life, and social life.

(e) Practical tensions: piety, spirituality

Here the crisis was intense. Those pious Jews who wanted to be converted to the new faith had to achieve an unbelievable transformation in themselves: they had to modify even their conceptions of the divine and the holy, of spiritual life, the rites to be performed, and so on.

There was a tension in ways of 'thinking about' God. They had to try to treat with the same deference a God of fear and a God of love. In fact, pious Jews were accustomed to worship a powerful and dominating God, threatening and vengeful. If they came over to Christian faith, they now had to recognize the presence of this same vengeful God in the humble image of the child in the cradle or on the tree of Golgotha. Psychologically, they felt torn apart: these people were brought face to face with the absurd, the intolerable. 'A scandal for Jews . . .', St Paul would say on their behalf. However, despite everything, the apostles of the new faith persisted in demanding this dualism in belief. St Paul is a living witness to it.

The situation presented to believers coming from the Greek world was not much better. Those wise men who revered – in a more or less confused way, and through various representations, though all of a transcendent kind – the existence of a mysterious Logos, the expression of the rationality of the world, would have to accept – as St Paul also put it – a 'folly': that of recognizing this same Logos, powerful universal reason, under the features of the frail child of Bethlehem and the crucified figure on Golgotha. It was no longer possible to trick them and to substitute one representation for another. They were asked, similarly, to order their religious faith round this twofold image of the deity; to match the same burning faith in the transcendent God with a faith in Christ, God incarnate. The inner crisis was inevitably terrifying: to begin with, at any rate, few would tolerate it.

A tension also arose in ways of 'serving God'. From now on, how was God to be addressed? Was it necessary to keep the reverent and deferential tone which prevails, for example, in the Psalms: 'Out of the depths I cry to you, Lord . . . If you keep an exact count of our iniquities, who can stand before your judgment?' Or, on the contrary, was it necessary to speak to God with confidence and love? 'From now on, say, Our Father who art in heaven . . . forgive us our sins.' If we refer to the texts of prayers from this period, we can see clearly that two forms of them were in competition: believers tried to reconcile them as best they could. In fact they did not succeed in synthesizing them, in joining them in one logical harmony. As we shall see later, it was impossible, in the first centuries, to keep to the principle of bipolarity when it came to religious lyricism. One of the poles, that of faith in God, had a clear priority over the other, that of faith in Christ. The passage from one to the other was only made very slowly, over the course of the centuries.[27]

We find a similar tension in the choice of rites and places of worship. What was to be done? Should Christians keep the ancient Jewish rites, which were aimed at offering reverential worship to the Lord of men and worlds, whose name could not even be pronounced? Should they continue to assemble in the temple, or in the synagogues, at a respectful distance from the 'Holy of Holies', chanting the Psalms of King David ('I will go to the mountain of Zion . . .', 'I will sing your glory for ever . . .')? Or should they assemble in an intimate way, to repeat the gentle 'sayings' of the inner master Jesus, lovingly preserved, surrendering themselves to the tender glow of shared memories, enthusiasms maintained and thanksgivings performed? The believers of the first generation were led to divide their time (and their hearts) between these two types of behaviour. Should they celebrate Pentecosts or hold fraternal agapes? Both types of behaviour were in competition in the primitive church. In fact, as far as we can judge from the historical information which has come down to us, the primitive communities tried to manage two kinds of rite and practice, in parallel, dividing their religious devotion between the rites of a triumphal (one would now say triumphalist) liturgy and those of an intimate liturgy, adapted to the modest circumstances of the life of Christ. It seems that the equilibrium was maintained during the very first generations. In due course, a chance event changed the balance, for a while, in favour of an intimate liturgy. Quite simply, this was the destruction of the Temple in Jerusalem by the Romans (in AD 70). Believers no longer had a 'high place' in which to celebrate the glory of God. The celebrations of God had to take a more reserved form. However, as we shall see, the problem of choice presented itself afresh when, thanks to Constantine's favour, it again proved possible to worship in the grand manner, and those Christians who were nostalgic for the temple could find compensation in the processions made possible by the size of the Roman basilicas, 'reconverted' for worship. The triumphal forms of worship regained all their vigour, and the intimate (I was going to say 'pitiful') worship which arose out of faith in Christ, the humble carpenter of Galilee, who died on the cross in Jerusalem, was again absorbed by the sense of triumph in powerful traditions like that of Byzantium: Christ was seen 'enthroned' on his cross, in royal garments, and the crucified one of Golgotha became the prestigious Pantocrator of Byzantine domes. However, whatever the momentary success of the attempts at unification around one or other of the two poles of Christian piety, those of the glory of God or the humility of Christ, in fact the fundamental bipolarity was maintained. In these different circumstances – and without doubt in order to put one more obstacle in the way of attempts at reduction (to one or other of these poles) which the first heresies surreptitiously introduced – those in authority in the growing church preferred to run the risk of incoherence and possibly to incur the accusation of contradiction, endeavouring by every means to maintain – for the moment at any rate – the twofold approach which I have described, of both triumphalism and intimacy. It was said of the first Christians both that 'they were constantly in the Temple', and also that they met in humble agapes 'to break bread together'. The two liturgies continued side by side . . . for the moment, at least (as we shall see, an attempt at a synthesis would be made only in the 'Carolingian mass', in which the two 'logics', triumphalist and intimate, were combined in a difficult compromise).

Finally, a tension arises in seeking to live the spiritual life. The contradiction between the two logics can also be felt in the sphere of the inner life which the believer is invited to practise day after day. It can be felt as much among the pious Jews who became Christians as among those who came from the world of Greek wisdom. By which inspiration was the human soul to live? Tradition replied, 'by the fear of God'. The perfect man is the one of whom it is said, 'He is just and God-fearing.' Now under the influence of the teaching of Jesus, people came to say that God is no longer to be feared, that he is 'gentle and merciful'; that he must not be dreaded, but loved. God the Father, a 'paternal' God, was substituted for the vengeful God. In these conditions, how were people to live the spiritual life? To which God were they to dedicate themselves? Even though it was repeatedly said that of course this was the same God, it did not alter the fact that he was seen under such contradictory and opposed aspects that even religious consciences were perplexed by them. Should one fear or love? Should one live in the fear of sin, or entrust oneself to the divine mercy ('where sin abounds, grace abounds even more')? Think of the inner crises which the people of the first Christian generations must have experienced! The writings of the apostolic period (the first and second centuries) bear traces of them and reflect their echoes. If we read them again with a critical eye (preoccupied by the problem with which we are concerned at the moment), we can feel this constantly: it is only necessary to reread St Paul, in particular, in this connection; or the letters of St Peter and St James; or the writings of St Polycarp, St Ignatius of Antioch, and many others (St Irenaeus, for example).

The tension makes itself felt in all the spheres of spiritual life. What is the loftiest attitude? Contemplation, which is directed towards God, or action, which is directed towards Christ? ('Woe to me if I do not preach the gospel', as St Paul said.) Which is the most 'urgent' virtue, the one which has priority? The faith which 'lives from God and for God', or love, which 'lives from Christ and for Christ'? An underlying tension nagged at the conscience. Whereas pious Jews, like the wise Greeks, felt that their spiritual life was perfectly unified around contemplation and faith, the believing Christian felt 'divided', stretched: he had to live oriented on two poles: contemplation and action, faith and love, both at the same time. In the spiritual order, his task thus became more arduous, but in spite of the difficulties this bipolarity established itself, little by little, as a fundamental characteristic of Christianity. Cost what it might, the faith of the believer had to be directed with equal fervour towards the triumphant God and the humiliated Christ. It was certainly a gamble, but that had to be maintained.

(f) Practical tensions: morality

Among the first Christians, there was also marked tension in the moral order, both in personal morality and in social and political morality. What human model was the believer of the first centuries to take as his inspiration? Should he take as a model the great figures of the Old Testament like the prophets; the righteous men like Job, Boaz, Mordecai and others, who all acted as 'heralds of the Most High God', and made themselves defenders of order and peace in a society which had to be 'conformed' to the orders of God? Or on the contrary, was it necessary to take as a model this Jesus of Nazareth and his closest disciples, who were on the side of the oppressed, the persecuted, those 'outside the law'? ('The prostitutes will enter the kingdom of heaven before you.') Should order be defended or challenged? What was to be done?

Could the Christian also look for his sources of cultural and ethical inspiration in Greek wisdom? This was the major problem for all those who came from the pagan world. Think of the tensions in the way in which they ordered their life which must have been experienced by these men coming from the highest circles of Greek wisdom. At the time they will have been from Stoicism, or certain Neo-Platonic groups, not to mention all the fine figures of the school of Alexandria. Just suppose, for example, that Marcus Aurelius were reading the gospel narratives or that Plotinus set about meditating on the Apostles Creed. What would they have felt? Tensions of the same order arose among all those cultivated spirits who were heirs of both Greek wisdom and the rules of thought of the Latin world (not to mention certain lofty traditions which had come from the East). We know very well that inner crises were experienced by men like Justin, Gregory of Nyssa, Athanasius, above all Chrysostom, and later – as he will tell us at some length in his *Confessions* – by St Augustine. He carried on the whole heritage of ancient wisdom and had to combine faith in God Most High (the God of his vision at Ostia) with faith in the God incarnate in the child of Nazareth and the man of the Passion.

This moral and cultural tension was also extended into the social and political order. Was the new Christian to serve order and peace (and here in particular Roman order and the *pax Romana*), or was he to challenge this order and put in its place the one which welled up in every heart? Was he to take up the struggle for justice? ('Blessed are those who suffer persecution for justice.') We know of the difficult position in which the future martyrs found themselves when they came before official tribunals. Most of the time they were accused of disturbing 'public order', in the sense that they did not always, and in everything, obey the public authorities (they did not offer to Caesar the worship that was required of them). The accounts of the trials which have come down to us (for example, those of the martyrs of Lyons or the martyrs of Carthage) show the difficulties in the pleas they had to attempt. In the name of their ancestral faith in one God, Lord of men and societies, they had to respect authority ('All power comes from God,' they said, following St Paul), and yet their faith in Christ caused them to challenge laws which went against their conscience. The discussions were often tortuous and difficult. We can see very clearly how they were, if one dares to put it that way, 'caught between two fires', the fire of their love for a higher God, Lord (and therefore inevitably regarded as 'guarantor') of societies, and the fire of their love for Jesus Christ, who called them to another kingdom ('my kingdom is not of this world'). We can find the same debate, the same tension, again in their attitudes towards material concerns, for example, towards money. Was it necessary to give up everything and have everything in common in the name of charity; or were they to respect the customary rules of exchange and service which were themselves modelled on justice? Difficulties arose on all sides. What I have called the 'bipolarity' of faith, faith in God and faith in Christ, could be felt everywhere, and produced tensions which had repercussions in moral and social life. Yet life had to go on: was it, then, always going to be necessary to give oneself over to perpetual compromise?

3. The difficulty of reconciling belief in God and belief in Christ

It seems certain that primitive Christianity experienced this tension between the two forms of faith as a kind of brute fact, which had to be accepted for what it was. Perhaps Christians shared the secret hope that the intellectuals or the men of the spirit would end up by finding a way to a reconciliation which ultimately would quite certainly commend itself as the result of an elemental need for logical coherence – at the levels of both personal and social logic. For the moment, the faith of the primitive church took the form of a kind of incandescent wave which was carrying along both traditional materials and new material; it postponed till much later the task of analysing and then purifying this wave. Meanwhile the wave spread; but as it spread, it tended to divide into different channels.

(a) Priority to faith in God

This spiritual current remained very strong. It came from the contemplative Jewish tradition. That tradition in fact underwent a renewal. The worshippers of the supreme God, though they had once withdrawn to Mount Carmel and elsewhere, had not disappeared completely. Beyond the tribulations of the exile to Babylon they can be found represented in various forms right down to the eve of the Christian era. This contemplative tradition is expressed in the Essene communities which flourished some decades before the coming of Christ. We can imagine their influence on some of the first Christian communities: those which 'gave themselves over to fasting and prayer' and which, from all the evidence, lived more from the event of Pentecost than from that of the death and resurrection of Christ; who lived more from the coming of the Paraclete than from that of Christ. For them, the coming of Christ had only been an episode – I was going to say a vicissitude – which had no other purpose than to prepare for the coming of the Holy Spirit, that is to say, to announce the great return of humanity to God (in a perspective oriented on the parousia). In this current of religious thought, all the world is waiting for a 'great return', the great return not only towards God, but to God. This is the current which gave birth to the astonishing adventure of the Stylites, the mystics of Upper Egypt, who were called 'God's fools', and who, in the worst of ascetical exercises, prepared for an imminent encounter with God (it should be noted that they do not make any appreciable personal reference to faith in Christ).

In the same vein (that of the contemplatives of Mount Carmel), we shall later find in the West a mystical current essentially based on the exaltation of faith in God. It emerges with a handful of monks grouped around Cassian, on the coast of Provence, and takes root at Lerins, with St Honorat. This current won over Gaul with St Hilary of Arles, St Loup and St Cesarius of Arles. Centres of contemplation also developed under the influence constantly diffused from Mount Sinai, with the monks of the Monastery of St Catherine, and beyond that in regions of the Near East like Cappadocia and Phrygia. Soon the whole of the Eastern church followed suit: it preserved as a precious gift this pre-eminence of contemplation and this sense of divine transcendence.

(b) Priority to faith in Christ

In this spiritual current there is certainly no question of diminishing faith in God in any way. However, we might say that at a psychological and even a social level, little by little this faith in God came to be hidden under faith in Christ: more attention was given to the latter than to the former. The goal of religious life is no longer so much to go directly to God (if that is possible) by contemplation, as to seek to encounter him indirectly by identification with Christ (it being understood that Christ is God). This current developed from the first centuries onwards. Those who took it up were the first to call themselves 'Christians'. We can see them doing anything to achieve this identification with Christ of which they dreamt: the identification of their thought with the thought of Christ, of their will with the will of Christ, of their love with the love of Christ. They took over a saying of St Paul (who, as I remarked, had prepared the way for this spiritual current): 'For me, to live is Christ'. We can even see the formation of doctrines intended to coordinate the different aspects of this attitude: this is how the first 'christologies' appear (which go on to complement the ancient 'theologies'). In this current are found men like St Athanasius, St Cyril of Alexandria, St Gregory of Nazianzen and St Gregory of Nyssa among the Greek thinkers; and among the Latin fathers, men of sound doctrine like St Augustine, St Jerome and St Hilary of Poitiers. Later, this tendency was again heightened in a meditative figure like Pseudo-Dionysius, whose major preoccupation was always to seek to penetrate the mystery of Christ, so as to be able to arrive by means of this mystery at the mystery of God.

During this time, others sought to penetrate the mystery of Christ, not by spiritual life but by practical life, and in particular by charity. What they wanted to revive – also in order to reach God – was the charity of Christ: his charity towards the poor and the forsaken of every kind. Some sought to identify themselves with him through apostolic zeal, going from town to town to spread his word and, by doing this, to implant the kingdom of God, in effect extending his own ministry in Judaea and Galilee. Others sought to identify themselves with his sacrificial action: they kept their eyes fixed on the agony of the one who, on Golgotha, offered his life for the salvation of sinners. They formed groups of penitents in the cities around the Mediterranean, or in solitude went deep into the deserts of Egypt or Cyrenaica where they lived the life of anchorites, hermits thirsty for penitence, like St Antony, who withdrew to Mount Kolzum in Egypt. This tradition of penitential heremitism (as distinct from that of the Stylites) was perpetuated in the great orders which soon came into being (from the sixth century on).

We find the same attitude and, ultimately, the same reasoning behind these various approaches. We seek God, like our predecessors, but while they had to make the difficult – and ungrateful – approach through contemplation to find him, it seems to us easier to seek him through Christ, since Christ is 'God present among us', and we have been able to see him, hear him, touch him. To find God, we have to do no more than to make Christ live again in us, thinking his thoughts, performing his actions, loving in accordance with his love. Caught up in this approach, the believer inevitably comes, little by little, to concentrate all his spiritual life on the person of Christ: Christ becomes a real 'pole' of his spiritual life. Gradually he becomes the chief end.

As a result, we shall not be surprised soon to see the birth of a real cult of the worship of the person of Christ. It begins with veneration, veneration which was extended to his 'sayings', then to 'remembrance' of him, to the images which he had left in the memory of those who had known him. An ancient tradition was concerned that people should begin to make portraits of him (at the beginning of the second century) which were then reproduced (this is the origin of the oriental tradition of icons). The places which he marked by his presence become the object of real veneration: Calvary (with the relic of the 'true cross', which soon came to be rediscovered, during the fourth century, by the agency of St Helen, mother of Constantine); the Holy Sepulchre; a little while afterwards, the site of Bethlehem (above all with St Jerome), and so on. Articles of clothing and shrouds were miraculously rediscovered and became objects of veneration. Special importance was attached to a 'remembrance' which, by the will of Christ, was destined to perpetuate on earth his saving and redeeming action, the breaking of bread and drinking of wine according to the rites which he himself initiated not long before his death. This celebration soon came to occupy a very important place in the religious life of the first Christians. 'They met for the breaking of the bread.' In its way, this remembrance 'reactualized' the presence of Christ on earth. When the sacred words had been pronounced on the bread and the wine, all the faithful knew that Jesus was again among them. They quickly took up the idea that from that point on Jesus would be among them only in this form; that is why a veritable cult, not only of veneration but also of adoration, grew up around the bread and wine, said to have been 'consecrated'. This would later be called the eucharist.

Little by little the cult was organized around Christ, his person and his message. A religion of Christ was developed. Pagans, whether Greek or Latin or from elsewhere, sometimes regarded it as a new variation of an oriental cult (cults from the East were all the fashion at that time, whether of Isis, Osiris or Mithras), and sometimes as idolatry. However, no matter who the observer was, from a social point of view he would make the same observation: this worship of Christ was added to the worship of God, from the end of the first century onwards. The two were combined: with difficulty, but inexorably; and the first Christians came to be equally loyal to their faith in God and their faith in Christ. Martyrs died both for God and for Christ. Both the historian and the sociologist may be amazed at this development, but the fact cannot be denied: people lived out one and the same unique religious faith, ordering it around two spiritual 'poles', God and Christ. It gave rise to tensions, but did not tear people apart.

From the point of view of social psychology, this was the situation created by the arrival of Christianity in the Mediterranean world at the time of Tiberius. A new religion was born which, with variants, set out to order religious fervour, in the unity of one and the same faith, around two poles: a transcendent God and a person who was known through history, Jesus of Nazareth. The first Christians came to live out this bipolar faith, often in tragic intellectual and moral conditions. Their faith was immense. They did not always understand, but they knew that they were confronted with the greatest of mysteries. And they bowed down and worshipped. It would be good to be able to dwell on certain specific cases here, to analyse – I almost might say, 'psychoanalyse' them – and to try to enter peoples' minds to relive the agonies which must have been caused. Beyond doubt, all that would excite the psychologist, the sociologist, the philosopher, the theologian, the spiritual man. However, I must restrain myself. So I shall dwell only on one case, albeit a characteristic one: that of St Augustine.

Here was a man who enjoyed the legacy of all ancient culture. He had read all the Greek writers (even if this was through Latin translations) and all the Latin writers. He had tried Plato and his *Dialogues*, the best texts of Aristotle; he had experienced the intellectual adventure of the Neo-Platonists. He had taken a delight in reading Cicero, Virgil and Tacitus. He was a great humanist. Along with all of Graeco-Latin wisdom (he was not a Jew and so had not entered into the Abrahamic heritage), he believed in a supreme being, Lord of men and worlds, the supreme truth of the universe, the Logos (or Word) which illuminates the universe and truth, just as it also illuminates every thinking man who faithfully looks for the great secret of the world. He is what one would call a very great man: he points forward to future great men like Montaigne, Pascal, Goethe. Now this great man encounters the Bible: '*Tolle et lege*, take and read.' His first reaction is that of mistrust: compared with Plato, Virgil and Cicero, this book is badly written. What trust can be placed in it? What goodness, and above all truth, can come out of such a conglomeration? Yet we know what happened. Augustine encounters Christ in the silence of Cassiciacum, and from that point on, for him Christ becomes the supreme guide, the one to whom he owes everything and to whom he gives everything. In the religious life of Augustine, Christ occupied a new pole around which all his inner life was ordered: thought, love, will and being. The *Confessions* give us a marvellous account: there is a break with an ancient humanism and the adoption of a new humanism. Augustine abandons 'the old man' and 'puts on the new man'. All his life is as it were polarized around Christ. So a perceptive observer could detect the inner tension which arose in this man between the two poles around which his faith was ordered: faith in God and faith in Christ. We can feel him torn between fear and love: fear of the sovereign judge, who cannot but take a stern view of his past errors, and the love of Christ the redeemer, who 'forgets and pardons'. He does not know whether he should tremble or allow himself to be swallowed up in love. The tension is constant. However, we do well to recognize that his oratorical skill – made up of a love of paradoxes and an interplay of contrasts – was shown at its best in this contradiction: think of the fine variations provided by this theme of God who is both dreaded and adored, feared and madly loved, evaded and at the same time sought again! In short, Augustine, making a virtue of necessity, converted the tension into an oscillating movement (I was going to be anachronistic, and call it a dialectic) and tried to find acceptance in the contemplation of this God who was at the same time both distant and close at hand.

However, even if rhetorical virtuosity allowed Augustine to give the impression of reconciling the irreconcilable, the tension was not any the less real; gathering up the data of faith in a general and confident way – we should not forget that he was converted through a mystical experience and not at the end of a rational process – he accommodated himself, intellectually and spiritually, to this tension, to the way in which he divided his faith; and he accepted this faith with a total inner submission.[28] Nevertheless, for him, and even more for the average Christian, the problem remained a formidable one: from now on faith had to be ordered round two poles. The task did not seem easy. However, let us continue to be objective. Primitive Christianity, that of the first centuries (from approximately the first to the fifth) posed this problem to the faithful: for the moment, at any rate, until clarifications were introduced, they had to live out two types of faith, or more exactly one faith which was refracted in two directions: faith in a transcendent God whose judgments were feared and dreaded, and faith in a God incarnate in Christ whose yoke was easy and whose burden was light. The first Christians lived patiently with this tension . . . waiting for better times when they could hope for harmony and unification of their understanding, their affections and their will. Later centuries certainly gave them satisfaction . . . but in a quite unexpected way.

II

Theocentric and Christocentric Belief

By its very origins, then, Christianity proves to be a bipolar religion. In his social and psychological attitudes, the Christian must put his trust, with equal intensity, both in the transcendent God and in Christ, God incarnate. The Christians of the first centuries accepted this challenge, and tried to accommodate themselves to it as well as possible, maintaining a kind of psychological and social equilibrium between their aspirations and their devotions.

However, before long this equilibrium was disturbed. That was inevitable. Two distinct types of behaviour came into being at the heart of the Christian community, which at times were juxtaposed and at times superposed; sometimes they were even opposed, until one or the other gained the upper hand. Before studying this conflict, it will be useful for me to describe the two attitudes which made themselves evident and which, for the purposes of this analysis, I shall term theocentricity and christocentricity.

These two terms are not my own. They are well known, and have been used often. They were put forward for the first time by Abbé Bremond in his famous work *Histoire littéraire du sentiment religieux en France* (published in eleven volumes between 1916 and 1932 by Bloud and Gay). Bremond introduces them in volume III, which he devotes to Bérulle and the French school of spirituality (this volume appeared in 1921). Useful comments on the meaning which he attaches to these terms and the way in which they can be used appear on pp.23–9, and I shall summarize them here. It is a matter of denoting and understanding two attitudes, two forms of spiritual life, which can be lived by the Christian. The first is that which gives priority to faith in God and which shapes behaviour in conformity to this option. As Bremond remarks, 'One may call it by a barbarous, but almost necessary name, *theocentric* . . . God is our end' (p.23). The second is that which gives priority to faith in Christ and the spiritual behaviour which derives from this option. Using a similar philological structure, this may be termed *christocentric*. For convenience, I shall adopt this terminology from now on. By the term 'theocentricity', then, I shall indicate the spiritual attitude which develops within Christianity from the moment when, of the two poles offered to the religious fervour of the believer, attention is directed towards belief in God. This gives rise to a specific attitude which, as we shall see directly, presents particular permanent features. By contrast, I shall use 'christocentricity' to denote the spiritual movement, the spiritual current, which also develops within Christianity and which is formed from the moment when attention and fervour are directed more essentially to faith in Christ. So another specific attitude develops which also has permanent features. We shall see how these two currents flow side by side, sometimes come together and sometimes separate, and are often in opposition, at the risk, in certain periods, of excluding each other. However, before describing this subtle interplay and these 'interminglings', I must give an *a priori* description of each of the two currents. We have to see how each one of them at the same time determines: 1. two general orientations of faith and morality; 2. two forms of religious sensibility; 3. two styles of religious practice; 4. two general currents of spirituality; and 5. two types of religious action, in the political and social spheres, all of which presages two futures.

1. Two general orientations of faith and morality

I think that I have established, or at least recalled, that the first Christians were faced with the need for a 'duplication' of (and, as we are well aware, not a choice in) their faith. They had to believe simultaneously in a transcendent God and an incarnate God, who was one and the same God. In this way two 'styles' of faith were born.

(a) Theocentric faith

The adoption of a priority for theocentric faith determined a 'style' of faith with a specific content which gave rise to a specific attitude. In the first place, the content of theocentric faith seems to be of exceptional excellence. This faith seems to present the mind with the highest object of thought to which the human spirit can devote itself. The spirit is raised up towards consideration of a being, a supreme being, the first and last object of all contemplation. If it is properly lived out, this apprehension of the supreme being sets in motion a process of complete polarization in the mind: anyone who has discovered the existence of this supreme being cannot but think of him, live for him, act for him. Theocentricity is by nature exclusive. This is what the philosopher, and after him the sociologist, is led to recognize.

It seems that such theocentricity was the spontaneous reaction of primitive, or proto-historical man. It was the reaction of the earliest figures of the Bible, from Adam to Noah, from Abraham to Job. With the nuances introduced by polytheism, it was the reaction of the heroes of Homer and later of Virgil. The 'pious king David' made his thanksgivings rise to heaven, and 'pious Aeneas' offered sacrifices. All relate their being, their action and their life to the deity. This theocentricity illuminates the great minds of Greek and Latin antiquity, as of the world of the Bible. It serves as a term of reference for great minds, from Plato to St Augustine, from Aristotle to Descartes, from Descartes to Kant and Kierkegaard.[1] And as we shall see, that will remain true until Marx and Nietzsche.

If we look closer, we see that theocentricity is an attitude as old as humanity. The Sumerians turned towards Marduk, the all powerful, just as the Semites turned towards Yahweh, the One who Is. As we can sense through the Upanishads of the Indian tradition or the Discourses of Confucius, the Asiatic spirit also has a disposition towards theocentricity. Granted, the expression of this disposition is more obscure than in Western traditions, but it is real nevertheless. All these human beings from the earliest traditions relate their thoughts and actions to a superior reality. They take on theocentric features. And the striking thing is that this disposition is exclusive: there is a single polarity. The sacred figures who come to interpolate themselves between this final goal and simple mortals never play more than the role of guides, of leaders: they are there to lead men towards the divine pole. They may be the prophets of the Old Testament; the *vates* of the religious traditions of Greece and Rome; religious reformers of India like Buddha, or Chinese reformers like Confucius or Lao-Tse; but none of them seeks to monopolize for himself the faith of his believers. All 'lead' them towards something greater than themselves, and efface themselves before this distant grandeur. We shall find this orientation everywhere down to the seventeenth and eighteenth centuries. The great Christian thinkers are fundamentally theocentric: St Augustine and St Thomas, St John of the Cross and Bossuet. All relate to God. Both their thoughts and their actions are related to him: they do everything *ad maiorem Dei gloriam* (St Ignatius of Loyola). The Christian laity have the same spiritual and moral attitude over the long centuries: life is related to God, from the cradle to the grave. This is the essential feature of the 'peasant's creed' (as it will be of the 'craftsman's creed'; we shall see, however, that it will no longer be that of the 'worker's creed'). The secular thinkers, the great philosophers, the great scientists during the fifteen centuries of Christianity which lead from the first ages to modern times are all faithful to this same theocentricity. Let me recall some names. This theocentricity is certainly dominant in Thomas Aquinas, whose major work, the *Summa Theologica*, is composed in such a way that one can see that everything comes from God (Parts One and Two), and that everything goes back to God (Part Three). It is striking in Descartes. All the Descartes specialists know that in his system (and also, it must be recognized, in his private life) he relates to God, to God *causa sui*, the first principle of excellence and truth. It is to God that I must relate my thoughts if I want to be assured of their truth; it is to God that I must relate my volitions (to God himself, 'perfect will', since the God of Descartes is above all 'will'), if I want my will to have any consistency and to be ordered around the good. It is also to the 'God of Abraham, Isaac and Jacob, to the God of Jesus Christ' (whom he does not want to recognize – surely wrongly – in the God of the philosophers and wise men) that Pascal wants to relate all his thoughts, his affections and his actions, by a mystical ardour (following his 'night' of 1654). It is to this transcendent God that Malebranche – at the end of his *Search after Truth* – relates all his intellectual and personal convictions; to this God, the guarantor of the universal harmony of the worlds, that Leibniz relates all the operations of thought and action which are interchanged between all these 'monads' disseminated through the world. Finally, it is to this God, the supreme legislator of consciences, that Kant relates all human thought, even if mankind discovers him only through its actions and its moral life. All these great figures relate to God and all are dependent on God. Like the prophets and the religious masters, they too practise an exclusive and unifying theocentricity.

This theocentricity also shines through the attitudes which the men of the Middle Ages and the Renaissance were led to take up, under the influence of these speculations, in the moral and practical order. In fact theocentricity determines a particular way of thinking about practical problems. Ordering thought in the direction of a unique principle, regarded as the cause of all good, leads men to think that everything comes from this cause, that everything comes from 'on high', or at least from the one who is the Most High. Thus men become accustomed to a hierarchical conception of values: if we recognize that everything comes from on high, we have to admit that authority comes from on high, wisdom comes from on high, and so on. The great mediaeval writers in fact say that the contemplation of God produces in the human mind a sense of wisdom and thus of 'rectitude': contemplation of God leads, as the great scholastic writers will say, to an 'architectonic' which must give its style and attraction to human action. This contemplative vision of God results in the practice of the virtues, whether theological or cardinal. Thus God becomes the single pole around which life and action is ordered. 'In him we live and move and have our being' (Acts 17.28). We rediscover this disposition of the mind, in which the spirit and life are as it were illuminated by the presence of God; in which the soul lives in accordance with 'the will of God', in the great spiritual figures of the centuries of traditional Christianity: St Augustine and St Thomas, St Bonaventure and St John of the Cross. We also find it in the great Christian thinkers of the classical period: in Bossuet (one has only to re-read his sermons or his funeral orations, in which the departed is set before 'Him who reigns in heaven and on whom all empires depend'), or in Racine ('Yes, I come to adore the Eternal in his temple').

This perspective certainly leads to a hierarchical conception of authority, both moral and political. The monarchy derives its power from this God, Lord of men and worlds; it disposes of a power of divine right. The members of society have rights only through participation in this power, which is held to be guaranteed by the divine power. Magistrates administer justice 'in the name of the almighty God and sovereign judge'. We shall see all this in detail later on. Even the scientists feel themselves put under this régime of hierarchical authority and hierarchical truth. It goes without saying that their discoveries can only prove to be in conformity with purposes which have already been made known (in scripture) by God.[2] The laws which they discover in nature can only be 'the purposes of God'. As Newton put it, God governs the world as 'a king governs his kingdom'. To study the laws of nature is to study the laws laid down by God; and Newton intersperses his scientific explanations with thanksgivings for the will of God which he sees expressed in gravitation or the phenomena of light. It is the same for Malebranche ('of the Academy of Sciences'), and later still for Ampère. Going even further, certain philosophers see the purposes of God in the laws of the spirit and thank him for perfections the human logic of which he has guaranteed. 'You have made him little lower than the angels', they go on to say with the psalmist.

I should point out in passing that this way of relating everything in human thought and action to God should not be thought inevitably to lead to cultural and moral slavery. Far from it. On the contrary, God is praised for having in this way liberated man from the slavery of ignorance and folly. Every discovery of his thoughts is an 'illumination', and every revelation of his will a 'liberation'. For with the author of Ps. 118, these great worshippers of God readily repeat, 'The law of God is a light for my footsteps; his commandments are a support for my will'. In fact theocentricity gives rise to the delineation of an authentic humanism. It brings out in man an intellectual and moral 'rectitude' which makes him a being who is proud of his origins (divine), his capacities (illuminated by divine grace) and his successes (hallowed by the divine omnipotence). This theocentric humanism was the driving force of the Middle Ages: it stimulated the builders of cathedrals, and those who discovered new worlds (lands of God, to be explored for the greater glory of God and the well-being of men). We can still find living expressions of this, above all in wide sectors of the Anglo-Saxon world: the authorities govern in the name of God ('In God we trust'); justice is administered in the name of God ('You will be hung from the neck until you are dead, and may God have mercy on your soul'); temporal, material and financial success is held to be 'a gift from God' and calls for thanksgiving ('Thanksgiving Day'). It can also be found in the Latin countries, among those social strata of the populace who have kept close to nature, among peasants of the traditional kind (those who bless bread and pray at Rogationtide: those of the Le Nain brothers, or Péguy . . .).

(b) Christocentric faith

The expression of christocentric faith is very different. In what might be called the order of faith proper, reactions differ both in the content of this faith and the way in which it is lived out in practice. People here no longer make evocative meditations on nature or on the order of things. The starting point is reflection on historical facts, events produced in human history. This already requires the adoption of certain presuppositions.

Thus the first requirement is that one should believe in history, or more precisely in historicity, and should do so with all one's power because that is where salvation was to be found. Furthermore, it is supposed that one might expect something valuable and determinative from human witness, handed down through the ages. This reference to history, this total reliance on history, was something quite new in the West. It did not occur to the Greeks, for example, at least to the Greeks of the classical period, that one could receive apodeictic instruction, laying claim to absolute value, from a historical witness. History, 'this empirical routine', as Plato called it, can only produce 'narratives', and then 'opinions', and then 'myths' (just as the story of Diotima, a woman of Mantinea, enshrines some pious traditions concerning immortality). Historicity surveys the domain of *doxa*; thus it is unreliable. Besides, people generally see no meaning in history: the peoples of the East are unaware of it; the peoples of ancient Africa do not set much store by it; the civilizations of pre-Colombian America scorn it. The sense of historicity was born in a tiny people, in a very special culture, the Jewish people. Here, rightly or wrongly, there came into being the idea that the events experienced by a society (with very rare exceptions they did not dare to talk of events experienced by an individual) could be placed end to end to form a coherent ensemble. This idea – quite preposterous, when one thinks about it – that events could be added together to give rise to a history whose meaning could be discerned was in fact born among the tiny people of the Jews, because they had been taught that the events of their life were dependent on a superior will. This being the case, they were led to regard each event as the expression of an intelligent will, and then to look for its meaning. This idea would not have occurred to a Greek, since he would never have had the idea that the events happening to his people could be guided by an intelligent will (he would have thought, rather, of a blind destiny . . .). No other people had this idea: neither the Persians, nor the Japanese, nor the Chinese, nor the Malayans, nor the Eskimos, nor the Aztecs. . . The Jewish people were the only ones, and from this they were led to 'rationalize' the course of events, or more precisely to sacralize them. But that is a specific, particular fact, which does not have a scientific value or a universal philosophical value in itself. Everything goes to show that it is necessary first of all to believe in the God of Abraham and in the message which he wants to hand down to Abraham's posterity, in order to believe in the 'noetic' value of historicity. It is from the moment when one believes in sacred history that one begins to believe in the sanctity of history. Thus there is an option to take here which, after all, remains the object of a personal choice and which could not be imposed in the name of free reason. Besides, consideration of the world of cultures – made in the name of social psychology, in accordance with the method which I have adopted in this study – clearly reveals that the cult of history, or more simply the sense of historicity, has extended very precisely through those regions which were affected by the influence of Judaism. This is true geographically and chronologically.

In these conditions, one is forced to recognize that the sense of historicity owes nothing to the speculations of unaided reason: philosophy does not discover it spontaneously within its sphere of observation; and science (mathematics, physics and chemistry . . .) has remained a stranger to it. It is a cultural phenomenon bound up with distinctive conditions which govern a particular people. It cannot be given a universal value. Thus, to return to the specific problem which concerns us, there could be no question, through reason, of founding belief in God on historical witness. This would be the reaction of a truly philosophical and scientific mind. I have been concerned to recall these facts – to some degree exaggerating their features – in order to show more clearly the intellectual revolution involved in adopting belief in Christ, conceived of as God incarnate in history, or more exactly (to avoid the Hegelian-type interpretations which some people will be tempted to dream of), Christ conceived of as God, incarnate 'through' history, or 'to some extent' in history. Those who wanted to open themselves to such belief had to undergo a real intellectual revolution. If they came from Judaism, they had to renounce the idea which they had of divine transcendence (it would be the same for those who came from Islam). This operation was already very difficult to perform. It was even more difficult for those who came from the world of Greek wisdom and its modern heirs. They had to perform a twofold operation. Certainly, they also had to abandon some of their ideas about divine transcendence; in addition, however (and that was perhaps even more difficult, because it was so much more obscure), they had to disturb certain foundations of their rationality and accept – why and how is a mystery – the need to accord a minimum credit, which steadily had to become larger, to historicity. They were to obtain from history their education in wisdom (and that was a scandal!), and perhaps even the key to their salvation. In effect, those who put their trust in Christ had to tell themselves that their personal destiny would depend, for ever, on events which took place centuries beforehand, the narration of which had been handed down with some difficulty. Paradoxically, it was from that time that they received the consecration of their eternity. Clearly, this option is a dramatic – I was going to say a superhuman – one. However, that is what the first believers, Greeks or Jews, had to do even before putting their faith in Jesus Christ. Why, how, after what reflections, did they come to make this step? We do not have to investigate this subject here. I am not making a philosophical or theological analysis. I am simply stating the facts: I am conducting an investigation governed by social psychology. So I must stress again: clear-headed and sensible people put their trust in Christ as God incarnate in history, and they had to set this faith alongside that which they had in a transcendent God.

However, other elements of tension emerged. This faith in Christ came to determine a new pattern of religious behaviour; the content of this faith brought change. It was a matter of no longer having 'religious' faith (let me emphasize this point: 'religious' faith, not secular, which is simply a form of trust) in a being transcendent over the world, invisible, who cannot be represented by an image, in a God 'whose face you cannot see and live'; but on the contrary in a God who had become immanent in the world, whom people had seen in his human guise, 'whom we have seen and touched'. This was Jesus of Nazareth, 'who was born and suffered', at the time of Tiberius, who died at the age of thirty-three, and so on. He was a fully historical person. He was not even an apparition or a myth; he was a personage of flesh and blood. That was the stake. In the case of Jesus it was a question of introducing completely new epistemological data which needed to be taken firmly into account. It was a matter of believing it possible that a historic fact could give rise to themes of 'meta-historical thought'; that physical figurations could give rise to 'metaphysical' notions; that the moral rules formulated in a particular country, in a given century, could give rise to values which could be projected into eternity. Now this man from Galilee had said: 'I am the Way, the Truth and the Life.' He spoke with the same authority as the voice which resounded on Horeb and which gave commandments on Sinai. To have faith in him, then, supposed that one allowed that the immanent can become transcendent, that the contingent can become necessary, that the temporal can become a vector of eternity. At various levels there is a radical mutation of the data which the human mind has at its disposal. The secular can find itself sacralized; history can take on the garb of the values of eternity. This is metaphysical – it might be better even to say 'epistemological' – conversion, since it is not only a question of the content of knowledge but also of the mode of knowledge – this is the conversion to which the Christian dogma of the Incarnation invites us. This is the intellectual and spiritual *metanoia* which is required in the first place by faith in Christ as God incarnate.

Another attitude in the practice of faith also makes itself evident. Here the sense of wisdom with a transcendent focus which, as I have said, is characteristic of the theocentric attitude, tends to disappear. It gives place to what St Paul appropriately calls 'folly'. Since this is a matter of now referring to a historical and not a metaphysical model, people are drawn to give priority to circumstances, the concrete, what is lived, over the rational and the scientific. They come to meditate on the specific circumstances of the life of Christ: his 'sayings', his actions and gestures, his reactions to specific situations are the objects of study and meditation and then become moral criteria. It is no longer a matter, for example, of thinking about the problem of God 'in itself', but of verifying how Jesus of Nazareth thought of it. Truth is attained 'in the second degree': what is true is what is true for Jesus. 'They told you . . . I told you'; and it is what Jesus said which counts from now on (even when that overthrows our ideas or our convictions). The principle of christocentricity basically modifies and changes the conceptions which we have of the truth: it is no longer a matter of going by the evidence, but by the content of a testimony. The role of the 'inner master' is no longer played by personal reason, but by the word of Jesus, 'the divine master'. At the least, it is taken for granted that one portion of historicity has been sacralized, that which contains the actions and deeds of Jesus of Nazareth. Here history takes on the beginning of sacralization. Let us suppose that from now on (though I shall return to this at length), this process, once set in motion, can only develop: if one portion of history is found to be sacralized, why not extend the potentialities of this sacralization? So we can see that step by step, under the progressive influence of this christocentricity, people would come to sacralize not only the historical events inherent in the mission of Christ, but all those which surround it, before him and after him. Thus they would sacralize the past of Christ (that happened above all at the beginning of the twentieth century), but sometimes also the times which announce him ('the steps of the legions marched for him', (Peguy). Gradually, then, people would be led to sacralize the chief periods of history; from there some even went on to the complete sacralization of history (with Hegel). Under the influence of christocentricity, the 'diachronic', to use structuralist terminology, tends to get the better of the 'synchronic'.

Christocentricity also exercised its influence on another aspect of the attitude of faith: how one conceives of access to the truth and to truths, both speculative and practical. An 'intimist' conception of access to the truth is substituted for the hierarchical conception of access to the truth ('truth comes from on high'). If it is true that historicity has a certain element of sacralization, each human being – who incarnates a piece of historicity – must be able to find in himself a piece of truth, at least the piece appropriate for him, the piece which is made for him, 'his truth', the only thing which matters completely. This means that the subjective quest for truth takes the place of the laborious but confident quest for objective truth. If each person carries within himself a piece of this sacral historicity, it must be possible to find it, by means of a great inner effort at sincerity; and *ipso facto*, sincerity comes to replace truth. As we shall also see in detail, this is what happened when in Christianity christocentricity began to supplant theocentricity (a little after the Renaissance). The appeal to 'free examination' was substituted for the authority of controlled knowledge, and to this free examination each person could submit the most intimate areas of his being. I shall show how in effect christocentricity demanded this kind of attitude in certain churches of the Protestant tradition (as one might have expected). This change in attitude towards access to religious truth in turn determined changes in the intellectual attitude of the believer. In particular, we shall see the rise of a certain distrust of reason, at least of abstract reason (an attitude which can be discerned in Luther and his intellectual heirs). If one holds that every religious truth finds its source entirely in the Christ, a historical person, who lived a specific existence in a known country and in a clearly defined period, one will naturally be led to favour the historical, the concrete, what is lived and felt, in a word the existential, to the detriment of the rational (I shall have to return to this point). Among other consequences we shall see how the apologetic peculiar to Christianity evolves towards historical and concrete forms. It is no longer a matter of proving the existence of God, then the divinity of Christ, and then that of the church. The pattern followed is almost the reverse. The starting point is the beneficial presence of the church in the world; from there a line is drawn back to Jesus Christ and finally to God, the reference to God forming part of the 'revelation' made by Jesus. God, 'known only by Jesus Christ', as Pascal put it, is already involved in this direction. Finally the very conception of 'salvation', 'soteriology', is fundamentally modified. Whereas in the theocentric perspective, salvation is gained by 'adherence' to God, obtained by contemplation, in the christocentric perspective salvation is obtained by adherence to Christ through love. Here I can only indicate some innovations on the theoretical level; later we shall see how things develop in practice. As someone put it: 'For us, truth is not a principle but a man': an audacious doctrine, but one which cannot but fail to run grave risks when it is formulated.

In the moral order, christocentricity also introduces important modifications in connection with behaviour. As we shall see, reference to a God of love replaces that to a Lord God. The divine attributes are modified: stress is no longer placed on the omnipotence of God, his justice, his strictness ('I fear God, dear Abner, and have no other fear'), but rather on his goodness, his mercy, his forbearing towards sinners. The believer no longer lives under the same regime; he has passed from the rule of fear to that of love. The style of moral imperatives begins to change. Whereas in the theocentric perspective the will of God is presented in the form of imperatives to which one must submit, in the christocentric perspective one can feel the spirit of the beatitudes: the will of God is felt as an invitation to the good: 'if you want to be perfect, do this'. We have passed from the imperative to the conditional.[3] I shall analyse these developments at length from the point of view of social psychology. We shall see as a result the development of two religious sensibilities.

In general terms, then, one might say that faith takes on two very different 'styles', depending on whether it is based on theocentricity or christocentricity. In the first perspective, faith in God is surrounded with reverential fear, obedience, respect, the spirit of submission; in the christocentric perspective, by contrast, faith in God is coloured by familiarity, simplicity, a certain style of freedom, of confidence. The predominantly theocentric religions, like Judaism and Islam, keep harsh and rigid features. Christianity – which its adherents have to live out simultaneously through two types of faith – practises both styles at once, accentuating now the one and now the other, depending on times and periods. The Christian has both to fear God and to love him, to be in awe of his justice and to count on his mercy. He is in a state of perpetual tension, or rather perpetual oscillation, between these two poles. That is what we must analyse further.

2. Two forms of religious sensibility

The religious sensibility of the Christian, and particularly of the Catholic, is extremely complex: all the analysts have noted that. At the extreme, one could even say that it is riddled with contradictions, often cruel ones. We may try to disentangle them, employing for the most part the resources of phenomenology and possibly also psycho-analytical considerations.

(a) The fantasies of Christian consciousness

In Christian consciousness, the interplay of fantasies is particularly complex: we can sense the constant competition, alliance and sometimes clash between the fantasies which arise from the theocentric pole and those which arise from the christocentric pole. It is important first of all to sort them out.

So, we can begin by associating with the theocentric pole the feelings which arise in the awareness of the Christian that he is by nature only a 'miserable creature' in the face of the majesty of his God. These feelings are manifold. We should note the feeling of radical precariousness ('I am the one who is not, faced with the one who is', said Teresa of Avila); that of human fragility (of 'dereliction', as the Christian Kierkegaard put it). It is also necessary to allow a prominent place to the feeling of 'perdition'. The Christian feels in a state of abandonment: left to his own resources, he has the impression of going to ruin and death. Hence the theme of 'salvation', which is steeped in theocentricity. The Christian, according to traditional conceptions, feels himself to be in the situation of a shipwrecked mariner, whom the waves are ready to swallow up, and who can only escape by the intervention of divine grace: so he is always looking for his 'salvation'; he puts 'his trust in the divine mercy'. On the other hand, still in the theocentric perspective, since he is called in contemplation to come face to face with the infinite grandeur of the 'thrice holy' God, he can only realize his own wretchedness, his inadequacy and hence his 'sin'. The authentic Christian can only call himself a 'sinner'; inevitably he is burdened with a 'guilt complex'.[4] And from this perspective he seeks to discover means of purification (by repentance and also by penance). More profoundly still, he carries with himself the feeling of a gigantic failure on the part of humanity, understood in universal terms. This feeling of failure is combined with mysterious nostalgia for a 'lost paradise', following an initial fault. 'Man is a fallen god who remembers heaven' (Lamartine). This also sets in motion a reflex action of mistrust in specifically human enterprises (whether scientific, technical, economic or financial); and the success of these seems to be accepted only to the extent that it can be demonstrated, by certain expedients which it is important to find, that here man is furthering the plans of the Almighty God and co-operating with his glory.

However, these sentiments and fantasies, which might be thought to be a great drain on human energy, are happily compensated for – again in the theocentric perspective – by other fantasies which generate more energy and vitality. The believer who has 'put his trust in the Lord' will, by contrast, feel himself to be strengthened in his own dynamism. If he knows that his enterprises are blessed by God, he will devote all his strength to them. By prayer, he thinks that he can obtain the omnipotent aid of this God, whom he knows to be Lord of men and worlds. So his faith can 'move mountains'. Anyone who has 'built his house on the Lord' knows that it is indestructible. Even the worst trials will not defeat him, not even evil or suffering. For – and this is the staggering psychological interpretation – suffering itself, which was such an obstacle to human optimism in ancient civilizations, is here 'taken over' for the benefit of human vitality: the Christian learns that suffering is sent to him by the Almighty to test his faith and that, if he accepts it, he will have his 'recompense' in this world or, failing that, in the next. Here suffering is detached from the negative realm and reinserted in the positive realm (to use the language of phenomenology). This happens to such a degree and to such effect that despite trials, and beyond their overwhelming perspectives, for Christians – still in the theocentric perspective (things will be different from a christocentric perspective) – life can be regarded as a fine adventure. Whatever happens, whatever is accomplished, can be regarded as being written in the eternal designs of God, thus contributing to his glory. The only cry which may be uttered by the Christian, at the end of his existence, is the acclamation of a triumphal *Te Deum*.

By contrast, the fantasies which emerge from the christocentric perspective are quite different. Here the believer feels himself to be involved intimately with a historical person, whose infinite goodness and understanding are brought into the limelight. Thus his awareness will show feelings of confidence, which are often tinged with affection (pious souls speak of Christ as the 'good Jesus'). A number of affective states develop around the image of Jesus, as we shall see: pious literature, popular imagery, hymns (and even 'cantatas', like those of Bach), translating the affective states literally 'with love', and always filled with tenderness. This affectiveness dominates the commentaries made on the figure of Jesus. One popular feature is to relate the sensitivity accompanying his action: the movements of Jesus through the Galilean countryside, his involvement in the day-to-day life of men (the wedding at Cana, or, more sadly, the death of his friend Lazarus).

In another sphere, certain human values are 'taken over' by christocentricity in quite a different way from what is possible in theocentricity. Suffering and the fear of death receive a different meaning, and are lived out through the affections in a different way. Suffering, accidentally inherent in creation, takes on the sense of a mystical component which is added to the sufferings of Christ (at least in the Latin tradition; the Eastern tradition persists in regarding the sufferings of Christ as a historical accident: the Byzantine Christs 'are enthroned' on the cross as on a throne of glory; and the crown of thorns becomes a royal crown). In the Latin Christian tradition, suffering acquires an authentic positive value. 'A day without suffering is a day lost,' Teresa of Avila will go so far as to say. According to this tradition, suffering is rehabilitated as a redemptive value by mystical association with the sufferings of Christ. The believer is invited to make a real 'transference', amounting ultimately to an 'identification' with Christ. The same thing happens with reactions to death. The Christian must seek to identify his death, when he sees it approaching, with that of Christ, in the intention of making it, too, into an offering which, still in the sense of an identification with the Christ, will bring him the privilege of a glorious resurrection. Here we have an essay in the 'sublimation' of death. In fact, christocentricity develops this dynamic of sublimation in a fundamental way. It is necessary to identify with Christ, with his thoughts, with his ardours, with his sufferings, with his death, in such a way that our similar states of awareness are in turn 'sublimated' by the effect of his saving mediation.

Finally, under the effect of this polarization on christocentricity, the Christian soul awakens to the sense of a universal love. In fact the love of Christ extended to all men: righteous and sinners, whether faithful to God or not, sons of Abraham or strangers to Judaism. In the same way, the Christian soul has to extend its love to all men, without distinction. This gives rise in the affectivity of Christian awareness to a kind of capacity for universal sympathy (an *Einfühlung*, the Germans would say), which can even extend beyond men, to animals and plants (as we can see, for example, in St Francis of Assisi). Under the inspiration of christocentricity, the Christian soul will truly become what Bergson calls the 'open soul': open to all men and all worlds.

In this way, Christian awareness, required to order its affectivity around the two as it were divergent poles of theocentricity and christocentricity – finds itself subjected to inner tensions which are difficult to bear. Depending on the orientations which it may adopt (according to circumstances, or sometimes moods), the Christian soul can feel itself driven at the same time towards both confidence and mistrust. Its theocentricity could make it confident in the divine omnipotence, while its christocentricity could lead it to a kind of mistrust of itself and of human beings confronted with the spectacle of evil in the world and the lack of love among men. From the first point of view, it will be led to share in a deep-rooted optimism (being confident in a God – who is perhaps to some degree Leibnizian – the ordainer of 'the best of all possible worlds'); from the second point of view, it will be led towards an incurable pessimism, confronted with the apparent ineffectiveness of the redemptive work of Christ (think of the pessimism of the great 'christocentric' figures like Mauriac, Bernanos, Graham

Greene, for example). Christian awareness will be constantly torn between these two interpretations.

There is another form of emotive tension: the tug-of-war between a sense of fear of the transcendent God and familiarity with Christ. Some approach the divine mystery with 'fear and trembling' (Kierkegaard); others with a joyful confidence (St Thérèse of Lisieux). Is there an infinite distance between God and us, or an intimate proximity? Over the course of the ages, and in essentials, Christian consciousness is constantly torn between these two conceptions. Depending on his or her spiritual temperament, each one leans in one direction or the other. The dilemma has never been resolved.

There is yet another object of tension: reactions towards the changes and chances of life. Here Christian awareness is also very divided. It is divided between the taste of success and the taste of failure. The theocentrics value success above all: it is a gift of the omnipotent God, as we have already indicated. Given temporal or spiritual success, they raise a song of thanksgiving to God. By contrast, souls prone to christocentricity regard success with suspicion, and prefer failure. They have their eyes fixed on the failure of the cross, which hides the secret of the true 'success' of Christ. 'If a grain of wheat does not die, it does not bear fruit.' In that case human success is suspect, and by contrast they rejoice at the failure of their enterprises, sometimes with a touch of sensual delight (which some might perhaps call 'masochism'). In the face of these contradictory attitudes – which we can rediscover throughout the history of Christianity – the social psychologist is somewhat dismayed. He gains the impression of incoherence.

(b) An essay in psychoanalysis

The analysis which I have just made is at the level of ordinary psychology. We can try to go a little deeper by resorting to the keys offered by psychoanalysis – adopting the necessary methodological caution. Like all human awareness confronted with basic choices, Christian awareness is at root governed by complex states which are centred on the interplay which I have just described between the tendencies ordered around theocentricity and those ordered around christocentricity. The tensions and contradictions which I have indicated are in fact intertwined in an extremely complex way below the level of awareness of the Christian believer, in complexes of impulses and inhibitions, fantasies, derivations and sublimations, the causes and effects of which are very difficult to grasp. Let us make the attempt nevertheless. First of all, we see that the Christian who wants to live out his religion in an authentic way is necessarily seized by anguish, over his spiritual security. If it is not to end up in illuminism or to remain blissfully unaware, Christian awareness cannot put itself in a position of security. Faith in God can certainly arrive at that point by the paths of mysticism; but faith in Christ will restrain the believer from pursuing this road. In fact faith in Christ creates a thirst for personal perfection and a need for the salvation of others which brings about perpetual dissatisfaction, bordering on anguish: 'How can I feel reassurance when I think of all the wretchedness of the world?' ('While even dogs are being beaten somewhere in the world', as one spiritual authority of our time remarked.) This feeling of anguish is also reinforced by that of failure, the permanent failure of all enterprises to achieve the perfection expected of them. A demanding super-ego (as Freud would put it) constantly reminds the Christian of the vanity of his efforts; in fact he must hold in front of himself either the image of a Father thought of as perfect (in the theocentric perspective), or that of a brother, regarded as the perfect model with whom identification will prove impossible. Besides, when christocentric inspiration is the predominant fashion, this attempt at identification becomes one of the permanent facts of the Christian life. It is sought as an end, 'it is no longer I who live, but Christ who lives in me', as St Paul said; however, in the event failure is inevitable; and this failure leads to 'repressions'. These in turn can give place to sublimations, which can transform themselves into mystical aspirations, for example (thus the Curé d'Ars, despairing of ever being able to lead all his parish to Christ, seriously dreams of seeking refuge in the contemplative life, in a monastery). On the other hand, it has been noted that this failure to identify with Christ at the same time contributes to a guilt-complex in the conscience, which can lead to self-accusation. However, it is here that sublimation – for example, by prayer – can offer a way out.[5]

We must also consider carefully the way in which Christian awareness can experience inner development over the course of a human life. Given the tensions between the two poles, God and Christ, what is the long-term aim for the Christian soul over a whole life? Some seek to rediscover an unalterable happiness, a 'place' where they will enjoy eternal happiness: perhaps certain analysts will see here the echo of a need to return to the mother's breast, the anticipated image of which is provided by some cell, or even by some 'return to oneself'. In that case numerous obstacles will present themselves along the way (Jacob had to struggle with the angel): it will be necessary to go through experiences of 'dark nights', cruel experiences, even if they are sometimes compensated for by views of what Freud calls 'oceanic' horizons.[6]

By contrast, others are attracted – again in order to free themselves from their complexes of failure – by promises of communion (and thus of sublimation) offered to them by occasions for loving exchanges with their like: these are the 'apostles'. Some of them seek to extend their mysticism to all men: they make themselves heralds of God the Father. This is the mysticism of St Bernard leaving on crusade. Others are inspired by the love of Christ, God the brother, to share their sympathy (their *Einfühlung*) with all mankind, calling them universal brotherhood. And if one or the other should fail in their enterprise – which in the majority of cases is foreseeable – we can see them blaming and accusing themselves: their imperfection is the cause of the failure, because 'the grace of God never fails' (in that case they risk falling victim to what might be called the complex of the 'worthless servant', who calls himself the 'off-scourings of the world').

However, whether they retreat in their inwardness or become open and outward-looking, these forms of awareness – and as such, it does not matter whether they are oriented towards Christianity or not – find themselves up against the three profound impulses which Freud has designated as the instincts of *eros*, *thanatos* and reality.[7] Christian awareness – experiencing the inner tensions of the bipolarity which I described above – will perhaps find these conflicts more intense than others. Faced with the instinct of *eros*, the Christian consciousness has a difficult role to play. At all costs it must make use of this instinct, but it may not submit passively. Faced with eros, appearing in a subtle proportion which will vary depending on whether the option is theocentric or christocentric – a Christian can adopt three different attitudes. He can attempt to bring it under control, and in a cruel game 'of love and death' try to turn it back on itself, to make it an instrument of self-accusation, giving place eventually to sublimation: this is the example shown us by St Augustine after his conversion, then by Luther, and nearer to our times by Christians like Mauriac and Graham Greene. He can also attempt to divert it, above all in the form of filial submission to God the Father: in that case we shall see *eros* turn into 'devout love' (in a secular setting into courtly love): we have an admirable example of this in St Francois de Sales and by the faithful readers of *Introduction to a Devout Life* from the seventeenth century to our day. Finally, the Christian soul can try – this time under the direct influence of christocentricity, to achieve, in a direct and spontaneous way, a radical 'sublimation' of love which will then produce agape, i.e.

diffusive love, love without frontiers, and ultimately without an object: this is the psychological evolution that we shall find realized in St Paul, the 'passionate' man who became the universal apostle; in St Francis of Assisi, who became, if we can put it that way, 'the universal lover'; in Père de Foucauld, who became 'the universal brother' (note here the specific slant of the term 'brotherhood').

Confronted with the death instinct (*thanatos*), which Freud describes as an impulse that tends to destroy what is by blocking off what should be – Christian awareness reacts differently, depending on whether theocentricity or christocentricity is the predominant influence. Under the influence of theocentricity, some note the imperfections of the creature as over against his creator; however, recognizing the inescapable character of these imperfections, they reconcile themselves to them. They are the 'resigned ones' who accept 'the will of God', resigned to evil, to suffering, to misery: they are the occasion for talk of a 'Christian optimism'. Others (more under the influence of christocentricity) will rail against the imperfections of creation (which comes from God) and indefatigably seek to correct it (in the name of Christ). They protest, they challenge, they fight: they struggle desperately 'against evil', calling in question the creation of the Father, in the name of the Son. They are the occasion for talk of a 'Christian pessimism'. They carry on untiringly this fight against everything that is 'evil', this fight against everything that their death instinct exposes for their condemnation; and if they feel that the fight is unequal, and that they can only fail in their task, they turn their faces to the cross of Christ.

Finally, faced with the instinct of reality, which Freud describes as an impulse, working on the level of the id, that causes the consciousness to record its clashes with foreign objects and to try as far as possible to accommodate to them – the Christian will also have variable reactions depending on whether the option is theocentric or christocentric. Sometimes – and this will be more in the context of a theocentric attitude – he will feel inclined to bow before the facts, seeing them as expressions of the superior will. In that case he will adopt an attitude of submission and prefer to modify his desires rather than the world order (as Descartes would put it): and here we would speak of 'Christian realism'. At other times, faced with the cruel realities of life, the Christian will try to reject them, to remove them, to put them beyond the sphere of apperception. (With Baudelaire, he will say 'What is all this that is not eternal?'). And he will do his best to substitute dream visions (analogous to the dream visions of English pre-Raphaelitism) for these painful realities. Here we would speak of a 'Christian idealism'. This will clearly inspire some more christocentric interpretations (one might think of the pages which Renan devoted – in his inimitable way – to the one whom he called 'the sweet dreamer of Galilee').

I could extend these analyses further, but this is not the place for them. However, it is important that we should remember certain lessons. The tension between theocentricity and christocentricity produces manifest psychological effects. The principal tension arises from the permanent confrontation – in the Christian sub-consciousness – between the image of God the Father who is venerated, and from whom one must keep a respectful distance; and that of the brother Christ, whom people seek to imitate and approach, but with whom they despair of identifying themselves. The Christian is strongly attracted by each of these two poles; he is even torn apart. He does not know whether he should move away from his term of reference or go towards it: withdraw from the omnipotent or approach the well-beloved. He is on the rack, torn apart.

In fact every Christian will try to make his 'own' Christianity; he will allow this or that tendency to develop, with the awareness of falling short of fulfilment. That must be said openly. This is the situation which has been bequeathed by the Christian revelation to all those who want to live by it. The bipolarity which we have discovered in the texts, in the institutions, and then in the traditions is also maintained in feelings, even to the most intimate depths of awareness. It is now important to study the effects of this in a sphere which is extremely interesting to social psychology: that of reactions to moral and spiritual authority. (I shall speak of political authority later on.)

(c) Two typical reactions to moral authority

Theocentricity and christocentricity determine two attitudes to moral authority. Before defining them, I must recall that social psychology can teach us about different forms of authority. Roughly speaking, there are two types of authority, that of the father and that of the hero.[8] The authority of the father which arises from the family nucleus takes the form of a protective tutelage to which trust and respect are accorded: its 'model' is diffused in those societies which, generally speaking, have preserved a pattern of family life. By contrast, the authority of the hero arises in civil society; this is the authority acquired by someone who has performed an exploit which is useful to the group and who commands the admiration of all; it takes the form of an appeal to adventure and it calls for trust in the capacity of the guide and in the competence that he has shown. The authority of the father is founded on nature; that of the hero is founded on the facts. The former is stable and has the attraction of conservatism. The latter is mobile; periodically it has the need to justify itself; it leads to risky adventures. The authority of the father brings security; that of the hero never ceases to be disturbing, but it is stimulating. Depending on circumstances, these two types of authority can be found in all societies: political, economic and cultural. They also recur in religious societies.

These two types of authority present themselves at the heart of Christianity and in Catholicism in particular, and as one would imagine, the father authority is dominant where theocentricity is prevalent, whereas the hero authority is prevalent in conjunction with christocentricity. And of course the two models compete with each other. According to the theocentric perspective, oriented on the worship of God the Father, obviously the father authority is established and affirmed. This type of authority (i.e. moral authority) appears quite clearly in the very text of the universal prayer of Christians, the 'Our Father'. The authority of God is explicitly designated as that of a Father. This Father is 'in heaven', but he retains the characteristics of an earthly father: he is good and is a protector. People want his glory since, as in every family, it redounds on his children. They want his beneficent power to develop. 'Your kingdom come, your will be done.' By the very fact that it is a father's will, his will cannot but be good (which will not necessarily be the case with the authority of the hero). People ask him, like a good father, for daily bread, for inner peace through forgiveness, and for protection against evil. Now if we consider the symbolism by which this idea of the Father God is evoked, we see that it is a direct transcription from the traditional image of the *paterfamilias*. The image of a respectable old man (think of the frescoes on the ceiling of the Sistine chapel) is presented for the worship of the faithful. The attributes of paternal respectability are conferred on him: dignity, advanced age, calm and tranquil power, an entourage of servants, a noble abode (on a mountain, in particular), the possession of a certain power over the elements. The major features of the *paterfamilias* can be found in these often naive images. Literature confirms the tendencies of the imagery. Readers will know the famous verse by Lamartine, which address the Father God in these terms:

> O Father whom my father worships,
> Whom we name only on our knees,

Whose terrible and sweet name
Made my mother's face frown.

All the literature of the great centuries of the West describes God in this way in heightened terms, as head of the family. The authority which emerges from the Father God in all these texts is that of the *paterfamilias*: the same rights and the same duties – if one may put it that way – are conferred on him.

If, by contrast, the christocentric perspective is adopted, the very type of moral and religious authority changes completely. The model adopted is then that of the hero, the hero who has gone through every cataclysm (like Hercules among the Greeks), or who has taken up the challenges of mediocrity and abandonment (like Hermes or Apollo). This image of the hero can be found in all the cultural traditions, from Gilgamesh to Aeneas and from Joshua to Jonah. Now it is to some degree under the guise of the hero that the first Christians came to imagine Christ. In fact his mission seemed like that of the conquering hero: certainly he was an unfortunate hero (and attractive because of that), but he finally triumphed over adverse forces. He was given a mission; he encountered the worst obstacles, but finally he triumphed over them. He overcame the angry waves, he conquered sickness, he faced human perversity, and finally, as a supreme triumph, he conquered death! The Christ is the greatest hero of all time. That is how he has been seen since the beginning of Christian awareness. That is why he aroused boundless admiration, and his authority was founded on this admiration. He was hailed with formulas addressed to the triumphant hero: 'Sun of justice', 'Light from the East'. He was depicted in the guise of a fighter and then of a conqueror (see the Christ of the last judgment in the Sistine chapel). He was hailed by religious literature as the perfect man, the 'glorification of humanity', and by sculpture and architecture as the Pantocrator, or as the 'le Beau Dieu' (of Amiens); he is the triumphant figure on the tympanum of cathedrals. And people awaited his return like that of the conqueror returning from his adventures: Maranatha! The authority which emerges from this model is that which emanates from the hero. He has challenged the forces of evil and come out on top: one can have trust in him. One must follow him as one follows a supreme guide. He enjoys a charismatic authority. However, his heroic mission changes meaning according to the taste of the time. When the theme of salvation is in vogue, he is acclaimed as a saviour; when fashion is for order, he is hailed as the Christ king; when it is for liberty, he is hailed more as the liberator. According to the myths in vogue in a particular period, the sense of the mission of the Christ hero changes. At a later date we shall study the evolution of these myths – from the viewpoint of social psychology – and in doing so we shall see the evolution of the images which people made of Christ (see the later chapters, which are devoted to the triumph of christocentricity). The type of authority which I am describing determines a particular type of submission. Someone who follows Christ as hero will not follow him with deference but with enthusiasm and fervour; he will follow Christ as one follows a hero: he will put his thoughts in tune with Christ's thoughts, bend his will to Christ's will, kindle his love in the heat of Christ's love. It is a matter of being won over by psychological fascination, of being 'captivated': as people will say, the Christ has me wholly in his grasp.

These two types of authority come to be juxtaposed in Christian consciousness, and – as I shall also show – at certain periods we shall see real conflicts between the two social logics which emerge from these two conceptions of authority. The partisans of moral order hurl themselves on the partisans of perpetual progress, as we shall see. For the moment, we can conclude that there is room in Christian consciousness for two sensibilities: a sensibility inspired by theocentricity, which is characterized by the sense of order, of confidence in a Father God, the omnipotent protector, and of filial submission; and a sensibility inspired by christocentricity which is characterized by a certain sense of dissatisfaction, of perpetual disquiet and permanent contention. The two tendencies will subsist over the centuries at the heart of the Catholic church, come what may.

3. Two styles of religious practice

Bipolarity, theocentric and christocentric, also determines two styles of religious practice in the church, i.e. two ways of conceiving institutions, two forms of worship (which are perpetually in competition) and two great types of spirituality.

(a) Two conceptions of religious institutions

The adoption of the theocentric perspective on the one hand calls for an administrative and hierarchical conception of the church entirely based on the sense of the authority of the Father. The reference to the model of the father calls for authority as an absolute principle, from which everything comes and on which everything depends. There is a repetition of the Pauline formula 'All power comes from God.' Furthermore, the supreme authority in the Catholic church is designated by the significant name of 'Holy Father'. Both his designation and his installation are surrounded with all the evocative symbolism of the model of fatherhood. Sacralization is achieved by the secrecy of the designation, the fasting and the proclamation, and the decorum surrounding the actions and deeds of the person elected. This symbolism tends to give rise to sentiments of 'filial' attachment on the part of the faithful. On the other hand, this supreme authority calls for legal and moral functions which express the feeling of a real fatherhood exercised towards subordinates: the preservation of the heritage ('You are Peter, and on this rock I will build my church'; 'Keep the deposit of faith'); assurance in the government of a sphere (the theme of infallibility); and the feeling of durability across the centuries (if the Father dies, an heir takes up the succession).

There is another feature which goes with institutions inspired by theocentricity: the sense of hierarchy. The will of the Father (to be precise, of God the Father) must be handed on to his immediate neighbours and then to those who are in contact with them, and so on. The impulse which comes from above has to be handed on by degrees down to the lower levels; in that case authority is exercised in a hierarchical way. However, we must be careful here: that does not mean that this authority will be despotic. On the contrary, it can prove to be very paternal, that is to say, characterized by love and good will. The 'Pope' (equivalent to the term Father) can prove to be a benevolent protector of his faithful, whom he regards as his children. It will be the same for the bishop with his priests, for the priests with their parishioners; and of course for the Father Abbot (Abbas also means Father) with his monks. The chief criticism which some people make is that here, by the nature of things, there is a tendency towards paternalism: the father authority risks regarding his faithful as children, no longer in the filial sense of the term, but in the psychological sense, that is to say, as 'infantile' beings.

According to the christocentric perspective, things take on a different appearance. Here authority loses its sacral character, its mythical 'aura'. It has to have some degree of justification: it, too, has to have passed its test, whether by the verdict of the electorate (who make it clear by means of the size of their vote who has the most credibility, or by the spontaneous choice of public opinion, which elects by acclamation). Transmission of authority by natural heredity (hence willed by God) or moral authority (according to the traditions which are derived from the distant will of God) is replaced by designation through visible and human means, since the inspiration in everything is the visible and human model provided by Jesus of Nazareth. He certainly designated the first authority which he instituted, that of Peter, but he did so according to human modes, as the texts prove. This authority was conferred following a brave testimony of faith and not some divine intervention (there were no tongues of fire). The christocentric conception of authority calls for a designation in human terms. It follows that every institution which is derived from this will also adopt a very human style. It is no longer a matter of transmitting a legitimacy, but of inaugurating a power. There is no more hierarchy (since there is no longer a 'hero' at the source), but a distribution of tasks according to competence and opportunity. The authority of mission is transformed into the authority of service. In the imagery of the hero, anyone given a task justifies his function by his success: if he fails, he loses his claim to keep his post. Actual success forms the basis of legitimacy. Thus the foundations of society are completely changed, and more particularly those of religious society. To put it simply, authority no longer comes from above, but from below. In fact, if success is the foundation of legitimacy, who can be judge of this success, if not the interested parties themselves, among whom the person concerned exercises his role? These are the interests which, in the last resort, make themselves judges of the legitimacy of their leader. The movement which animates societies – and let us recall that here we are talking of religious society – is no longer deployed from the apex to the base, but from the base to the apex. The creative and regulatory impulses come from the base.

These are the very different conceptions of social life and its internal rhythms which originate and develop within the Catholic church from the beginning. From this we can guess at the tensions which will arise, in particular, between the two forms of authority and government. This tension has lasted for two thousand years, and it has given rise to the innumerable compromises in which conciliar decisions and canonical texts abound. In fact no real reconciliation is possible: here two social logics come together and clash. We shall find this clash at every level. It can be seen in the election of the supreme leader, the Pope (by a method to which people have devoted great ingenuity in trying to reconcile the theocentric and christocentric privileges which must both be connected with the person to be elected); it can also be seen in the status accorded to bishops, which has constantly varied over the centuries, oscillating between theocentric conceptions (the power of divine law) and christocentric conceptions (the power of service). The rites which surround these different designations give a good indication of the embarrassment of the organizers: one feels that they constantly oscillate in their concern over representation between the divine origin of the power to be accorded and its human expression: there is constant hesitation between ostentation and simplicity, between a sense of mystery and clarity. Every member of the church experiences this tension in the daily exercise of his mission, whether he is the Pope, a bishop or priest, or the layman with his apostolic mission: is he a man of God or a man for men? And each one tries to live out, as best he can, the consequences of the interplay between these two contradictory logics. There will be a good deal to say about this theme at the appropriate point. Here I shall simply introduce a number of aspects of the problem.

(b) Two sorts of worship

We shall see the development of two sorts of worship, depending on whether the inspiration is theocentricity or christocentricity. They have different characteristics: each has its own style of expression and even its particular inspiration. The theocentric perspective inspires a type of worship ordered around God the Father. Thus this worship aims at giving glory to the divine majesty. It has the utmost magnificence and a taste for the triumphal. 'Nothing is too beautiful to pay homage to the greatness of God', repeated the saintly Curé d'Ars, who bought the most sumptuous ornaments and decorated his little church in the richest fashion possible. In this case, the style of worship borrowed the essentials of its procedures from Jewish worship in the Old Testament (which was integrally theocentric, and for good cause). In particular it took over the sense of the majesty of the temple, this temple which originally had to be unique (since there was only a single God to worship and this God willed to be worshipped in Jerusalem): the future 'synagogues' – a Greek expression, and therefore in itself decadent – were only staging posts, intended to maintain fervour for the worship of the Jerusalem temple. Also from the Jewish tradition, it retained the idea that in this temple the centre had to be formed by a privileged place, the holy of holies, where there was a mysterious manifestation of the presence of God, and into which only the High Priest and his assistants penetrated. The temple is the 'place of the glory of God', and the place where God has deposited his thought in the form of the Torah. The faithful never penetrate this holy place; they stay in the outer courtyard. Now growing Christianity took over this biblical heritage in connection with the cult. The cult had to revolve around a holy place. The lessons come from the biblical tradition, but also from Christ himself, since as far as we know he respected the rules. He spoke 'in the courtyard of the temple': no one tells us that he was ever allowed to go into the holy of holies. That seems to be constitutive of Christianity: from the beginning, it seems to have been taken for granted that it would develop, sociologically speaking, around a holy place. We shall have occasion to see this in detail in the historical investigation which I shall make in the next chapter. Here I shall keep to the sphere of general trends demanded by a certain social logic. I shall therefore take it as established that the idea of the sacred is utterly characteristic of the theocentric tradition. This sense of the sacred was extended to cult objects and to people consecrated to the cult. The leading idea is that in the city there has to be room – and a central place, a place of honour – for a precinct devoted to the deity, and that in this place there is a secret area, particularly holy, which is visited only by consecrated men. As we shall see, we come across this idea again in the construction of buildings for worship across the centuries,[9] in the churches and cathedrals of the Middle Ages, with the arrangement of all the architecture around a 'choir', which only 'men of God' can enter, and which is soon surrounded by a protective grille (or a sumptuous rood): this was the holy of holies of Christian churches.

We may also understand how, according to theocentric logic, cultic rites – as I shall also have occasion to show historically – are also aimed at paying homage to God the Father. The liturgy has to be stamped with respect and deference. The specific approach of the faithful takes on the appearance of processions visiting the 'ancestor', the venerable Father, albeit invisible. Processions are organized, offerings are brought, and hymns are sung to the glorification of the Father. The smoke of incense rises to the skies – the symbolic abode of the Father of all the ages – the wreaths of which carry upwards the supplications of the children of this Father, who remain on this earth. By its very harmonies, the music which accompanies these manifestations of deference and veneration has to maintain in the soul a sense of reverence: use is therefore made of music with order and harmony, i.e., the Gregorian chant, the hymn of adoration *par excellence*. The priests charged with this worship are above all 'men of God'. Their whole lifestyle has to be theocentric. In this respect they are the heirs of the priests of the temple of Jerusalem. All their being has to be directed towards God: their mode of life (celibacy) serves to express the choice which they have made of exclusive service to the divine being, transcending the world: their general appearance reflects their mission; their dress allows them to be identified easily, with a reserved way of speaking and distinct manners.

As for the very essence of worship, according to the theocentric perspective it takes on a characteristic form which is also inspired by the Bible. The major object of this worship is adoration. God the Father has to be hymned for his own glory (by the very effect of enthusiasm, in the etymological sense of the word, which seizes those who find themselves confronted abruptly with an object of inaccessible grandeur): the human soul utters Hosannas, Alleluias and other Hallels of mystical exaltation. God the Father is thanked for his goodness, his largesse, which is manifested in nature or in the life of men. He is also prayed to, supplicated, adjured as dispenser of all good things. Another important feature is that the human soul also sees God the Father as the sovereign judge of consciences: it is then led to ask pardon for imperfections experienced or regretted. All these reactions, of adoration, of thanksgiving, or repentance, and so on, ultimately contribute towards the creation of a triumphalist spirit in the believer. The believer is proud of his faith because he is proud of his God. He knows that he is the faithful follower of the mighty God, of God Most High, the Omnipotent; so he has the feeling of enjoying a privilege: he has the inestimable chance of 'knowing the one true God'. He feels that he is the object of a divine election. Certainly he gives thanks for it to heaven, but he does not forget to manifest it on earth among his kin, those who 'do not know the true God'. His pride in his faith is translated into a certain assurance in social matters, as we shall see; but also in a more material way, in his concern to construct for the worship of the God of Majesty buildings which are as sumptuous as possible. (This is also a feature, in certain regions, of the houses of the ministers of this God.) The whole of religious behaviour is aimed at 'the greater glory of God'.

By contrast, according to the christocentric perspective, things change direction completely. Worship is called on to take quite a different form, as is the behaviour and practice of believers. Here it is a question of setting in motion a quite new form of worship, a worship which can be addressed to what one might call a Brother God. There is no precedent in this sphere as far as we can tell. Greek mythology did not provide any model of this kind (despite what was thought by certain Christian humanists of the fifth and sixth centuries, like Juvencus, Paulinus of Nola, Ausonius and some others). It was important to open up new ways. First of all, people looked for appropriate places of worship. Alongside meetings in the temple there were meetings in private places, without any particular cultic aim (a little later, the need for security forced a 'descent' into the catacombs). And there people met, not to celebrate the glory of God, but to commemorate the 'passage' of Christ among men. To do this, prescribed actions were repeated, like the breaking of bread ('Do this in remembrance of me'). Here there were no sumptuous ornaments, but working clothes. As I shall show at length in the next chapter, at these meetings people found themselves among Christians, in simplicity and brotherhood. According to the logic of christocentric worship, meeting had to be above all a sharing: a sharing of the word (the reading of texts about the ministry of Jesus or the letters of the apostles); sharing of goods (by mutual offerings); sharing of sentiments by spontaneous songs, stripped of all aesthetic elegance. Here there were no recognized clergy, 'clerics', 'men of God', charged with a sacred ministry. The community organized itself in accordance with the way in which the spirit moved it: only those were prominent who could pride themselves on having 'known the Lord . . .' or, in default of that, on having known someone who had known him, and so on. In this perspective the notion of priestly caste inherited from the Old Testament (cf. the Levites) gave way to the notion of a shared priesthood: 'You are a royal priesthood, a holy nation' (St Peter).

The centre of gravity of religious consciousness is displaced. Faith is directed towards Christ. It is the Christ whom people set out to worship as the expression of supreme perfection. It is the Christ who is venerated, by virtue of the infinite merits which he has acquired through his sacrifice on the cross. It is the Christ to whom people pray by virtue of the power to intercede with the Father which he has earned. A cult of *doulia* is organized, which tends – ultimately – to change into a cult of *latreia*. However, I am not yet introducing facts; I am merely indicating trends. The germ of them is to be found in the initial option, and they develop according to their own intrinsic logic.

Simply because it was addressed to a person known under his human aspect, worship of Christ took on a deliberately anthropomorphic form. Real worship was offered to the Love of Christ, to the redemptive mission of Christ, to the mysteries surrounding his death and resurrection, and then his ascension into heaven. It was then necessary to sacralize his thoughts and his actions, to make them into 'sacraments', agents of the future sanctification of the disciples, and it was there above all that innovations were needed. The notion of 'sacrament', that is to say, the sanctifying action obtained by recourse to tangible signs (and no longer to simple adjurations addressed towards heaven), was totally unknown to the Graeco-Latin world and even, it seems, to the Jewish world. It had to be accepted that water could become an agent of sanctification, and even of eternal salvation, on condition that it was administered in accordance with the thoughts of Christ; that bread and wine could become the direct intermediaries of a 'communion with the deity' if they were consumed in accordance with the rites envisaged by Christ, and so on. There was even a deliberate shift in respect of the cosmos: sanctification, which up till then consisted in escaping from the world of the senses, could henceforth be obtained through it, provided that certain conditions were observed. The world of the senses was rehabilitated in a strange way, at least in certain of its aspects: the new mystique of the incarnation was developed. Another new fact which also came into play in the development of the new form of worship was that one could (and indeed had to) talk to the spiritual Christ in all confidence; it followed from that that one could speak to God as one spoke to Christ, that is to say, with confidence. The tremblings of Job, the stammerings of Jeremiah, are no longer in place; the soul is invited to enter into 'dialogue' with the Christ, and by doing this it believes that it can come into contact with God himself. However, the quality of faith, or, if one prefers a different term, the style of its expression, began to change. The affirmation of the faith lost its triumphal character; by contrast it became intimate and discreet. In fact the God of Jesus Christ is a 'gentle and humble God'. The image which the first Christians used to foster their religious fervour would be that of the child of the cradle at Bethlehem or of the crucified man on Golgotha. The psychological attitude which derives from this change of reference gives place to the birth of a completely new type of faith. This faith is secret, intimate, unquiet, searching; it is the faith of the Christmas shepherds, the fishermen of Galilee, the sick people of Judaea.[10] As a result of these changes of imagery, or better of model, in worship the lowly figures increasingly gain the upper hand over the glorious ones. It is pointed out that the true glory to be attributed to God is to be sought more on the side of simplicity, of modesty; and, moving on a little further, on the side of failure. Some people begin to say that the glory of God shines forth in the self-denial of his faithful, in their apparent failure 'in the eyes of the world', and so on. These themes are not developed explicitly, but they flourish among the more christocentric writers, for example even with St Paul. All this means that intimacy and quiet is cultivated more than triumphant celebration.

However, although it is relatively easy to make an analysis of these two 'logics', the one derived from theocentricity, which leads to triumphalism, and the other derived from christocentricity, which leads to intimacy, it is much less easy to live them out simultaneously. Yet that is what was demanded of the Christians of the first generations. They could not renounce either one or the other, at least to begin with, nor did they want to. Hence the tensions that can be felt, especially in the way in which worship came to be organized. We have the impression that two forms of worship come face to face, or at least are juxtaposed. Christian worship is constantly 'balanced' between two tendencies: on the one hand to show the grandeur and the majesty of God, and on the other to show his lowliness and humility. The Christian liturgy of the first centuries – and this will go on for several centuries – will be triumphal or intimate depending on whether it is inspired by one source or the other: it will let loose great organs, or confine itself to the murmur of a silent prayer. The tension will be perpetual, with periods of alternation of which I shall take account later on, when one of the tendencies gets the better of the other. The choice of places of worship bears the mark of this tension. Sometimes they take on a majestic form, the better to hymn the glory of God; sometimes they are humble and modest, the better to represent his lowliness. Sometimes the tension makes itself felt within one and the same temple: an intimate corner is preserved within a church of grandiose style and adornment, or the faithful are invited to meditation and to humble and silent prayer. In the course of time, believers certainly get used to this tension, but the impartial observer, whether or not he or she is a believer, cannot but note it and even see it as a contradiction. A believing Jew or Moslem, a Buddhist or a Shintoist will be disconcerted by these contradictions and will see in them a kind of inability to get out of a mysterious dilemma. The tension will even make itself felt within the symbolic figures of worship and the objects used there. Thus in Byzantine churches we find the crucified Christ adorned with signs of triumph: royal crown, sumptuous robe richly embroidered, and so on. The contradiction is flagrant: an infamous gibbet is treated as a throne of glory. There is another instance in the West: the eucharistic bread, the sign of intimate love and memorial of an ultimate sacrifice, is regarded as an object of glorification in the triumphal procession of monstrances on Maundy Thursday, or at Corpus Christi (note the theocentric French name, Fêtes-Dieu). Around this humble bread of sacrifice the gold gleams and the jewels shine. The cups of sacrifice become sumptuous pieces of jewellery. In this way one could cite numerous examples of the ambiguity which surrounds the essential expressions of worship and have done so since Christian antiquity.

A specialist study could be made in this connection of the centre piece of Christian worship, the altar where the mass is celebrated, and later on I shall have occasion to make a few comments. For social psychology, from a purely technical point of view, this is a privileged object for observation. We have to begin from the recognition that this is the centre of gravity of all worship, and goes right back into antiquity. Every form of worship presupposes an altar-stone on which the High Priest officiates: that is true from the times of Noah, Melchizedek and Elisha, down to cathedrals and modern basilicas (not forgetting the 'non-confessional' altar of the 'meditation room' of the United Nations). Every cult needs an altar stone (one could easily show the deliberate significance of this 'stone furniture', but I must refer the reader to the works of Jung in that connection[11]). Now this stone altar is, first, an instrument serving to glorify God. To this end it is retained in Christian churches, in that they are heirs of the theocentric cult of the Old Testament. However, other events, which took place at the beginning of the Christian church, introduce a new meaning into the use of the altar, which, come what may, people endeavour to bring into later practice. It has been said that the sacrifice of the new covenant is the sacrifice of Christ, and that this sacrifice of Christ finds its memorial in the consecration of the bread and wine of the eucharist. But where is this eucharist to be celebrated in places of worship? Is it necessary to reserve the traditional altar for theocentric celebrations of a triumphal kind, and to celebrate the eucharist on the fringe, in a different and more modest part of the church? It is quite clear that there was hesitation in the first cultic celebrations. The period in the catacombs of Rome favoured compromise. At that time the eucharistic sacrifice was celebrated on the tombs of the martyrs (as a tribute to their heroism) and no longer on an ordinary table (or some *trapezon*). After the peace of Constantine, something of this practice was maintained. Someone had the idea of putting bones of martyrs under the altar stone: in this way a compromise was found. The glory of God was celebrated on the altar stone, and at the same time there was a celebration of the sacrifice of Christ on the relics of his martyrs. Theocentricity and christocentricity were in juxtaposition. But the compromise remained fragile, and the intentional (and functional) significance of the altar always remains ambiguous in Christian tradition: is it the place of the glory of God or a table of sacrifice? The two ideas are in competition.[12] The model oscillates from the baldaquin altar of St Peter's in Rome to the simple wooden table of a suburban chapel. Furthermore, at present, with a strange incongruity, the two models in the churches continue to be in competition: two altars (one to the glory of God and one in memory of the sacrifice of Christ) are often juxtaposed in the choir. One could not think of a better way of translating the perplexity of Christian consciousness over the matter of worship.

In the same way, two types of liturgy eventually come into confrontation, representing two religious motivations in Christianity. One can constantly sense the juxtaposition of a liturgy of the glory of God with a liturgy of the lowliness of Christ. The two social logics are in competition. The liturgy of the glory of God, which seeks to be the heir to the Old Testament, is aimed at giving ceremonies the maximum of splendour: the priestly vestments are the most sumptuous possible; gold and marble shine, great organs ring out. Sometimes the greatest geniuses of the time are called on for their contribution, Bach with his *B Minor Mass* and Beethoven with the *Missa Solemnis*, and so on. And while the harmonies resound and the decorations gleam, a celebrant reads the texts and repeats the words which report how the incarnate God, the Christ, was 'made obedient to death, even the death of the cross', and goes on to the remembrance of the humble eucharistic meal eaten around a table in communion with the redemptive sacrifice. The juxtaposition of these two types of liturgy and the competition provided by two obviously divergent social logics represent the basic ambiguity of Christian worship (when it does not pose problems for unbelievers, who complain of duplicity and hypocrisy). Without doubt the logics are in subtle competition, and one cannot see *a priori* how this struggle can be resolved.

Finally, I should point out that this tension is experienced more deeply still by those charged with perpetuating the church on a human level, i.e. the bishops and priests. There, too, two models are in confrontation. According to the model inherited from the Old Testament, with a theocentric orientation, the priest is the man of God, charged with maintaining his worship on earth, inviting men to hymn his splendour and his glory. He is the incarnation of the priesthood 'according to the order of Melchizedek', a priesthood perpetuated by the priests of the temple of Jerusalem, a priesthood also practised – in quite a different way, but with identical intentions – by the priests of the great Graeco-Latin religions (priests of Cybele, priests of Apollo, flamens of Jupiter, for example). This is the priest as he is usually thought of by public opinion in our Western societies: the man of God, guarantor of the chief covenants and witness of the great actions of life. However, the christocentric conception invests the same person with quite a different mission: according to a widespread formula, he is to be 'another Christ'. In his way he is to prolong the priesthood of Christ, and that represents the humiliation of God, his lowliness, his sacrifice. From this point of view, then, the Christian priest must make himself the agent of the redemptive sacrifice, take on 'the sin of the world', and in his own way live out the passion of Christ. We can imagine the terrible tension which he will experience in himself. Must he be the man to the glory of God, and therefore adopt a respectability and a dignity which will impress on everyone the respect due to his mission, or must he be the man of immolation, humiliated and sacrificed like his master? Both types of priesthood are possible.[13] What is difficult is to live them out simultaneously. This division is sociologically impossible. Each Catholic priest must try as best he can – and will manage with more or less success – to embody both these types of priesthood in himself, the biblical priesthood and the priesthood of the gospel. Bishops come up against the same difficulty in perhaps an even more pointed way: historically they are the heirs of the high priests of the temple of Jerusalem (and also, sociologically speaking, heirs in the Latin church at least of the imperial prefects, 'defenders of the city', like St Loup and St Germain, and like St Augustine); but at the same time they are the successors of the apostles, poor disciples of a sacrificed and humiliated Christ 'led to death like a lamb to the slaughter'. Now they are called to live out these two models at the same time, and history shows that their task will not be easy. They are confronted with a radical practical contradiction, and it is hard to see how they can resolve it. It is impossible for them to find a compromise. All that remains for them is to take a resolute decision for one or the other of these two logics, and to do that either as a result of their personal sensitivity or as a result of circumstances. In fact history shows that they have practised alternation: depending on the period, bishops act as high priests, defenders of the city, or as successors of the apostles of Christ, who died for men, presenting themselves as candidates for martyrdom.

In this way one could multiply *ad infinitum* analyses of the tensions inherent in these cultic practices. We do not have to pass judgment here. It is enough to take note of them as the facts which go to make up the inner life of Catholicism. This is the assertion that the sociologist can make. But the expression of these tensions does not stop here. They can be felt right down to the deepest areas of inner life. So I must also talk about spirituality.

(c) Two currents of spirituality

There are many different schools of spirituality in the Catholic church, but the alert observer will easily perceive that in the last resort their differences depend on the initial option chosen for the inner life of the church: theocentricity or christocentricity. In effect, spirituality is shared by two basic currents: one tends to direct souls towards the contemplation of the transcendent God; the other seeks to lead them more towards the 'imitation of Jesus Christ' and spiritual activity in human society. Now the church has never wanted to dissociate these two currents. It invites its faithful to live out these two orientations, to conform to the demands of these two logics. Thus contemplatives are asked to have a concern for action and active Christians to have a constant leaning towards contemplation. This is peculiar to Christianity and in particular to Catholicism; it does not recur, at least with the same degree of tension, in any other religion. It is therefore important to make a rather closer analysis of these two vectors of spiritual life.

According to the theocentric interpretation, the Christian must devote his energies to the quest for contemplation of the transcendent God: outside the contemplation of God, nothing counts. The attitude *par excellence* will be the silent contemplation of the majesty of the thrice-holy God. It is expressed in the great contemplative tradition inherited from Mount Carmel and the patriarch Elijah; then lived out on the 'holy mountain'; perpetuated by the Essenes; maintained, as I have shown, by the desert fathers; and taken up subsequently by all lovers of solitude and silent contemplation: disciples of St Bruno in the desert of the Chartreuse; disciples of St Teresa of Avila and St John of the Cross on the heights of Castille and in all the Carmels of the world; disciples of St Benedict on the heights of Monte Cassino and then in numerous places of silence and peace. All these spiritual groups have a theocentric inspiration; they devote themselves entirely to the contemplation of God. Furthermore, they give themselves over – albeit in different degrees – to penitence. Their reaction is understandable. These are the ones who are 'thirsty for God'; they note that if they do not get on as far as they would like towards the perfect encounter with God, it is because an obstacle has been put in their way; this obstacle is the body and its carnal desires. So why should they not seek from now on to reduce the dominion of this body, to keep it subservient, to tame it and become its master? In the end, some of those with excessive desire for God will even seek to destroy themselves; this will be the case with the Stylites of the Egyptian desert in the first century, then later with certain Catharists, and in a way with the Jansenists. Finally, let us note that if the apostolate is not completely lacking (how could contemplatives, madly in love with God, not want to see all humanity seized with this thirst for contemplation?), at least it does not take the form of direct activity. It is a matter more of witness: the one who prays, by his private and public prayer, gives a living testimony to the divine transcendence. He pleads for God. In that case he wagers on the receptivity of his brother men to the message that he thus addresses to them, expecting them to give an apostolic form to his witness. God does not demonstrate himself; he shows himself. Hence it comes about that contemplation is regarded, and even proclaimed, as 'the soul of all the apostolate' (Dom Chautard).

By contrast, the christocentric inspiration leads to quite a different conception of the spiritual life. Here, the principle of the religious life is participation in the saving action of Christ the redeemer. Thus attention is directed much more towards men than towards God, towards the wretchedness of men rather than towards the glory of God. Henceforth the essential of religious life consists first in seeking contact with men, to gain their sympathy, and once this sympathy has been gained, in leading them towards Christ the saviour and towards God. The road to be travelled is certainly long, but the true apostle is indefatigable. Besides, again following the logic of christocentricity, the spiritual life can also consist in seeking to live out directly the 'states' of Christ (that is, his states of mind) in human society. We shall see at length how the French school of spirituality develops this theme in the seventeenth century. However, well before this period, others had also thought to make the Christian life an 'imitation of the life of Christ'. This is the case with St Francis of Assisi and his disciples. Later, putting the accent above all on action, St Ignatius of Loyola and his disciples of the Society of Jesus seek to be 'apostles of Christ' in every sphere, trying to pursue the work of preaching and transformation that he undertook in Galilee. However, again I am only indicating the general trends which must inevitably develop in the spiritual order from the choice of the christocentric interpretation. I shall establish the facts in due course.

Finally, let me add that in the realm of the spiritual life there is a constant tension even within the Christian soul. For if the different schools of spirituality represent the different orientations that the Catholic church can offer to its faithful, the apparent specialization of the schools is quite relative; in fact every Christian is called to be both contemplative, like Elijah or St Bruno, and active, like St Paul and St Ignatius Loyola. He will feel himself divided, torn, stretched between these two appeals. Christ himself did not make a mystery of the paradox to which he would invite his disciples: 'Be in the world as though you were not in it'; that is to prescribe, *a priori*, a tension such as one will not apparently find in any other religion. The twofold spiritual attitude which it implies ('Be men of God', but also, 'be men . . . for men') is visibly inherent in Christianity, and is so by the very will of its founder. Perhaps there is a paradox there, and some might call it illogicality. At all events, it is a fact inscribed in history: Christianity carries within itself this 'congenital' contradiction. We simply have to take note of it.

4. Two types of political and social action

The bipolarity peculiar to Christianity, its theocentricity and its christocentricity, also determines two conceptions of social life, and the same nagging tensions can be rediscovered here. First, let us recall that Christianity felt authorized to venture into the political and social realms, although it was essentially a religious movement. It is in fact of the nature of a spiritual movement, whatever it may be (for example, it happens with Stoicism or with Islam) to want to project into the temporal realm the best of what it feels it possesses in the spiritual realm. As everyone knows, there are no limits to the diffusion of the good. Christianity was able to maintain this appeal. Not many decades after its foundation, people wanted it to teach the best way of governing the state or improving society. That is only normal. But difficulties arose for Christianity when it realized that the spiritual bipolarity on which it rests could only lead to divergent practices.

As I have already pointed out, the theocentric inspiration, where faith is ordered entirely round the cult of God the Father, makes it defend a very 'paternal' (not to say 'paternalist') conception of authority. From this point of view, the Christian is led to support all the types of authority which have a 'paternal' style, i.e. which are based on respect for the leader, obedience to his will and reference to the notion of order. So this kind of Christianity results in the favouring of governments with a monarchical structure, or which propose an institutional presidency. Some historical successes may be attributed to the effect of this kind of reaction. To quote some at random: the Byzantine empire in its best periods; or the Holy Roman Empire, which survived down to the Austro-Hungarian empire at the beginning of the twentieth century, the last empire based on Catholic principles. Generally speaking, this type of government would correspond to what J. Maritain termed a 'sacral regime' (in his *L'Humanisme intégral*). At all events, theocentric inspiration led people in all circumstances to defend the restoration of order, the peace which springs from this order, and harmony among citizens.

It is the same in the social sphere. Theocentricity leads to the defence of social systems which are modelled on patterns of the image of the father. In this case, the Christian pays respect to authority ('All authority comes from God', a thesis confirmed by St Thomas). This respect is paid successively to the feudal lord, because he has received the investiture marked with a sacred sign (the dubbing of knighthood or its derivations): it is given to the owner of a business (the word 'patron' comes directly from the word *pater*). This appears very plainly in the social régime of the Middle Ages, the régime of the corporations: all production is achieved and directed in accordance with a system of hierarchical responsibility (grand master, master, craftsman, apprentice), and the relations between the agents of production are marked by respect and submission. The predominant sentiment which governs all social relations is that of respect, and the predominant virtue which gives its quality to men and makes them estimable in relation to others is nobility: nobility of rank but also nobility of heart, nobility of sentiment.

By contrast, christocentric inspiration dictates virtually opposed attitudes in connection with political and social problems. I have already indicated some of its features. Here the Christian is inspired by his sympathy for the brother Christ. The charter to which he refers is no longer the crude Decalogue proclaimed on Sinai but rather the Beatitudes pronounced under the sweet sky of Galilee. 'Blessed are the poor in spirit', 'Blessed are the peacemakers', 'Blessed are those who suffer persecution for justice.' In this case the political and social régime of which the Christian dreams will be a régime based on individual liberty and no longer on order; on equality and no longer on competition; on brotherhood and no longer on submission. In other words, democracy blossoms in his thoughts. He no longer dreams of a holy empire founded on sacrality and order, but of a republic founded on human dignity and brotherhood.

In the social sphere this option gives place to similar developments. The dream of a universal brotherhood begins to haunt men's spirits and above all their hearts. The ideal society will be egalitarian: 'There will no longer be either slave or free man.' Relations sustained by force, wherever they manifest themselves, must disappear. There is no more 'dialectic of master and slave' (Hegel), since men are called to a single vocation, that of 'service', some in the position of leaders and some in the position of executants; each one brings his skill and dedication to the realization of the common task. This is the ideal which the christocentric inspiration maintains in the heart of the 'militant', in politics or in society. The ideal goes on to produce a kind of permanent contestation of the established order (itself the heir of theocentric conceptions: we can imagine the internal conflict which will tear apart the militant Catholic from now on). But we do not have to develop these perspectives here.

What emerges from these brief analyses is that the two political and social tendencies are radically different. Tension within Catholicism will remain very strong in this area, by reason of the specific character of the options which have to be chosen. If the Catholic is inspired by the theocentric tendency he will call himself above all a friend of order and peace: he will be led to be conservative. If, on the other hand, he is inspired by the christocentric pole of his faith, he will act in perpetual confrontation with institutions, and disrupt them (he may even be a revolutionary). These two tendencies are inscribed on the very heart of Christianity. One may read and reread the gospels in vain, but it is impossible to eliminate this intrinsic contradiction. As he reads, the believer may feel himself led to adopt the attitude of the conservative, who calls himself the friend of order and authority ('Render to Caesar that which is Caesar's'; the centurion's commendation of obedience, and the later word of St Paul, 'Slaves, obey your masters, as Christ'). Equally, he may feel himself led to the revolutionary attitude, always tending to demand more justice, equality and brotherhood. Both lessons are in the texts; they stand alongside each other without ever really coming together. The fact is undeniable.

5. Conclusion: two futures

I could prolong these analyses even further. They would only confirm us in this perspective. Christianity is a religion which rests irreducibly on a bipolarity: faith in a transcendent God which inspires thoughts of order, harmony and power; and faith in Christ, God incarnate, which inspires thoughts of liberation, universal brotherhood and sacrifice. These two tendencies are immanent to Christianity: they cannot be challenged. That explains why Christianity has always nursed within it two hopes, and has always given birth to two futures.

By the faith in the transcendent God which it has inherited, it has attained to the mastery of contemplation, wisdom, order and harmony. It is concerned for the 'will of God to be done on earth, as in heaven' (that is to say in an absolute way). It dreams of establishing the city of God on earth, as St Augustine would say. In being the vehicle of this faith in God, it will always and everywhere be a force for order and peace (at least if it remains faithful to its mission).

However, its faith in Christ, in God the brother of men, will at the same time give it another dimension. In that case, it will be led to exercise a reforming influence, not to say a revolutionary one. It will constantly put in question established situations; stimulate spiritual, social and even aesthetic initiatives.

Christianity carries these two forces within itself, and that is congenital. It has to accept them to make its members true followers. It is easy to see that in the course of history it could not remain in this uncomfortable position and constantly accord the same attention to both forces: there would be times when equilibrium was disturbed. In the course of events, one of the two forces would inevitably get the better of the other. In fact, the whole history of Catholicism embodies the alternation of these two forces. So at this point it will be useful to make a rapid survey of the stages of this interplay. Only after this retrospect shall we be in a position to understand the actual situation today in the Catholic church.

III

The Theocentric Tradition
(Fourth to Seventeenth Centuries)

It can be foreseen that, depending on the period, one or other of the two poles of Christianity, theocentricity or christocentricity, will become predominant. In fact a historical survey of the last twenty centuries shows that we can discover three successive periods. In a first period – that of primitive Christianity (first to fourth centuries), which I analysed in Chapter I – there was simply an awareness of the situation which had been brought about in Christianity, in its deepest structures: namely, that it was based on a dual polarity. This was no more than a growing awareness, which could not but cause hesitations and expectancy (I shall go on to discuss once again, briefly, this state of hesitation). We shall then discover that subsequently a second period takes shape, in which the tendency towards theocentricity begins to affirm itself and even become dominant: this period begins with what is conventionally called the 'peace of Constantine', in the fourth century, and extends right across the Middle Ages, surviving down to the seventeenth century. Finally, after a period of new hesitation, or more precisely, of oscillation (which will not last more than half a century), this time we see christocentricity affirming itself in a growing way, above all towards the end of the seventeenth century. It affirms itself to such a degree – to the detriment of theocentricity – that after the eighteenth and nineteenth centuries it ends up by occupying almost the whole sphere of the social awareness of Catholicism in the twentieth century. This affirmation will even be so strong, towards the middle of the twentieth century, that it tends to eliminate all theocentricity among certain Christians: we end up with a 'Christianity without God'. These are different stages which it is useful to retrace if we are to have a good understanding of the contemporary situation of Catholicism.

1. Jewish Christian origins: theocentricity confirmed

First, we must return to the situation prevailing in the first centuries. I have recalled the doctrinal data relating to this period. We must now return to them to study their consequences for social psychology. In terms of social psychology, the starting point for Christianity is evidently to be sought in the social matrix in which it was formed, i.e. the Jewish faith.

(a) In theology

Christianity was born in the Jewish world. Its founder, Jesus, was himself a Jew and to begin with, at any rate, shared the convictions of his people. That is why we find the same acute sense of divine transcendence among the first Christians. To put it without any paradox, Christ himself is theocentric (and not christocentric): all his thoughts and actions are directed to the glory of God, the worship of the 'Father which is in heaven'. 'No one knows the Son – no one knows who is the Son – except the Father' (Matt. 11.27). 'No one can come to me unless the Father who has sent me draws him' (John 6.44). The spirit of God must come after him, at Pentecost, and not his own. The Christ never presents himself as coming to inaugurate a new religion of which he will be the centre, and where the worship of God will be attenuated for his benefit. His mission consists in leading men towards God (and not just towards himself, as a historical figure). St Clement of Alexandria sums it up very well: 'What is the meaning of this instrument, the Logos of God, the Lord, and his new song? To open the eyes of the blind and the ears of the deaf, to lead the crippled and those deprived of their rights, to show God to insensitive men, to stop corruption, conquer death and reconcile disobedient sons with the Father' (*Protreptikon* I, 6,1). What the first Christians saw in Christ was not the principle of a new religion; it was rather the occasion willed by God for renewing traditional religious life.[1] Furthermore, in this way they summed up the essentials of the messianic hope sustained by Judaism. Through the coming of Christ they awaited the coming of the Spirit of God. If the Christ was born on this earth; if he had lived and taught there for more than thirty years; if he had suffered martyrdom and death; if he had triumphed over death by a glorious resurrection, this was not so much to lay the foundation for a personal work as to prepare for a much more important work than all these 'episodes': the coming of the Paraclete. What they waited for was ultimately the inbreathing of the Spirit of God which was to renew the face of the earth. The birth of Christ, the

Transfiguration, the Passion, the Resurrection at Easter, constituted the preparatory phases for the final event, Pentecost. At least in the Roman Catholic church, we too readily forget that all the messianic expectation had only one end in view, the coming of the Spirit of God on this earth. That remained the profound conviction of the first Christians, and we must never forget the fact. That was the essential content of the faith of the twelve apostles and their first disciples. To use the terms I have chosen, we might say, without a shadow of doubt, that the first Christians (those of the first twenty years) had a deeply theocentric faith: they were well aware that the adventure which they had experienced and to which they had committed themselves for the future, had only one end, the glory of God. In their eyes, Christ himself, in his person and his mission, was to be subordinated to this mission. Christ had come on earth to prepare for the coming of the Spirit of God and consequently for the kingdom of God, where this spirit would reign. To be precise: there is not a trace of christocentricity in the very earliest church. There the Christ is not yet the object of direct worship. He is the infinitely beloved spiritual master, whose disappearance is lamented ('Men of Galilee, why do you wait like that for the one who has left you?'). He is the one who has taught the ways of God, who prepares for the coming of the Spirit. But it is the Spirit who will soon sanctify all things. And the salvation of the world, the salvation of humanity, will begin at Pentecost (and not at Easter).[2] That was clearly the faith of the very first Christians.

Soon, however, modifications were introduced into this faith. To begin with, they were imperceptible; then little by little, as we shall see, they came to determine a new orientation. The essential problem is to give an exact standing, in the sphere of faith, to the person of Christ. Now new developments took place in this connection, and as far as we can judge, they were above all the work of St Paul. It seems that it was St Paul who came to modify the status accorded to Christ: instead of mediator, according to St Paul, he became the very revelation of God. From then on the major event was no longer the coming of the Spirit but the coming of Christ. Easter gradually 'dethroned' Pentecost. This is a serious matter, so we must look at things more closely.

In these years at the beginning of our era, messianic expectation was intensified. The Essenes expected a king, a priest, an exceptional prophet; some even looked for a speedy return of Elijah. Paul certainly frequented these milieux and shared in their hopes. He too looked for the Messiah with exceptional fervour – that is certain. His zeal in persecuting the first disciples of Jesus of Nazareth proceeded from this fervour; and it was this which led him to attack the one whom he took to be an impostor. Then came the famous episode on the Damascus road (round about AD 35). A voice from on high pointed out his error. 'I am Jesus whom you persecute.' It was a voice from on high which spoke, and Paul knew Christ only through this voice. In that case, to make the point again, his knowledge of Christ was integrally supernatural. For him the Christ was necessarily not a being whom he had known historically, but an essentially mystical being. Because, so far as we are aware, Paul had never known Jesus in a concrete way, he would never have had a problem in imagining him as a divine being. In his eyes it would be appropriate, therefore, to imagine the Christ not only as a mediator between God and man, but also as the very presence of God among men. That is why, in his eyes, there was no problem in Jesus himself becoming an object of worship. He had to be adored as a divine person. In consequence, the coming of Christ was no longer to be considered as an episode leading to a more important event, the coming of the Spirit of God. It was appropriate to consider his coming as an end in itself; in itself it was the revelation of God among men. Here was the Christ who 'came to renew the face of the earth'. With St Paul, if one may put it this way, Easter overshadows Pentecost. Far from being the end, the coming of the Spirit is only the means by which the apostles will receive the necessary strength to announce the real event, the coming of Christ. What counts from now on is to proclaim 'Jesus Christ' (and no longer the coming of the Holy Spirit). Here we have a tangible 'displacement' of the focal point of faith. From now on, we can imagine a worship of Christ which could develop in competition with (or, if one prefers it that way, as a complement to) the worship of God. It is here, at this level, in these fundamental intuitions of Paul's faith, that I would place the very first roots of a future christocentricity. Certainly Paul, as a good Jew of his time ('Are they Jews? So am I') is and remains profoundly theocentric: all his faith is placed in the God of Abraham, Isaac and Jacob (by his contacts with Greek thought he accepts even the faith in the unknown God which is professed by pagans, cf. Romans 1.15–20 and the Areopagus speech in the Acts of the Apostles). However, we must recognize that he introduces a degree of direct worship of Christ into religious awareness, and will make this very much felt in his epistles. He thinks that Christ is due adoration, worship and reverential fear in the same way as God. These theories are still imprecise, even in Paul's thought: it will be necessary to wait for the conciliar definitions of the fourth and fifth centuries for the necessary precisions to be made.

However, we must record in all honesty that this interpretation proposed by St Paul was not always accepted without difficulty. Some of his contemporaries are reluctant about it. For example, it is thought that we can find reluctance about it with St James, the brother of the Lord.[3] The Christian community in Jerusalem certainly proved reluctant, as did the Jewish-Christian communities of Transjordan (after the emigration of 70). Nevertheless, such was the spiritual influence of Paul that his views established themselves: the mystical character of his faith in Christ (let me stress once again he only knew Christ in a uniquely supernatural way, on the Damascus road, and in further visions which 'transported him into the third heaven') soon won over a large part of growing Christianity (his personal influence on St John also seems to be proven).

So the influence of Paul was considerable, and it contributed very effectively to the birth of an authentic cult, a cult of *latreia*, and not just *doulia*, in respect of Christ. Still, it nevertheless remains true that the faith of the first Christians remained on eminently theocentric lines. The texts from the end of the apostolic era show that the faith of believers was directed essentially to the thrice-holy God, the transcendent God. The Book of Revelation is quite significant in this respect. Thus the reactions of the people who figure in this book lead them all to give glory to the eternal and omnipotent God. The good deeds, or more often the misdeeds, which come home to roost with the living, are the effects of the divine sovereign judgment. Certainly, in all this the Christ plays a prominent role. He is the lamb without blemish, which was slain. He is the intercessor in prayer. He is the agent of the chief works of God, breaking the seven seals, etc. However, we must recognize that the Apocalypse, which officially brings the divine revelation to an end, is profoundly marked by theocentricity. Christocentricity only appears there as a stepping stone.

If we now look at the period immediately afterwards, that of the Fathers of the Church (and here I am thinking of the Fathers of the second, third and fourth centuries) we see that here theocentricity largely remains predominent. The essential, primordial and (for some people) unique aim of the virtue of religion is to give glory to God: that seems to be self-evident. The reference to Christ has the effect of an 'additive': one appeals to Christ to pray better to God. Prayers must pass *per Christum dominum nostrum* to reach God. One can always note slight nuances among the Fathers. The Greek Fathers are manifestly more theocentric; the only thing that counts is the glory of God. If the life, the sufferings and the death of Christ are to be taken into consideration, this is to the exact degree to which these events can help us approach God, to praise him better and to love him better. Everything is focussed on the divine majesty. We find more nuances among the Latin fathers. Faith in Christ can take on merit in itself. We can see a slight trend in favour of christocentricity.

The official thought of the primitive church maintains a constant equilibrium between the two tendencies. This is already visible in the different creeds (or declarations of faith) which came into being from the second century on, like that of St Irenaeus, and then those of Origen (in his *Principia* I), and Tertullian. As for the text which circulated at that time under the name of the Apostles' Creed (there are five different versions of it which can be found in Jerusalem, Caesarea, Antioch, Alexandria and Rome), it is a masterpiece of equilibrium between the two tendencies: theocentricity and christocentricity are divided, almost equally, in the faith of the believer. He has to believe in one God, maker of heaven and earth, 'and' (here appeal is made to a simple coordinate conjunction) in 'Jesus Christ his only Son'. Towards the end, 'I believe in the Holy Spirit' is added with the same simplicity of tone; that is to say, the three beliefs are to be put on the same footing. In the Nicene Creed (fourth century) the same balance is respected, but with a slight reinforcement of the affirmations about the Holy Spirit (Council of Constantinople in 381), which could contribute to reinforcing the theocentric tendency to some degree. As for the Athanasian Creed (or at least the creed attributed to Athanasius), it was formulated after the controversies about the person of Christ occasioned by Nestorius and Eutyches (which I mentioned earlier); thus it is not surprising that the dogmatic affirmations in it about the relations between the Father and the Son are very precise. Essentially, the declaration is about the Trinity. Christ is presented as being the incarnation of the second person of the Trinity: *Jesus Christus, Dei Filius, Deus et homo est*, says the Latin text. It is even made more precise: *Deus est ex substantia Patris ante saecula genitus; et homo est ex substantia matris in saeculo natus: perfectus deus, perfectus homo*. Here, it must be confessed, it is difficult to make a division between theocentricity and christocentricity. The Athanasian Creed – where we find again all the official teaching of the councils (in particular those of Ephesus and Chalcedon) – maintains a perfect equilibrium between the two underlying tendencies. On reading these texts, the believer feels himself led to put his faith with equal fervour in God and Christ. However, if we look closer, we shall see that it is faith in God which remains the archetype, the unalterable model. The believer must first of all live faith in God, and then extend that to Christ. Christ is said to be 'God of God, light of light', which means that he is regarded only as a mediator between God and men. His person, his role, his mission cannot in any case be detached from the divine reality in one way or another. Everything is centred on God: we are in a theocentric climate.

(b) In practice

Even if Christ is said to be God, *Deus perfectus*, we do not see the immediate rise of a strictly christocentric worship. The prayer of the first Christians is addressed to God, and only 'passes through' Christ (*per Christum*). It is only very slowly and at a late stage that prayers are addressed to Christ himself. The foundation of these prayers is provided by the psalms, which are necessarily theocentric (it is in hymns that the first traces of christocentricity will appear). Here is the text of a prayer inspired by the psalms which will be in use towards the fourth century:

> Blessed art thou, Lord God of Israel our Father, for ever and ever.
> To thee be magnificence, power, glory and victory,
> To thee be praise, for all things which are in heaven and on earth are thine. Thine is the kingdom. Thou art above all the princes.
> In thy hand is might and empire over all things.

Reference is also made to the most triumphalist passages in the Bible, like the prayer of David (I Chron. 29; I Chron. 14) or the famous prayer of Esther (Esther 14): 'Mighty God, above all others, hear the voice of those who have no other hope than thee.' However, little by little, nuances appear in the texts. So the biblical formula 'Lord God of our Fathers' begins to be replaced by the gospel formula 'Our Father who art in heaven'. At other times reference is made to the texts of the biblical prayers which appear in the gospels, like the Magnificat, the biblical prayer put on the lips of the Virgin Mary on the day of the visitation; the text of the Benedictus, a hymn given to Zechariah; or the Nunc dimittis, attributed to the old man Simeon. Although they come from the gospels, all these texts are very theocentric: they make no reference, at least explicit reference, to Christ. The allusions to Christ only make a first appearance in the texts of the Prefaces, and then only from the fourth century on: the Christ is always invoked only as mediator: *per Christum dominum nostrum*.

A very interesting case to study, because it is full of significance (for the problem that concerns us), is that of the texts of the religious office referred to as the mass. To take up the history of the text of the mass is to take up the whole history of the relations between theocentricity and christocentricity. The mass is as it were the 'geometric point' of the tensions between these two poles. In principle, the mass renews the memorial of Christ's last supper (on Maundy Thursday). But just as, in turn, this last supper occurred in the context of the celebration of Passover, it is ultimately the celebration of the Jewish Passover which forms its sociological foundation.[4] There one rediscovers the same fundamental facts: acknowledgment of faults, the reading of texts, the chanting of prayers, acclamations. The whole event is fundamentally theocentric. It is against this background that we should see the rites evoking the role of Christ in the celebration of Maundy Thursday. Here are the components of the paschal meal, the significance of which was translated into the memorial of the sacrifice made by Christ himself, comprising an offering, a consecration and a communion. From the point of view of social psychology, here we find both logics, one on top of the other. Two interpretations are in competition: the commemoration of the Passover (that is to say, the flight from Egypt) and the eucharistic memorial (that is to say, the farewell meal of Christ). Furthermore, this last rite in turn contains two others more or less in their integrity; the rite of the meal of friendship in which people share their faith and brotherly love, and the rite of the memorial of a sacrifice (where the sacrifice is given material form by the separation of the body and the blood under the forms of consecrated bread and wine). It follows that in the religious service which will later be called the mass, not two but three logically distinct currents come together and are imposed on one another. To put it briefly, these are: 1. the perpetuation of the paschal meal, eaten in haste by the Hebrews, with readings and symbolic references to the sacrifice of a lamb; 2. the idea of a reunion of friends, where agape reigns and where kisses of peace and salutations are exchanged: 3. the rite of the sacrifice of Christ, with oblation, consecration and communion. It will be noted that if the first element is specifically theocentric, since it is devoted to the glory of God, the second and third are more specifically christocentric. A socio-psychological analysis of the composition of the actual rites of the Catholic mass could always reveal the superposition of these three components. They call for three logics. In fact we see that each requires different developments, at each stage, according to its particular needs. From the first centuries, there has been a vivid awareness of the composite character of this gathering for worship. Tensions can be seen in connection with it. Some people wanted to retain its original biblical character, which was profoundly theocentric. That is to say, they wanted to continue to make it a reunion in which one found oneself among believers, above all to hymn the glory of God and give thanks to the Eternal (hence the originally Greek name which was soon given to it; eucharist, thanksgiving). Others insisted on the other logic, which was inspired by the idea of a brotherly meeting, of a meal where one shared offerings (at that time people spoke of agapes). I should mention that this point of view gained too much importance, so that the authorities in the primitive church even had to intervene to slow down its extension.[5] As for the third idea, that of a meeting held as a memorial of the sacrifice of Christ, it only made its mark slowly (very probably under the influence of the disciples of St Paul, and in terms of the mystical christocentricity which inspired it). Beyond question, in the course of the first three centuries there were hesitations over the matter. But we can detect a visible resistance from theocentricity: many communities sought above all to perpetuate in these gatherings the spirit of what the Jews practised at the temple, that is to say, to give the priority to prayer, adoration and thanksgiving. The tendencies towards christocentric interpretations found it difficult to find a footing. Besides, they would almost completely disappear with the age of Constantine, which here as elsewhere was to mark a return to integral theocentricity.[6]

However, we must return to another matter, that of places of worship. There, too, perplexity was great. I have already indicated the question: should the place chosen be the 'place of the glory of God', or should it evoke the humiliation of Christ? Should it be a place of 'triumphal' worship, or be modest and discreet? Opinions differed on this issue. Certainly events would soon favour the option for modesty: in times of persecution people met in cemeteries, and in the catacombs which had been hollowed out in these cemeteries. However, despite everything, the need to give worship more splendour made itself felt, and each time that the Christians could enjoy a respite from persecutions, they constructed imposing buildings, often above the catacombs, to be able to sing the glory of God worthily there. We have some revealing texts on this question. This is how a person in authority thought of the Christian assembly at the end of the third century (he is giving advice to a presbyter–bishop): 'When you gather together the church of God, regard yourselves as the commander of a great vessel, and arrange everything with prudence, ordering the deacons to put all the brothers in the place which befits them. First of all the church will be like a vessel, long and turned towards the east . . . The bishop's seat must be in the middle, with the priests sitting on each side and the deacons standing . . . and their care must be that the laity sit quietly and in good order in another part of the church; that women are separate and silent. Towards the centre, a reader placed in an elevated spot will read the books of Moses and Joshua, the Judges, the Kings, the Chronicles and so on. Another will sing the psalms of David and the people will chant the verses as a response. Then the Acts of the Apostles and the letters of St Paul will be read. Then a deacon will read the gospels.'[7] After a short homily from the bishop, the catechumens are sent out. Then begins the offering of goods in kind. Finally, after the thanksgiving of the Preface, they go on to the consecration of bread and wine. The description of this assembly for worship is interesting; it reveals that primitive Christianity is 'balanced' between theocentricity and christocentricity. People meet on the one hand to sing the glory of God, but also to commemorate the Last Supper (and hence the sacrifice of Christ). These two tendencies are, of course, championed by Jewish Christians and Gentile Christians respectively. The heirs of Judaism insist on the necessity, above all, of making these assemblies occasions for singing the glory of God, as their kinsmen continued to do in the synagogues (for want of the temple, which was destroyed in AD 70). By contrast, the Gentile Christians who met essentially because of their common attachment to Christ, and without reference to Judaism, only wanted to see these meetings as occasions for the mutual support of their love for Christ. 'Converts from Judaism and converts from the Gentile world were two religious races with different characters and different tendencies.'[8] Thus the Jewish Christians remained very theocentric, while the Gentile Christians had a tendency to orient themselves on a degree of christocentricity. This struggle for influence gradually made itself felt everywhere, in particular in the choice of readings for worship: were they to be texts of the Old Testament or texts of the New? It was necessary to make compromises and pass judgments (especially as there was the risk of apocryphal texts being introduced).[9]

The rivalry between the two trends can also be found in the composition of hymns, songs created to give lyrical expression to the faith of the first Christians. It is curious to note that in contrast to the psalms, which are quite naturally theocentric, the hymns prove to be emphatically christocentric. An offensive developed on this front. From the end of the second century onwards, certain hymns resolutely present Christ as God among men, like this famous evening hymn:

> Hail, gladdening light of his true glory poured,
> Who is the immortal Father, heavenly, blest,
> Holiest of holies,
> Jesus Christ our Lord.

Readers will recall the famous phrase of Pliny about the Christians: 'Christians meet on a fixed day to sing a hymn to Christ, as God.'[10]

If we turn to the way in which Christians were led to sanctify time, that is to say the day, the week and the year, we also find a kind of confrontation – again during the first three centuries – between theocentric and christocentric tendencies; however, the second hardly gets the better of the first. The sanctification of the day continues to be inspired by biblical themes: people recite psalms at different hours of the day (the monks preserve this usage). And there is hardly any explicit reference to Christ. The week also remains stamped by the biblical tradition: Christians continued to celebrate the sabbath. Only very slowly did they add to this celebration of the sabbath certain celebrations which took place on the first working day (the future 'Sunday'), in memory of the resurrection of Christ. The competition between these two days lasted for several centuries. For a long time the Christian year, too, was calculated on the Jewish year: celebrations were held on feasts which were related to God (very little account was taken of Christ): the great days of the year during the first four centuries remained those of Easter (a recollection of the exodus from Egypt, and not yet of the resurrection), Pentecost (harvest festival), and so on;[11] only slowly did annual celebrations dedicated to Christ make their appearance. Thus towards the end of the third century we note the timid appearance of a feast of the Epiphany, recalling the triumphal presentation of Christ to the magi, who had come bringing gold, frankincense and myrrh. Then, when we see the appearance of the festivals of Christ, they are indirectly integrated into Jewish ritualism, as for example with the Circumcision (on 1 January) and the Presentation in the Temple (on 2 February). Commemoration of Holy Week makes only a late appearance. Obviously, the calendar of Christian piety in the first centuries remained faithful to the demands of theocentricity.

A study of the vocabulary for designating Christ is equally interesting. It shows with what caution Christian piety came to give a basis to faith in Christ as God incarnate. The first formulas which go in this direction appear in the *Shepherd of Hermas* (in the second century, a time when this text was still part of the canon of Scripture). As we go down the centuries the formulas acquire more and more force; they become charged with veneration and soon with real *latreia*. However, the evolution is slow. Here are some characteristic formulas used to speak of Jesus. St Justin (second century): 'The angel of mighty counsel, the Man, the Christ, God, Wisdom, Star, the East, the Cornerstone, Virtue . . .'; St Clement of Alexandria (third century): 'The Pedagogue, the King, the Pastor, the Light, the Fountain, the Bread, the Blood, the Milk . . .'; St Ephraim (fourth century): 'the Emmanuel, the Star, the Prince, the East, the Admirable, the Second Abel, Melchizedek, Joshua, the Tree of Life, the Lamb, the Eye, the Leaven, the Salt, the Pontiff . . .' As we can see, the vocabulary is full of imagery. These images denote the slow evolution towards a real cult of Christ. However, popular piety remains theocentric. Adoration is directed to God. Christ is regarded simply as the mediator.

As for institutions, in these first three centuries they too remain clearly theocentric. The life of the church is articulated around people who are generally called presbyter-bishops: figures venerated for their age and long standing in the church, on whom hands have been laid to make them the authorized successors of the apostles. For convenience I shall call them presbyters, or simply priests. These priests, as much by their status as by their behaviour, and as much by the power that they exercised as by the dignity conferred on them, could consider themselves the successors of the priests of the Old Testament. They are priests 'according to the order of Melchizedek': their original model, sociologically speaking, is to be sought among the Sumerians. They are priests according to the natural law and, in addition, by divine choice. Hence the hesitation which arises among the apostles of Jesus: what is the real nature of their priesthood? To become priests of Christ, had they first to become priests of the Jerusalem temple? Apparently they did not think so. Christ was the one from whom they derived their power. However, if *de facto* they held their power from Christ, *de jure* they presented themselves as 'priests of God' and not, as one would have thought, as 'priests of Jesus Christ'. They claimed to hold the power of Jesus Christ, but this was power which came from God. Jesus Christ served only as an intermediary. There is surely no historical ambiguity on this point. The priesthood of the first presbyters was a theocentric priesthood.

Another fact is that the first places of prayer which were chosen were called 'houses of God'. The church, the *ecclesia*, the meeting-place, became a separate building, a house specially consecrated to God, all other secular usage being banned.[12] The priest dressed in special liturgical vestments, aimed at denoting the sacral character of his function. In Rome, for example, his garments were the tunic and the stole (a sign of dignity among the Romans of the time); the deacon was dressed in the dalmatic (a tunic originating with the Dalmatians), while the priest wore the chasuble, a mark of distinction worn by Roman magistrates. The rites had a solemn stamp: censing and benedictions. The sacraments retain a trace of biblical usage: oil, water, the laying on of hands. The formulas used remained profoundly theocentric. This is the case with the blessing of water: 'I bless you, creature of water, by the living God, by the true God, by the Holy God, by the God who at the beginning, with the help of his word, separated you from the dry element.' The texts of blessings concerning water (of baptism), salt, oil, ashes, incense for burning are all integrally theocentric; there is hardly any allusion to Christ. The only exception is in the blessing of fire, and more particularly of lamps, in connection with which there is reference to the 'light of Christ'.

In the practical sphere, that is to say, in daily life, the first Christians similarly remained very theocentric. They appeared to their fellows as 'men of God' rather than as 'men of Christ'. The conflict which developed with the civil authorities took place in the sphere of theocentricity: the first Christians called themselves worshippers of the true God. They were quite ready to serve order and peace (which come from God) if those in power did not force them to pay sacrilegious homage to Caesar. They were not objectors (they even served in the Roman legions, if necessary), but here too much was asked of them: they could not renounce their faith in the invisible God to serve idols.

As far as one can judge, Christians were persecuted as men of God and not as disciples of Jesus Christ ('a certain Chrestos', people would say with suspicion). They radiated faith in God. They even prided themselves on rivalling the Jews in this respect: they were 'every day constant in the temple', as much as and more than the Jews. We cannot say that what one might call a 'cult' of Christ was formed. Certainly a tendency developed which sought to blaze a trail. But we still have to wait a long time before it is expressed, because in the Constantinian era which would soon begin, far from diminishing, theocentricity began to grow stronger, and did so for a long period.

2. The age of Constantine: an assured theocentricity

If primitive Christianity remained fundamentally theocentric, it was above all because of its Jewish origins, though I have also taken note of the attempt to make an opening for christocentricity, which was obvious, if tentative. However, with the advent of the age of Constantine – that is to say, with the era in which henceforward Christianity would have civic rights and could develop in complete security – we see a new phenomenon. Theocentricity finds itself reinforced, no longer by reason of its Jewish roots but by reason of the fact that now at last it encounters circumstances favourable to its expansion. The hesitant christocentricity which we have seen emerging is swept away by a new theocentric wave, this time with a force of its own. In fact, Christianity becomes a great monotheistic religion presented to the whole of mankind (and no longer reserved for the Jewish tradition). What we have to describe here is the advent of a triumphant (perhaps even triumphalist) monotheism.

(a) The significance of the Constantinian reaction

People have pondered a good deal, above all in our time, on this Constantinian reaction. Some people have sought to present it as the beginning of a kind of corruption of the Christian message. But that is a partial view, which can only be sustained if we detach Christianity from its monotheistic roots. If it is true that the intimations of christocentricity which emerge then disappear for a long time, and that worship of Christ diminishes, by contrast, worship of God, the thrice-holy God, breaks out into the full light of day. That is the crucial issue, from both a historical and a sociological point of view. Let me recall some of the important facts.

In 313, by the Edict of Milan, the Roman emperor Constantine recognized the legitimacy of the Christian religion (his armies had triumphed over Maxentius at the Milvine bridge; and in this victory he had seen an intervention by the God whom his mother, St Helen, worshipped). From then on, and *for the first time* in the history of the world, the worship of the invisible God, transcendent over the world, became publicly possible. Better still, the greatest empire in the world recognized his omnipotence and officially subjected itself to his will and worshipped him. This was a stunning victory for the God of Abraham, Isaac and Jacob, but it was also the victory of the supreme transcendent being, glimpsed by Aristotle, over all the idols. This was certainly one of the great moments in the history of the world. For the first time the worship of the thrice-holy God left the boundaries of the Jewish people, and Jewish-Christian or Gentile-Christian circles, to spread out over all the earth. The *pax Romana* could finally give all people access to the true God. This is the prodigious significance of the Constantinian reaction. Sometimes people have thought to say that it marked the beginning of the subordination of Christian faith to a temporal power. However, the opposite is true. It was a liberation: at last belief in God could be expressed freely. Better still, it would benefit from the support that could be given it by Roman order in its gradual conquest of the universe. Furthermore, from the day on which the Edict of Milan was proclaimed, belief in God, and also in Christ, was to undergo a considerable expansion: history shows this.

The church developed (and with it other forms of monotheism, as for example Judaism). The development continued until the reaction prompted by Julian the Apostate, and then resumed until the arrival of the barbarians, when another task began. Great figures illustrate this period – figures who could never have appeared had the age of Constantine not been inaugurated. One might recall St Ambrose of Milan and his attitude to Theodosius, stamped with a majestic theocentricity: this was truly the 'man of God' speaking to the sinful emperor. One might recall the figure of St Augustine, who observed the action of God in the world and tried to retrace it in the *City of God*; the figure of St John Chrysostom who took the worship of the most holy God into the Byzantine world. Great religious figures will also emerge in the face of the barbarian invasions: St Loup, St Germain, St Hilary of Poitiers, St Trophimus of Arles, and so on. All present themselves as 'men of God' who want to defend the loftiest faith which has ever been lived out by men, faith in a transcendent God. They played a role analogous to that played by the prophets of Israel in the history of that people, when belief in God weakened, in favour of idols. It was before the faith of a 'man of God', St Remy, that the heart of the savage king of the Franks, Clovis, was humbled; he recognized the Lordship of the 'God of Clotilde'. The faith of all these men is first and foremost faith in God, in the transcendent God. Their faith in Christ is certainly great, and sustains their faith in God, but it only takes second place: that is a historic fact. This theocentricity will dominate all centuries from then on, in a stunning fashion. That is the real significance of the beginning of the age of Constantine.

(b) Constantinian theocentricity

During the age of Constantine, a new style of religious life took shape in Christianity. Beyond question, the clandestine atmosphere of the catacombs had favoured a kind of religious intimacy (which hardly accorded with a triumphal worship of God). This fact favoured a type of worship focussed on Christ, whose humiliations and oppression could be shared in this time of persecution. The martyr – and the possible candidate for martyrdom – could feel a spiritual affinity with the mocked Christ of the passion and the crucified Christ of Golgotha. Psychological conditions helped in this direction, and we have seen evidence of a degree of christocentricity, a certain devotion paid directly to Christ. However, with the age of Constantine, the psychological and social conditions changed. Belief in the omnipotent God could break out into the light of day; people could hymn the glory of God in public places. A new style of religious life was also born, which one can hardly imagine existing before. And yet – let me repeat this – it was the first time in the history of the world that people could vaunt the pride that they felt in putting their trust in the transcendent God, in a way which went beyond all racial or tribal bounds or constraints. The believer in God who hitherto had been living in an atmosphere of persecution, or at least of suspicion, could now give the dimensions of an empire to his faith; and from there, he could make it shine out on the whole of the known universe. What a development! At last the faith of Abraham was proclaimed on the Capitol, and from there it resounded to the ends of the world.

Try to imagine the intoxication which will have seized believers. The idols could fall; the moral and spiritual barbarisms could be thrust back. The kingdom of God was going to begin. This was the final triumph of the God of Abraham, the God of Isaac and the God of Jacob, and also, of course, of the God of Jesus Christ; but it was also the triumph – indirect, but nonetheless real – of the God of Aristotle. We must not forget that. The first Greek Fathers, in particular, were not wrong when from then on they took care to 'recover' (in the best sense of the word) all the treasures of Greek wisdom in favour of this advent of the true God (think of the efforts in this direction made by Gregory of Nyssa, Gregory of Nazianzen and many others). A new world was opened up, and everything had to be invented. It was necessary to invent a form of worship of God which would not just be limited to the horizons of Jewish tradition, but would be open to the dimensions of the whole world. It was no longer a matter of practising the worship of God in the fragile little communities of the clandestine churches of Ephesus, Corinth, Alexandria or Laodicea: it was a question of opening up to the worship of God the crowds who filled the market-places of the Greek towns, the Roman Forum, the cities of the Gauls, of Germania, Phoenicia and Northern Africa. And that was done as quickly as possible: in a generation or less. All the accoutrements of an official, public, universal Christianity had to be created. This was the religious work of the fourth century. Let me now run rapidly over its major features.

First of all we can see the appearance, in public, of a type of man hitherto unknown, whom one could call the 'man of God'. He was everywhere. He was to be found in business, in administration, in the magistracy, in the army (and not just in the hidden world of slaves and illiterates). His kind appeared quickly (as the 'pagans' went into retreat), even among the mass of population on the Mediterranean coast, as far as northern and eastern lands. His personality commanded respect: it was that of a man whose thoughts are entirely directed towards the adoration of the most holy God, to whom the realities of this world must be submitted; and that is why he would always work to display 'the glory of God'. This style of thought and life came to be projected in the institutions themselves. Here too a great work had to be done. These 'men of God', who now became the prime movers behind the city, had to work out a new model of society. Of course they could no longer content themselves with projecting the model of Jewish society, the only one which they knew, with its traditions, which were valid for the twelve tribes. Nor could they go on perpetuating the model of the Roman society in which they were born, for this bore too much the stamp of idolatry (emperor worship, for example), of pagan materialism and polytheistic superstition. They had to invent a law, a type of administration, a social régime, a form of justice, a legislation in conformity to belief in God. Another difficult problem was finding the formula which would make it possible to harmonize temporal power and spiritual power, that of the emperor and that of the pontiffs of the church. This difficult work was accomplished bit by bit. But it is clear that all the schemes are borrowed from the model inspired by deference to a Father God: all the social psychological models proceed from that. The notion of the father leader, not the hero leader, predominate. In that case society was conceived of as subject to the authority of a Father, a spiritual or temporal Father, depending on circumstances. It was intrinsically hierarchical, as is clear from the organization of cities, even after the passage of the 'barbarians', whether this is Lugdunum, Lutetia, Byzantium, or the cities of the Eastern empire. Thus post-Constantinian society was profoundly theocentric. Everything is related to the authority of God. Authority is exercised in the name of God; the virtues practised are those of respect and obedience, due to those who hold an authority which comes from God. Here is an instance which I have taken from Henri Marrou. In his work *Saint Augustin et l'augustinisme*, he describes the way in which the judge administered justice from the beginning of the Constantinian era:

> After Constantine, the empire recognized the competence of episcopal jurisdiction in civil trials, when one of the parties preferred to go there rather than to the tribunals. Now more and more the plaintiffs, even pagans, preferred to resort to the bishop as being a more impartial, juster judge. He was more human, and we can understand this when we recognize the barbarity of judicial procedures, the widespread use of torture (St Augustine at one point prides himself on never resorting to punishments more severe than whipping). For a bishop like Augustine, also to have to administer justice (especially if it was a matter of the most secular questions: inheritances, guardianships, questions of property, boundaries) was one of the heaviest of obligations; every morning at the end of the liturgy he took his place at his tribunal, hearing pleas until it was time to break his fast, which, on busy days, could well be prolonged beyond the morning, until the evening.[13]

This administration of justice gave way, little by little, to a new conception of law which differed notably from Roman law. We can see this with the False Decretals attributed to Isidore of Seville (towards 850), and soon in the first foundations of future canon law. An attempt was made everywhere to create a new order, and there was a desire that this order should be founded on a sense of God, on deference to the will of the Father God; there was a desire for the rise of a hierarchical order in all things. Reference to this order made itself felt (in this transitionary period between pagan antiquity, which was dying, and the Middle Ages, which were coming into being) in every sphere: the spheres of administration, of public functions, of military life, commerce and working life. In these centuries after Constantine an authentic theocentric civilization came into being. We cannot exaggerate – because of our ignorance – the extraordinary effort of imagination which was made by the creators of this new world. They gave birth to a civilization. It soon became mediaeval Christendom.

They could hardly count on Roman order to help them in their task, because that was in process of dissolution. Moreover, they could not be directly inspired by the thoughts of Christ, since he did not seek to involve himself in the realm of Caesar: he did not leave a 'model of society'. So what was to be done? We see that the only models to be followed were those of ancient biblical theocentricity, which holds sway in the Old Testament. If the model of political authority cannot be found either in Caesar Augustus or in the Christ of the Gospels, it has to be sought with king David, Solomon, and their successors. So the first societies in the new civilization coming into being are formed around the model of the sovereign in the biblical tradition, filled with the sense of God, the image and inspiration of confidence and peace, order and harmony. We already find this image at the very head of the church in the figures of the Popes, resplendent with pontifical power. We may think of great figures like Gregory the Great, or Gregory VII. We also find the model in the abbot fathers whom St Benedict put at the head of his monasteries, which were real cells of this nascent civilization, embodying the virtues both of the *paterfamilias* and of the high priests of the biblical tradition. Soon villages were organized along the same lines: around Christianized pagan places or around modest sanctuaries, housing relics or adorned with great saints like St Martin or St Aubin. A whole civilization developed under the aegis of theocentricity. Granted, worship of Christ was also a great influence, but it did not monopolize religious and social life to the same degree. We must admit frankly that in this period it remained subordinate to the worship of the Most High God: all thoughts, desires and actions are governed by faith in God. Excesses are possible, and we can see how this theocentricity degenerates into theocracy (excesses of this kind certainly emerge in Byzantium). However, the existence of these excesses only confirms our theory. On all sides theocentricity reigns supreme.

3. The Middle Ages: theocentricity triumphant

In the Middle Ages (in both the West, and in the East with the Byzantines), everything was related to God. He was regarded as the key to all knowledge, all action, all creation. Certainly there was constant reference to Christ, but Christ was regarded as the mediator. His function, his role and his mission were only significant in so far as they led to God, brought people near to God, achieved union with God.

(a) The Western tradition

The prevalence of theocentricity in every sphere: not only thought, but practical, moral and social life, and throughout mediaeval humanism, is so evident that we need only recall a few features to demonstrate the point.

First of all, God is the key to mediaeval thought, from both a philosophical and a theological point of view.[14] As I have said, this is shown by the general layout of St Thomas' *Summa Theologica*. The whole venture of the universe and of humanity is seen as a movement which comes from God and returns to God, passing through Christ. This is the movement which makes itself evident through the three parts of the *Summa*. Moreover, in the account which St Thomas gives of the totality of beings, everything is arranged around God. The God of St Thomas is the *ipsum esse subsistens*. He is enthroned above all beings, and it is from his creative omnipotence that everything proceeds. Immediately around him are the angels, pure spirits, themselves established in a hierarchy depending on their capacity for the contemplation of God. Then, 'a little lower than the angels', is mankind, in the first ranks of which are believers, those who hymn the glory of God and form as it were his terrestrial court, an extension below of the celestial court formed by the angels: these are the saints, the martyrs, the confessors and the Christian people. Then we have the mass of humanity, those who have yet to attain to the light of faith. Next, below that (well below that) comes the world of animals (not forgetting the monsters who can be put somewhere between men and animals) and the world of plants. Finally, serving as the foundation for all this marvellous hierarchy, is the earth and all that it contains. The earth is regarded as a solid pedestal (it does not yet revolve around the sun) on which God has placed his magnificent empire. We shall find this representation in men's minds and thought-patterns; we can also see it in all the imagery of the Middle Ages. We rediscover it on the fronts of cathedrals (on the tympanums of the narthex) and in the stained glass; we find it in the frescoes of the Italien Quattrocento; in Giotto, in Raphael and in all the painting of the time. This is also the vision which Dante describes in sumptuous terms in the Divine Comedy.

Now the whole of this universe is fundamentally theocentric. God is in the centre; better still, he is the apex. The Christ certainly has his place there: he sits just next to the summit. He is 'seated at the right hand of the Father' (and has his mother Mary next to him). However, the splendour of the glory which emanates from him is a glory borrowed from the Father. He is in turn the 'glory of the Father'. He is a ray of the divine majesty. And it does not occur to anyone to offer him autonomous worship which is not, consistently and immediately, a direct expression of the worship offered to the Father. The glory of God provides mediaeval religion with all its movement. There is nothing religious outside this glory of God.

Both mystical and spiritual life are alike entirely concentrated on this glory of God.[15] Above all in the first part of the Middle Ages, monastic life essentially has contemplation of the divine majesty as its object. That is the object of the fervour of the disciples of St Benedict and St Bruno, later the disciples of St Bernard, both Cluniacs and Cistercians. The aim of the disciples of St Dominic is to diffuse and radiate the glory of God ('*contemplari et contemplata aliis tradere*'). As for St Francis, he introduces a new note by proposing to hymn the glory of God in his creatures (see the Hymn of the Creatures) and no longer in himself. Here is something new which clearly puts in question the generalized theocentricity which was dominant at the time (did St Francis perhaps indirectly prepare the ground for a future christocentricity? I shall return to this question).[16]

Furthermore, the liturgy also took on an eminently theocentric form. In architectural constructions, everything is done to orient thought on the glory of God. Whereas the romanesque buildings were still arranged to house the congregation (I described them earlier), this is no longer the case with Gothic buildings. Here the construction is not so much conceived of to house the people as to 'house God'. The cathedral is above all the temple of God Most High. The audacious sweep of the vaulting, the skilful interweaving of the pointed arches at a great height, all conspire to lead the faithful to lift up their souls towards the God who is in heaven. Housing the people is only of secondary importance. What counts is to make the building a gigantic homage to God, of stone, of light and lines of perspective. The centre of the building is the choir, which is reserved exclusively for divine worship. The centre of this centre is the altar, where the worship is offered, worship which is made as sumptuous as possible. It is surrounded with decorations which are as elaborate as can be: a large number of statues, and very ornate furniture. Finally, the choir is surrounded with a grille, lofty and strong, often adorned with decorations, the role of which is to mark out the reserved, i.e. the eminently sacred, character of the sanctuary. The people are kept at a distance: they are confined to the nave and the aisles; later (this was not envisaged at the beginning), great organs were added, whose triumphant harmonies, filling the vast enclosure with sound, created among the people emotions which could arouse the soul to adoration and reverence towards the thrice-holy God. Finally, in these majestic places, a triumphant liturgy was celebrated, which translated into actions and words the sentiments of reverential adoration in the congregation. Pontiffs bedecked with gold and adorned with impressive mitres presided over processions and celebrations to solemn rhythms which were also hymns to the glory of God Most High.

Finally, in his personal life, the mediaeval Christian would subordinate his behaviour to an exclusive concern for the glory of God. The virtues which he practised were meant to create within him conditions for making his life a hymn, more precisely a hymn to the glory of God. By the practice of the cardinal virtues of courage, fortitude, temperance and justice, and the theological virtues of faith, hope and charity, the mediaeval man was 'formed' within in accordance with divisions which would make his heart a sanctuary where God was adored, in the same way as he was adored in the cathedral with its arcades of pointed arches.

This Christian humanism was projected on to the political, social and economic order. In the political order, theocentricity finds its natural extension in the theory of the divine right of kings. The 'most Christian' sovereign governs his people 'in the name of the omnipotent God'; he is the lieutenant of God 'who reigns in heaven', and whose reign is extended – by the secular arm – among the kingdoms of the earth. This is the way in which St Louis conceived of his form of government. Joan of Arc led her troops to the cry 'God must be served first'. Later, the sovereigns of the Holy Roman Empire would be crowned 'in the name of the holy and indivisible Trinity' (and the Treaty of Vienna would be made in these terms in 1815); it is by the grace of God and as defenders of the faith that the sovereigns of England ruled (and still rule: because the mediaeval conception of the monarchy is still alive there). The coronation (the eighth sacrament) is the foundation for their legitimacy; the unction gives divine power. The most spectacular illustration of this theory of the source of political power in divine power is beyond question the scene at Canossa. Conceptions are similar in the social sphere. All collective activities are conceived, at least theoretically, as having to lead men to the love of God and the glorification of God. The spirit of feudalism – and its social élite, the representatives of chivalry – is based on the idea that those in authority in the society of the time, the feudal lords, have the task of making peace and order prevail, so that the only kingdom which counts may be inaugurated on this earth, i.e. the kingdom of God. They feel accountable for their vassals, down to the last of their villeins, before God. All society is truly theocentric: relationships are regulated in terms of order and hierarchy. Finally, the last echo of this theocentricity is the institution of an original economic system which is also intended to lead men towards the divine perfection, recognized and sought after. This is the system of corporations.

All production aims at quality (and the supreme example of this quality is the masterpiece). The quality of work is judged by peers, who can appreciate the work from the context of the same craft. This quest for quality goes with a quest for perfection, and of course all human perfection brings its author nearer to the divine perfection. Happy the time when craftsmen and groups work only for the glory of God! Finally, it should be added that the poor are supported 'for the love of God', and the sick are cared for in 'hôtels-Dieu', hospitals.

To sum up: mediaeval humanism is eminently theocentric. All human reactions are aimed at bringing man to the contemplation of God, and all man's behaviour serves only to heighten the glory of God. The arts and literature echo this preoccupation. The style of architectural constructions – I have mentioned cathedrals – is aimed at lifting up the soul towards God. Sculpture gives the impression of beings turned towards the divine; the statues of Chartres are contemplative. Christ himself is presented in this attitude: the 'le Beau Dieu' of Amiens is rapt in contemplation of the Father. Literature in turn produces the same echoes: the *Divine Comedy* of Dante is a vast cathedral, whose naves converge on the sanctuary, this place of Paradise where the glory of God shines forth.

As a counterbalance, it must be noted that all through the Constantinian era, and in particular in the Middle Ages, the cult of Christ underwent a degree of attenuation in contrast to the first ages. There was comparatively little meditation on the life of Christ (at least not as much as there was in the very first centuries, and much less than there would be from the seventeenth century onwards, as we shall see). Certainly, the circumstances of Christ's life are evoked in the stained glass, and in the stanzas of the mystery plays which were performed in front of the cathedrals. However, these circumstances have no value in themselves (that was pointed out only in the seventeenth century); they are valid only in that they lead to the glorification of the Father who is in heaven: the glory of God shines out in creation, then in the incarnation of the Word, and then in redemption. An exception has to be made – and the astonishment with which it is greeted confirms its unexpected character – in the initiative of St Francis of Assisi. I have suggested that he could be one of the precursors of christocentricity. With him, in fact, the human life of Christ begins to be taken into account: he has meditations on the birth of Christ (with the custom of the crib), on the passion (with the practice of the Way of the Cross), and so on. With him begins a current, strengthened by notable piety, which contributes towards focusing attention on the historical figure of Christ and his humiliations. Furthermore, this introduces the beginnings of suspicion of the splendid architecture and art which theocentricity had hitherto required. However, this reaction remains marginal, at least in this mediaeval period, and the proposals of the *poverello* of Assisi have a somewhat esoteric influence. We also find an echo of similar hesitation in St Bernard: he, too, was divided between a taste for the splendour demanded by the glorification of God and a certain taste for simplicity and renunciation called for by a meditation on the life of Christ. He achieves a 'balance' between the splendour of Cluny and the tempestuous eloquence of his call to crusade at Vezelay on the one hand, and the renunciation, the silence and the oblivion of Citeaux (*O beata solitudo*) on the other. We must therefore conclude that if theocentricity was triumphant during the course of the Middle Ages, some suspicions of christocentricity can nevertheless be detected in it: as we shall see, they had to develop. However, for the moment we must look at theocentricity in the Eastern world, at Byzantium and among the Slavs.

(b) The Eastern tradition

Here theocentricity is not only widespread, but exclusive. Certainly Christ seems to play a considerable role: his image is everywhere. However, if we look at things a little more closely, we see that Eastern Christianity is integrally oriented towards the sole and exclusive glory of God. The East is essentially in search of mystical union with God. For it, Christ is a 'mediator'. However, we must be more precise about the position in the Russian and Greek churches.

It should first be noted that there is no explicit reference to christocentricity. The historical Christ is of no interest. One observer notes: 'The cult of the humanity of Christ is alien to the Eastern tradition, or rather, this deified humanity is garbed in the same glorious form in which the disciples saw it on Mount Tabor, the humanity of Christ which makes visible the deity he shares with the Father and the Spirit.'[17] It is God alone whom one contemplates in Christ.

Secondly, the cult of icons has a theocentric orientation. As everyone knows, icons present figures of Christ, of the Virgin and of certain saints (St John the Evangelist in particular); however, the icon *par excellence*, that which above all attracts the veneration of crowds and is regarded as the archetype of all icons, is the icon of the Trinity, Rublev's masterpiece. A critic describes it like this: 'The canon of this icon is established little by little; it is progressively stripped of all historical, realistic anecdotal elements, to culminate in the work painted by Andrei Rublev for the church of the Trinity of the Monastery of Saint Sergius. At the Muscovite Council of the Hundred Chapters, under Ivan the Terrible in 1551, the icon of Andrei Rublev was declared the iconographic canon *par excellence* of the church's representation of the Trinity.'[18] In fact, when all is said and done, the role of the icon in the Eastern Christian traditions is to exercise a seductive influence on human consciousness. It must captivate the soul, to induce in it mystical states, and, by so doing, put it in the closest contact with God. 'In its transformation of all flesh into a *sōma pneumatikon,* the icon participates in the breathing of the church moved by the Holy Spirit.'[19] The end in view is not the person of which the figure is a representation, but the mysterious divine presence. One might say that the icon serves only as an inductive agent: It leads to God.

Let me say a little more. In the Eastern churches – and this is true from the Byzantine period to our own days – religious practices are all aimed at establishing a mystical contact between the soul and the thrice-holy God, the 'Hagios Theos', the 'Athanatos Theos'. In the Eastern liturgies, everything possible is done to give the faithful the feeling of the mysterious presence of God: the officiants, whose vestments and actions evoke the splendour of the temple in Jerusalem, withdraw behind the iconostases at the most important moments of the ceremonies, just as the high priests in the temple withdrew into the holy of holies. The people are kept at a distance. All reverential attention is concentrated on the mysterious place where divinity is thought to reside. The continuity is visible between the worship of the temple of Jerusalem and that of the Greek or Russian Byzantine churches of the Eastern rite. The same logic (of course, a social logic) is respected there. The same theocentricity reigns.

In social life, Eastern Christianity has remained equally faithful throughout its history to the same theocentric inspiration. The priest is first and foremost the man of God; he participates in the order of Melchizedek before participating in that of Christ. This is a priesthood according to the natural law before being one according to the supernatural law. We know the respect with which the Orthodox priest is treated in Near Eastern societies. We also know the veneration which was offered in traditional Russia to this exceptional type of 'man of God', represented by the *starets*: people go to him to discover the mysterious presence of God in him. And it is with the glory of God that the monks of Mount Athos, and all the monasteries of the Christian East, are concerned.

4. The Renaissance: theocentricity suspect

If theocentricity is characteristic of the mediaeval spirit, as I have said, we can see how the first breaks in the cultural edifice of the Middle Ages would make themselves felt by a decline in this theocentricity. This is in fact what happens with the Renaissance.

(a) Incompatibility between the spirit of the Renaissance and theocentricity

As is well known, the Renaissance marks the beginning of a period when man claims his own liberty and independence and tries to make a world of which he will be the centre and the support. This movement cannot but lead to a decline in theocentricity. By emancipating himself, the 'son' withdraws from the authority of the father, even if this is the Father 'who is in heaven'. This rejection of the authority of the father rapidly makes its effects felt in the religious sphere, and then much later in the political and social spheres. In fact, in the latter, the skill of those in power allows them – by manipulating the movement to their advantage – to hold up this movement for some time to come (right up to 1789 in France, and the beginning of the twentieth century for Russia and the central European empires).

Of all the institutions, the Catholic church is the first to suffer the shock of the appearance of humanism (which from then on one could call anthropocentricity). To begin with, the Popes made an intelligent response towards it, trying to make use of the humanist movement to their advantage: this was the attitude of Julius II, Leo X, and their immediate successors. The church made itself patron of arts and literature. For the moment its theocentricity could be reinforced. The works of the great artists of the Renaissance, from Michelangelo to Leonardo da Vinci, from Bramante to Bernini, could be called in to support the great work of the glorification of the Most High God. The church 'espoused' its century. It became 'open' to the world. However, the experience was not to last long: the world was stronger than the church. A wave of paganism broke on Christianity. As could be foreseen, in the face of this disaster there was a violent reaction: an appeal was launched to 'protest' against such paganism. This was the Protestant Reformation, an undertaking led by Luther. Calvin and their disciples, and the venture ended up in a schism. What was the Catholic Church to do then? Reform itself, from within. That happened at the Council of Trent, the importance of which would be considerable.

(b) Reactions of Catholic consciousness

The reaction of the church was profound, and almost instinctive. It was being attacked at an essential point, over its faith in God; it responded by seizing on this essential and reaffirming its faith in God more than ever. The first action that we notice (again from the perspective of social psychology, which I have adopted), is a resolute reinforcing of theocentricity. Thus an effort was made in the church which consisted in rejecting the invasion of anthropocentricity and then commending a return to the most stringent theocentricity. This is the significance which can certainly be attributed to the great spiritual revival which started from Spain (a country perhaps less affected than others by the spirit of the Renaissance, simply for geographical reasons) and won over France and then Europe, and was embodied above all in the Carmelite reform. Another effort with quite a different spirit also developed, favouring mysticism and a return to theocentricity, beginning with the Rhenish schools of spirituality. To understand the evolution of these ideas in the church properly, we must take our bearings and look more closely at the three reactions which I have just recalled: the Rhenish school, the Carmelite school and, for the whole of the church, the spirit of the Tridentine reform. These are the three ways adopted by Catholic consciousness in an almost desperate effort to reinforce its theocentricity, which was threatened on all sides.[20]

The Rhenish school of spirituality – with precursors like Suso, Tauler, and masters like Meister Eckhart and Nicolas of Cusa – produced a reaction which was both subtle and very hazardous. First of all, let it be said that it accepted the spirit of the Renaissance entirely. Its masters wanted to be humanists, just as much as Erasmus or Montaigne. But they wanted to prove that despite the excesses perpetrated (above all in Rome and in Italy), it was possible at the same time to have faith in man and faith in God. Their reaction consisted in responding to the faith which had grown up in man by an increase of faith in God – trying in this way to 'baptize' the Renaissance. The case of Nicholas of Cusa is striking in this respect: he wanted to be as much a humanist as Erasmus and as much a mystic as St Bruno. The result was ambiguous, and the effort did not have a notable repercussion on the church. It remained somewhat marginal.[21]

This was not the case with the Carmelite school, which originated in Spain. Here we have a real return to the sources of faith in God: it went back, in fact, to the prophet Elijah and the contemplative life practised on Mount Carmel, twenty-five centuries earlier. First of all there was a deliberate rejection of the anthropocentric demands of the Renaissance. Furthermore, there was no question of turning towards the christocentric pole of Christian faith. There was a resolute decision – in an almost exclusive way – to rediscover the one theocentric pole. The ground had been prepared in the intellectual sphere by the works of the philosophical and theological school of Salamanca, and later by the writings of Suarez. The preoccupation affirmed here was to take up again the ancient contemplative tradition which derived from Mount Carmel. From the beginning, this tradition encompassed all the contemplative groups mentioned in the Bible: the 'sons of the prophets' and the 'schools of the prophets', the Rechabites, the Hasideans; later the Essenes and even the Pharisees. Pursuing this current, the Carmelite school, above all with St Teresa of Avila and St John of the Cross, sought to be essentially contemplative. It was directed towards 'God alone', loved, adored and praised for himself alone, for his pure glory. The ideal of Teresa, through the 'seven mansions' of the *Interior Castle*, is to arrive at a unitive life with God; and St John of the Cross thinks that at the climax of this ascent of Mount Carmel, to which he invites the fervent soul, one attains ecstasy in the one who is everything, in a contemplation of the eternal. In one case or the other, the appeal to Christ is certainly constant, but it is by way of mediation. The Christ is not the end in himself. He is the one who leads us to the Father. The end is this Father who is in heaven, and he alone. As we shall see, this spiritual current exercised a considerable influence in the Catholic church at the beginning of the seventeenth century: it was the last chance for exclusive theocentricity, which had reigned for so long.

The Council of Trent too – and, we must say, above all – tried to make a supreme effort to restore the earlier theocentricity in its fullness, after it had been so maltreated by the cultural evolution of the age. This Council – which, like all councils (it was the eighteenth), is in principle 'timeless', that is to say binding on a permanent point of doctrine – fulfilled a strictly historical role. It arrived 'at the right time' to bring correctives to the difficulties experienced by the church. The difficulties were all those which I have just indicated: the excessive anthropocentricity of the Renaissance; the excessively violent reaction which had appeared with Protestantism, and so on. Under the pressure of the needs of the hour, it thought that there was only one attitude to take: to proceed towards a general reinforcement of all the theocentric structures which had given strength to the church hitherto. First of all, theological dogma was strengthened: the production of the famous catechism, the so-called catechism of the Council of Trent, had this as its principal preoccupation. Faith in God was again presented as the corner-stone to religious life in Christianity. All other spiritual attachments are subordinated to it. There was also an attempt to strengthen the psycho-social structures which followed (as I showed earlier) from the theocentric option. There was a reinforcement of the sense of hierarchy, the practice of obedience; in the same spirit, there was a rigorous codification of the practice of the sacraments (beginning with the eucharist, i.e. the mass). Future clergy were called to prepare themselves methodically for their mission, considering this as an entry into 'orders' (note the term). Finally, in the spiritual realm, the council constantly laid stress on the role of divine grace at every stage of the economy of salvation. The Christian was invited more than ever to act as a 'child of God', who receives from the Father who is in heaven everything that he needs in the spiritual and temporal order. The reaction, then, was a lively one, and there is no doubt as to its orientation. Faced with the dangers of disintegration (internal disintegration through the paganism of the century, and external disintegration through schism), the official church responded by reinforcing its earlier positions, and reinforcing its intellectual and social structures which derived from theocentricity. This was the situation in the church at the end of the sixteenth century.

5. Intimations of christocentricity

If theocentricity remained triumphant and virtually exclusive throughout the church, and particularly in the official church, that does not prevent our seeing the dawning of intimations of christocentricity, that is, attempts at recentring faith on the person of Christ, and no longer on God. They represent the laudable concern to rediscover a new way for religious life. However, as we shall see, this crucial religious period for the church, which runs from the Renaissance to the beginning of the seventeenth century, immediately preceding the Grand Siècle, will end on a note of disquiet.

(a) Equivocal intimations

Despite the predominance of theocentricity, we can discover, here and there, some suspicions – albeit timid – of christocentricity. Some people begin to turn towards Christ, the God-Man, in an attempt to make him the prior object of their faith. However, these attempts will often take equivocal forms.

That will be the case, for example, in certain aesthetic spheres, where at times we find a kind of exaltation of Christ. But this exaltation takes quite pagan forms. Christ is presented as a kind of spiritual athlete who can impose himself on the world by his human vigour.[22] The humanism of the Renaissance is put in the service of faith in Christ. Numerous works of art exalt the Christ in his humanity. This is the case with the Christ represented with splendour as the sovereign judge at the Last Judgment in the Sistine Chapel (the judge is no longer God the Father).

A similar reaction begins in literature, at the end of the sixteenth century. Lefèvre of Etaples presents himself as *philosophus Christi*: the formula is ambiguous, to say the least: Christ is integrated into the line of the great wise men of antiquity. Montaigne evokes a figure of Christ who makes one think more of Stoicism than of the faith of the councils. Perhaps these efforts at integration were governed by a certain apologetic concern: people wanted to show that Christ is a superman and then try to reclaim the humanism of the Renaissance to the advantage of religious faith. In fact, however, they took the direction of a kind of Orphism.

Other attempts at christocentricity seem nearer to the tradition. Thus we can see the commendation of a return of piety and devotion towards the human person of Christ. This was the time in which the treatise written by Thomas à Kempis and entitled *The Imitation of Christ* had a wide circulation. The title was very bold for its day. Of course the author had lived a century earlier, but the work did not enjoy any success until this century. This case is interesting. We can see how the work was seen as a rather esoteric writing: in this period of theocentricity, an appeal to the 'imitation of Jesus Christ', though having some Franciscan echoes, could not but appear unusual. God alone should be the source of inspiration, and a model for life should be sought in his infinite perfections (as the current of Carmelite thought forcibly said again at that time), and not in Jesus Christ.

(b) A prophetic attempt: the Society of Jesus

St Ignatius of Loyola, who also came from Spain, reacted in his own way to the humanistic movement of the Renaissance. He also wanted to try to rehabilitate the spirit of the Renaissance, but he did so with much more finesse and subtlety than his predecessors. In his thought, as in his undertakings, he sought to make contact with Renaissance man, his desires, his ambitions, his projects. However, he did not aim to conquer him by attempting to outclass him, by presenting a superman Christ to him. He proposed to try to direct the humanist current towards a particular 'man' whom one could certainly say to have been fully man, towards Jesus of Nazareth. He compelled his contemporaries to recognize that Christ is ultimately more profoundly 'human' than is the man of Montaigne, Erasmus or Rabelais. The ploy was a subtle one: it plays on any sense one might have of human profundity. It was a kind of pious one-upmanship. The spiritual skill of Ignatius of Loyola and his Jesuit disciples was to take the Renaissance at its word and also to argue for man (by the quest for culture, knowledge and art), and then, using these ends as means, to show that if one pursued the same aspirations as the humanists of the Renaissance one would end up with a great discovery: real humanism is that of Jesus Christ. Carried out well, this tactic of apostolicity should lead souls to Christ, and then, through Christ, lead them to God. It was an audacious and subtle approach. It announced the themes which would soon develop in the seventeenth century, and would lead to the elaboration of future christocentricity. Here Ignatius of Loyola served as a precursor.

(c) The situation in the Reformed churches

I am concerned only to study the situation in the Catholic church, but in passing I can point out the attitude which was taken by the chief Reformers and the founders of the Reformed churches, in the face of the Renaissance and its paganizing humanism. This is because they are indirectly a reaction against Catholicism. If it was necessary to break with the humanism of the Renaissance to remain faithful to God, it was better to break with the Renaissance, and to attempt a reform in depth, which would direct man immediately towards God, without passing through humanism. This was the basic reaction of Luther, for example, in his work *De servo arbitrio* (1525), where he appealed in pure faith to the saving grace of God. In his *Institutes of Christian Religion* (1536), Calvin develops his theory of predestination, which is clearly theocentric, to the utmost degree. The initiative for salvation comes from God and God alone; human merits do not carry any weight.

Everything comes from God and everything returns to God. Success in both the temporal world and the spiritual world is the gift of God. The famous *Book of Common Prayer* of 1552, dear to the Christians of the Reformation, has an eminently theocentric spirit. The soul turns constantly towards the Eternal: the Eternal One is its end and its happiness. Of course, Christ is frequently invoked, but as an intercessor: it is his merits which allow us to approach the divine majesty without too much unworthiness. As for the churches of the Reformation, they are above all temples of God. There is no altar of sacrifice. From the perspective of social psychology the centre of the building is the pulpit, the seat of truth. However, one of the theses of the Reformers could serve to support a degree of christocentricity, namely the attention given to the reading of the Bible. The reading of texts is psychologically favourable to the rediscovery of the historic person of Christ. It was probably also this practice and its logical developments which gave birth, in the nineteenth century, to liberal Protestantism and the christocentricity which it defends. However, as a whole, the religious movement which arose from the Reformation remained very profoundly theocentric. That can be verified even today.

6. Tensions

At the end of the sixteenth century, then, the positions held by theocentricity were very strong. However, certain tensions emerged in the first decades of the seventeenth century. Different spiritual currents appeared which were to come into collision. These currents of thought were sub-conscious: soon they would come clearly into the light of day. Let me recall the chief of them.

As ever, tending to reinforce theocentricity, in the first place we find Carmelite spirituality. At the beginning of the seventeenth century it underwent an astonishing reinvigoration. From Spain, the reform movement of the Carmelites reached France, and then other countries. How can we forget in this connection the name of Madame Acarie, who worked so hard to found Carmels in France? All the Carmelite convents became centres of contemplative life and spiritual influence; they practised an exclusive quest for God and his august presence. To this current we could add the renaissance which took place at that time in the Carthusian monasteries in various countries of Christian Europe: in France, in particular at the monastery of Vauvert, near Paris; in Germany, in Cologne; in Italy, and even in Catholic England. We could add to them other movements which equally developed their activities in the direction of theocentricity, spiritual movements which, in

Italy, followed the lines of the thought of St Catherine of Siena and then St Charles Borromeo, Blessed St Angela of Foligno and the one who now continued in Spain the work of reform sought by St Teresa of Avila and St John of the Cross. The spiritual masters most in vogue were all theocentric. They wanted the soul to go directly to God. The best-known are Luis of Granada and Denys the Carthusian; Father Benedict de Canfield (of English origin) who frequented the salon of Mme Acarie, and from there exercised his influence on the French religious élite. This last supported 'the rejection of the humanity of Christ by going past it, to achieve pure contact with the deity'.[23] Here there truly was an exclusive theocentricity. The activity of St Francis de Sales at this time also pointed in the same direction. His *Introduction to the Devout Life* is aimed at helping the man of the world, steeped in the humanism of the Renaissance, to enter directly into contact with God, thanks to a quite theocentric practice of the values of this world, 'relating all to God'.

This theocentricity was apparently the approach of the majority of religious figures of this time (between 1600 and 1630). However, difficulties begin to arise in Catholic thought when we see a whole part of the educated world of this time soon abandon, purely and simply, faith in God, to adopt a kind of serene atheism, made up of refined humanism and a critical taste for independence of the spirit. This was the era of the 'freethinkers'. The crisis was a serious one: it is clear that this period at the beginning of the seventeenth century was a period of 'rapid dechristianization' in many countries of Europe (as an indirect result also of the wars of religion). What, then, was to be done to defend the faith? As I have said, in the previous century, faced with the schism of the Reformation, the Catholic church had reacted by strengthening both its intellectual and institutional structures in the direction of theocentricity. What was it to do now, confronted with this new danger, more profound even than schism, that of an incursion of atheism? Was it enough just to reinforce theocentricity a little more? That would be the first reaction, which was expressed, as I have said, in the Carmelite renaissance. However, another reaction soon emerged. It was no more than a trickle in these first years of the century: it developed considerably in the course of the century, as we shall see in the next chapter. What we have is a completely new attitude in the history of the Catholic church. It consists in arguing in the following way: if the thought of the time is no longer open to faith in God, perhaps there might be a possibility of opening it up to faith in Christ; then through faith in Christ one might end up bringing people to faith in God. That was in fact the dream of a number of audacious apologists between about 1610 and 1630. Let us look, they said, as much as possible towards Christ: let us turn our thoughts, our actions and above all our understandings towards him. Let us think intently of Christ: through our thoughts his presence will transmit itself little by little to our brother men, and through Christ they will return to God. This apologetic concern would guide people in one of the most astonishing reversals that religious thought has ever known (and here I am including all religions). It would lead them to a 'recentring' of the whole content of the faith of a religion. A move was made from one pole to another, from the theocentric pole to the christocentric pole. It was in this same spirit that the method of thought which would be called the 'method of immanence' arose, again with an apologetic concern. We are familiar with the principle and the approach which it introduces: let us make Christ known and loved as a historical person, and the atheist – who must be brought to God – will see clearly that no other human being has 'spoken like this man'; Christ must be considered to be the most accomplished of men, and as a result his message must be heard. Now the chief truth which this man taught was faith in God. So, 'believe in God'. Faced with the shortcomings of theologians, whom people began to treat ironically as 'beings who thought themselves more than man' (Descartes), and whose reinforced theocentricity no longer gained a hearing in an educated audience, and faced with the failure of philosophers who, like Descartes himself, tried to formulate new demonstrations of the existence of God, but only encountered scepticism in the salons and hostility from officials of the Catholic church, the representatives of this new apologetic method could pass themselves off as interesting innovators. This would be the case, for instance, with Pascal.

In fact, it is worth ending this rapid survey of religious thought on the threshold of the modern world with a look at Pascal. He found the best illustration for this situation of growing 'tension' between the first suspicions of christocentricity and traditional theocentricity, a tension which I have taken to be characteristic of this period (the beginning of the seventeenth century). In fact, with Pascal we still have the most confident affirmation of theocentricity, at the same time as the first echoes of a christocentricity in search of an identity, the possibilities and consequences of which cannot yet be assessed. What is Pascal's basic attitude? Brought up in the Jansenist tradition, he was therefore theocentric. In their piety the Solitaries of Port Royal are quite close to the Carmelites. They, too, want to live for the utterly pure and exhilarating 'glory of God'. They were seized with fear and reverence before the divine majesty. In the *Augustinus* of Jansen they learnt that the distance between God and man is infinite and can be bridged only by divine grace. Pascal shared in this elevated sense of the divine majesty (one has only to reread the *Provinciales* to be convinced of that). But at the same time he was a man of the world. He frequented the salons. He met the freethinkers; and he suffered to the depths of his being on seeing men removed from God and lost in the darkness of atheism (for in his eyes atheism is a fruit of ignorance). So it was necessary to instruct these poor people. How was that to be done? He went to meet them on the ground where everyone was accessible, the ground of concrete experience. Look in human history, he told them.[24] There was a man who lived in an exceptional way. And we know well that the majority of the *Pensées* are devoted to recalling the concrete facts about Jesus: the fulfilment of prophecies in him, his miracles, his resurrection. 'If you do not believe in God, at least believe in Jesus Christ,' he repeated to the freethinkers. He himself was won over by this approach: as is well known, he even came to contrast the 'God of Jesus Christ' with the 'God of the philosophers and wise men' (a dubious distinction). And in this way he thought that he could bring the freethinker, by Christ, to God. Pascal's attitude is enthralling: he invites men no longer to direct their attention to God but to Jesus Christ. This is an original attitude in the church. In this respect he plays the role of a forerunner. He announces the coming of a new era, when attention to Christ will replace attention to God. Theocentricity will soon give way to christocentricity.

IV

The Renaissance of Christocentricity
(Seventeenth and Eighteenth Centuries)

At this point we ought to take our bearings. As I have said, in origin the Catholic church is a religious institution, the faith of which is focussed on two poles. This faith must be directed with equal vigour to both God and Christ. That is a matter of fact. The church tries to accommodate itself to this bipolarity; in particular it endeavours to justify it in the dogmatic definitions of its Councils and its creeds. Then it attempts, not without difficulty, to see that it is lived out by the faithful. In fact, the faith of Christians constantly tends to lean towards one or other of these poles, so strong is the need for unity in the human mind. After a period of oscillation, in the course of the first three centuries, from the age of Constantine Christian thought leans decisively towards the theocentric pole, towards belief in God: this tendency lasts for more than thirteen centuries. Then, suddenly, the opposite tendency revives: in the course of the seventeenth century the Christian conscience experiences a powerful attraction towards the second pole, that of faith in Christ, and we see a renaissance of theocentricity. This renaissance is so vigorous that in less than three centuries this christocentricity gradually takes the place of theocentricity, at least in the advanced wing of Catholic thought, despite the constant resistance of those responsible for the doctrine and discipline of the church. The chief aim of this book is to demonstrate this development. The movement in this direction goes so far that some theologians even end up affirming a 'Christianity without God', an atheistic Christianity. In my opinion, the origin of this movement is to be sought in the doctrinal and spiritual evolution that begins with a theological school known under the name of the 'French school of spirituality', formed in the seventeenth century around Cardinal de Bérulle and some of his disciples. This school exercised a considerable influence in the Catholic church, and it led to the upheaval which transformed the inner life of this church, the effects of which we can see in our own time. So we must begin with a study of this school.

1. The French school of spirituality

Let me first recall our concern. Towards the first third of the seventeenth century, between about 1620 and 1650, a movement of spiritual renewal, with amazing doctrinal intensity, originated and developed in response to the need for reform which was making itself felt in the church. It spread into the most influential cultural and the most important political areas in the nation. Its reverberations were considerable.

Its remote origin is to be sought in the silence of the Carmels of Spain, from where it came to win over Paris and France, and went on to exert its influence on the rest of the Catholic world. It affected theology (at least what one might call spiritual theology), and from there spiritual life; then, step by step, it began to infiltrate institutions, impress its rhythm on the psychological and social life of the church, and prepare the way for the structural evolution (as always, I am talking of structures in terms of social psychology and not of doctrinal structures) which would end up in the renewal proposed by the Second Vatican Council of 1962–65. The effort of thought which lies at the beginning of this movement has been called the 'French school of spirituality' by reason of its historical and geographical origins. This name was proposed for the first time, as I have already indicated, by Abbé Bremond, about 1925, in his famous work in eight volumes, *Histoire littéraire du sentiment religieux en France* (see especially vol.III). The recognized leader of this school was a very great figure, Cardinal de Bérulle, and its most brilliant representatives were St Jean Eudes, M. Olier, Condren, and St Vincent de Paul.[1]

(a) The objectives

What was the basic motivation of this movement? From all the evidence, it was apostolic. I gave an outline of it at the end of the previous chapter, to which I must now return.

In the first place, it was a matter of the Christian thought of the time reacting to the humanism of the Renaissance. Men claimed to be able to secure their own salvation by themselves, simply through their reason and culture, without the help of divine grace. It was important to meet this challenge. As a first reaction, Christian thought was concerned to begin by keeping its distance from the philosophy taught in the Schools, i.e. Scholasticism. This Scholasticism was much decried by the men of the Renaissance: these men, nurtured on human experience, and having rediscovered the vigour of twenty centuries of Greek and Latin humanities – regarded the conceptual analyses put forward by Scholasticism as no more than verbal formalism (and doubtless did so in good faith: intent on human experimentalism, they only saw words, where ideas were hidden; though verbalism may have wrought some ravages). However, while giving the impression of departing from scholastic teaching – by apostolic opportunism – the Christian thinkers of the generation of Bérulle (we may recall the personal encouragement which Bérulle gave to Descartes) *ipso facto* found themselves cut off from the sources of theocentricity, at least in its philosophical form – and its support. Furthermore, partly by conviction and partly by opportunism, these 'new Christians' wanted to show that they were as humanist as the spirits of their time. 'Are they humanists? So are we,' they might have wanted to say. So they set out to show that the Christian is as humanist as the rest, and that as a result Christianity is itself a humanism. As we shall see, this is what led them to focus all their apologetic, and soon their spiritual life (looking towards the distortions which they would have to make in their theology), on the theme that Jesus Christ was the most human of men, that he was the first of the humanists, and that he should be revered as man. Did not he who was called the God-man humanize man? We can imagine the upheaval that was under way.

There was another preoccupation. The thought of the time claimed to be scientific. We are in the wake of the first conquests of science (the first statements of the laws of gravity, of light, of the pendulum, and so on), and on the eve of the depressing trial of Galileo. A reaction was needed. At that time there were those who decided to break with conceptual analysis, and thus with scholastic philosophy, to turn towards the prestigious method of 'experience', then flushed with its first success, and to do anything to make sure that faith, if possible, took an experimental turn. For that to happen, faith had to be based on facts. But what facts? Certainly, it was impossible to invoke the facts of the laboratory.[2] People therefore thought of invoking historical facts, because in their way these too are experimental facts, or at least they have been in their time. In my view, this is one of the reasons why the so-called 'avant-garde' Christian thought of the period decided suddenly to turn towards the person of Christ, known historically, rather than towards the idea of God, grasped conceptually. A reversal of interest had begun. Religious thought then fixed on Christ, to make him an object of its meditations and its speculations. The hope was to obtain from him, as a historical person, the religious certainties which were no longer expected from speculative reason, faith in the transcendent God.

Finally, a third consideration was involved, which this time would be purely philosophical. At that time doubt arose as to the capacity of philosophical reason itself. With some anxiety, people asked whether human reason – which at that time was leading so many distinguished minds to unbelief and to free thinking, as it was called at the time was really capable of pointing towards the existence of God. The reactions of the young Descartes in this respect are typical. Along with his age, he no longer believed in the 'philosophy which can give demonstrations of everything' and 'make itself felt even among the most ignorant' (he was evidently thinking of scholasticism, conceived of as a verbalism); he also believed that theologians – here, the dogmatic theologians whom he may have known – spoke of God without seriousness, as if they knew him personally, and he ironically says that they imagine themselves to be 'more than men'. He then tries – as a good Christian and a good Catholic (who remains attached to his faith, which is 'that of his king and his nurse'), to play his part in the defence of the faith – 'as the Council laid its obligation on all the laity' (here, of course, he is talking of the Council of Trent), and he proposes a new demonstration of the existence of God in his *Discourse on Method* and his famous *Metaphysical Meditations* (Meditation IV). He had received a great deal of encouragement to do this, in particular from Cardinal de Bérulle and his intellectual friends, after the memorable evening spent at the Apostolic Nunciature in 1627.[3] The efforts exerted by philosophical thought at that time are immensely laudable (they are the work of Descartes, but also of his pupils, regrouped by Mersenne, and a little later Leibniz and his German and French friends). What do they produce? People endeavoured to set in train a new demonstration of the existence of God or – as Leibniz said – to put forward a theodicy, i.e. a 'justification of God'. But these efforts were more brave than persuasive, and they caused perplexity because of their somewhat 'acrobatic' character. The specialists in this problem in fact knew that all the attempts at demonstration ultimately relied on what was called the ontological argument: one had a certain idea of God and then confidently moved from this 'idea' of God to his reality. In the next century, Kant did not have much difficulty in showing the emptiness of such an argument: ideas can only engender ideas, and one can never derive a reality, even that of God, from them. The 'connoisseurs' became well aware of this during the lifetime of various authors. And it soon appeared that while this philosophical thought gained undeniable richness in its discussion of man and above all in its study of the human spirit, it proved astonishingly defective and deceptive over the problem of God. People were therefore left with the idea that only human reason of the classical type, i.e. reason oriented on the real, 'realistic reason', could lead to God; but that was in the hands of the scholastics, and they had discredited its usage – at least, that is what was said. People were at a loss.[4] What was to be done? Faced with the deficiencies of traditional philosophy and the inadequacies of modern philosophy, believers might be tempted to renounce purely philosophical reflection. And we can understand how they wanted to turn towards the facts, the simplest facts, those reported by a text for which they still had the greatest respect, that of the gospels. Soon they contrasted the 'proud philosopher' (as the author of the *Imitation* puts it) with the 'simple' reader of the gospel. They began to say that this text was worth all the treatises of philosophy. This facile irony enjoyed great success. It was another reason for directing attention towards the story of Christ rather than towards the intellectual (or spiritual) contemplation of God. A new era was indeed beginning.

To sum up, three factors had an influence here: the trend towards humanism, a taste for experimental method, and distrust of philosophy. They had an effect on the seventeenth century, but as we shall have occasion to demonstrate, they have also had an effect right down to our days. In essentials, they explain the evolution from theocentricity to christocentricity. People in fact began to think that it is easier to approach Christ than God himself. Perhaps one was better advised to explore the thoughts of Christ (to be found in the gospels) than one's own thoughts . . . above all when they moved in the direction of a speculative God. In broad outline, that is the basic attitude adopted by the most perceptive religious minds at the time of the seventeenth century. And I think that this reaction explains the attitude of the great spiritual figures who soon appeared, Bérulle and his successors.

(b) New religious intentions

In fact, what the great spiritual figures of the time tried to do was to turn completely upside down the perspectives which governed approach to the Christian faith. According to the traditional conception – which I recalled in chapter III – the soul is directed primarily towards God, to recognize his existence, to hymn his glory and to try to reach him by contemplation and prayer. Then it appeals to Christ for help, from his example, his teaching and above all his redemptive intercession. The conception which now develops is quite different. The soul goes first to Christ: it learns to know him, by reading the Gospels; to love him; and finally to submit to his thoughts and his will. Doing this, the Christian soul believes that it is being set in a good intellectual and spiritual direction which must lead it to the supreme truths. It is among these that it will find the possibility of access to God, which of course remains the ultimate goal of its aspirations. So it is in Christ, by Christ and with Christ that it undertakes to arrive at God. This is the pattern of the new approach which was commended by the great spiritual figures of the seventeenth century. One might remark in passing that this way of reacting has become so natural in the modern Christian world (since as we shall see, the influence of the French School was considerable) that we believe that it has always existed. It would have astonished St Thomas Aquinas and the people of the Middle Ages, St Bruno and even St Bernard. It had its greatness: it prepared the way for the religious renaissance of the Grand Siècle. But it also had its weaknesses, as the subsequent spiritual history of the Catholic church will show. However, before studying this spiritual adventure, which we may call christocentricity (because belief in Christ forms the centre of the religious life, and belief in God is as it were extra for the believer), we must show its slow rise, in the spiritual currents which were in competition at the beginning of the seventeenth century, and which I have already mentioned.

These spiritual currents seek, as I have said, to respond to the needs of an intelligence in evolution, a culture thirsty for human authenticity and truth. I have already indicated the importance of the mystical current, of Carmelite inspiration. I must return to that. Starting from Spain at the end of the sixteenth century, it reached France at the beginning of the seventeenth. In this setting it acquired new vigour. It had influence above all in the intellectual world, through the salon of that cultured lady Madame Acarie (who subsequently became a Carmelite herself).[5] She had sent emissaries to Spain, to the reformed Carmelite convents (M. Gallemant, curé of Aumale, then M. Brétigny, who was to have a long encounter with sister Anne of Jesus, one of the best spiritual daughters of Teresa of Avila). A Carmelite foundation was soon planned, so that the spiritual renaissance which had begun in Spain could reach France. A historian tells us of the preparatory meetings which were held at the home of Mme Acarie, 'at which were present Gallimant, Brétigny, Duval, Bérulle and even Francis de Sales; and a Capuchin, Père Archange de Pembrock, who was the first director of Mother Angélique Arnaud.'[6] The influence of Bérulle in this group was predominant; and it was Bérulle who was soon put in charge of the foundation. He went to Spain and returned with six Carmelite nuns, led by Anne of Jesus. Thus the first Carmelite foundation in France was assured, and the movement could develop from then on.

However, a reaction of the founder, Anne of Jesus, should be noted at this point, because it was to have the greatest consequences. As I have pointed out, the spiritual milieu in which the Carmel was established was at this time deeply theocentric. This theocentricity was so strong that it astonished, even shocked, the founder, Anne of Jesus. For although she was a Carmelite, against all expectation – but by reason of her personal sensibility – she found herself drawn more towards 'devotion to Christ', and thus towards the beginnings of a degree of christocentricity. This is what this religious in fact wrote: 'I am concerned that novices should consider and imitate our Lord Jesus Christ, because here people think little of him. Everything is based on a simple view of God. I do not know how that can happen. Since the life of the glorious St Denis, who wrote his *Mystical Theology*, the whole world has continued to apply itself to God by suspension rather than by imitation. This is a strange way of proceeding, and in fact I do not understand it.'[7] On the other hand, the same religious deplores 'the abandonment of the imitation of Jesus at the expense of a "simple view of God", a practice commended by unreadable books.'[8] And under her influence the first Carmel established in France bore the name Carmel of the Incarnation, to show its concern for change. Why did this religious adopt this spiritual orientation? Specialists claim that it was because she was more the spiritual daughter of St Teresa than of St John of the Cross: the latter, resolutely theocentric, would not have oriented his disciples in this direction.

During this time, the other spiritual currents in France remained resolutely theocentric, as we have seen. The Carthusian Monasteries were theocentric.[9] The various spiritual groups inspired by the Rhenish and Flemish mystics then in favour were equally so. All the writings of Carmelite inspiration, of which a great many translations were made, from the Spanish, directed the piety of their readers towards theocentricity. In particular, there was much talk of an 'abstractive contemplation' of God, that is to say, an assiduous quest for God in the utmost humility of spirit. The fashion in the spiritual world was more for renunciation, for spiritual poverty. Everything heralded the imminent era of Jansenism (the *Augustinus*, written towards 1630, appeared in 1640). This sister Anne of Jesus must therefore have had a very personal propensity towards devotion to Christ for the order of things suddenly to be turned upside down. The future Cardinal de Bérulle – who was to 'orchestrate' all the spiritual development of the century – would come under her influence, and as a result his own spiritual life would undergo an astonishing reversal.

(c) The spiritual development of Bérulle

In his youth, Bérulle showed a spiritual disposition narrowly oriented on theocentricity. His first writing, the *Short Discourse on Inner Abnegation* (1597), is utterly steeped in it. He commends the quest of 'God alone', invoking St John of the Cross. In the group around Mme Acarie, he has an affinity to the school of abstract contemplation, and he draws his inspiration from the Rhenish and Flemish mystics. However, he soon experiences a deep inner change, which takes him from theocentricity to christocentricity. It is difficult to date this inner change, but at all events his biographers put it between 1601 and 1610. Cognet notes: 'At the time of the introduction of the Carmelites into France, everything suggests that Bérulle was still entirely taken up with the ideas of the abstract school.'[10] Now some years later, in 1608 to be precise, one of his spiritual charges, Mère Madeleine de Saint-Joseph, was giving her novices strictly christocentric advice. 'We cannot be mistaken: the authorship of such ideas derives from Bérulle. So we can be certain in placing this complete change of perspective between the years 1605 and 1606.'[11] Others are more precise: they refer to a retreat made by Bérulle in 1601, called the 'Verdun Retreat'.[12] According to his biographer Habert de Cérisy, this 'reconversion' is to be put round about the years 1605–6. However, everyone is generally agreed that it was accomplished by 1609. Furthermore, it is recognized that Bérulle himself regarded it as important, both for himself and for the future of the church. 'Bérulle,' wrote P. Cochois, 'was aware of having brought about a revolution comparable to that of Copernicus in astronomy.'[13] Among the influences on him, one can mention, as has been said, that of Sister Anne of Jesus, at the head of Carmel, of whom Bérulle was the spiritual director. People have also spoken of a degree of sensitivity to the spiritual difficulties of his time: Bérulle felt the need to react in the direction which I have described. He wanted to react to humanism and to respond to the need for experience and authenticity which made itself felt everywhere. If he recommended that people should turn towards Christ, it was because for a man of the seventeenth century it was no longer possible to go to God. Furthermore, preoccupations as to the meaning to be attached to the Christian priesthood in the modern city will also have played a part;[14] finally, the spiritual anxiety of the young Bérulle will have been quickened by his reading of St Paul at that time. He will have had an inkling of the interest that the rediscovery of the 'Mystical Body' could have for the thought of his time. As his biographer Orcibal wrote, 'Once the idea of the mystical body was introduced, Bérullian christocentricity could only become more precise.' Prejudice towards philosophers – despite his good relations with Descartes – could also have played a part. At least, that is the opinion of Orcibal. 'As for the philosophers whose authority the *Grandeurs* still invoke, the *Life of Jesus* sees only errors in them.'[15] In fact it is probable that these different factors would exercise a convergent influence, to contribute to the accomplishment of this 'Copernican revolution' which would change the face of the church.

How did this 'revolution' appear? Cognet sums up the situation in these terms. 'M. Brémond does well to describe it as a "Copernican revolution": it replaced the incarnate Word at the very centre of Christian piety. However, to describe it we must go further and say that for the "theocentricity" already familiar to the abstract school it substituted a "christocentricity" from which sprang up all the spirituality that we describe as christology.'[16] Aware of the importance of Bérulle in religious history, another of his biographers, M. J. Dagens, risks a comparison with the reform in understanding brought about by Descartes. 'Its consequences are as important for the history of French Catholicism as the night of Descartes' illumination was for our philosophy.'[17]

I think that these statements are not excessive, and that we have a 'Copernican' or 'Cartesian' revolution, whichever one likes to call it, because it would bring about considerable upheavals throughout the church. It is worth analysing the actual content of this 'revolution'. Its major significance has been well presented by L. Cognet. 'The incarnate Word is the essential manifestation of God: in him the incomprehensible God makes himself understood, the ineffable God makes himself heard, and the invisible God makes himself seen. So it is pure illusion to want to attain him outside this essential manifestation.'[18] The chief text by Bérulle to consult on this subject is the *Discours de l'état et les grandeurs de Jesus*. To illustrate Bérulle's thought, I shall quote a particuarly famous text, taken from that volume, which is typically characteristic of the style of Bérulle:

> From all eternity there was a God worthy of infinite worship, but there was not yet an infinite worshipper: there was a God worthy of being infinitely loved and served, but there was no infinite man or servant who could give infinite service and love.

> Now you, O Jesus, are that worshipper, that man, that servant infinite in power, in quality, in dignity, fully to accomplish this duty and render this divine homage. You are that man, loving, worshipping and serving the supreme majesty as it is worthy to be loved, served and honoured. And just as there is a God worthy of being adored, served and loved, so too in you, my Lord Jesus, there is a God adoring, loving and serving him from all eternity in the nature which was united with your person in the fullness of time (*Grandeurs de Jésus*, p.183).

In its compactness, this text sums up the whole of Bérulle's thought. It is in Jesus Christ that God is known in his true measure (which is infinite); it is in Jesus Christ that he is loved as he should be (which is beyond all possibility of loving). It follows that in knowing Jesus Christ we shall know God, and in loving Jesus Christ we shall love God. The object of all religious knowledge and all spiritual love can therefore only be Jesus Christ. Therefore the thought of the believer – if he wants to attain the truth – must be wholly and integrally directed towards him. To seek God outside Jesus Christ is to waste time and to mislead oneself. With Bérulle, we enter into a new conception of Christianity, a new way of living which one can call 'christocentricity'. All attention must be directed towards Christ; everything must come from him; everything must revolve around him. This is the 'Copernican revolution' proposed by Bérulle. It is no longer God who must be at the centre of the quest and of faith; it is the Christ. A decentralization has taken place. From now on, everything will revolve around the christocentric pole.

This is the opinion of the chief modern commentators on Bérulle. One of them, Father G. Rotureau, writes: 'Thus the incarnate Word is not only a model, a perfect realization of the ideal . . . He is both the ideal and the principle at the same time, and a principle which, in some way, simply makes up a single person with the one who believes in him. It is no longer so much a matter of imitating Christ as allowing oneself to be made by him, of allowing him to live in one. This has been called passive christocentricity.'[19] Thus the essential approach commended by Bérulle consists in putting oneself face to face with the mystery of the incarnation. 'The basic thesis of Bérullianism is to put the mystery of the incarnation at the centre of history and at the centre of the Christian life' (Cochois, p.56). And it is from there that one can arrive at the knowledge of God. The thesis goes a long way – and it will make some theologians frown: it is in the human nature of Christ that we can see not only the one God but even God the

Trinity. In fact Bérulle puts forward the curious argument that Christ is so much the 'revelation of God' that by analogy one can find in him all the attributes and processions of the divine being in their intrinsic perfection. In this connection, P. Cochois notes: 'Bérulle does not hesitate to consider the Incarnation as a second Trinity . . . For him there is a first Trinity, the Trinity of subsistence in unity of essence, which is the Father, the Son and the Holy Spirit; and a second Trinity, a Trinity of essence in unity of subsistence, which is composed of the body, the soul and the divinity of Jesus' (p.60).

From these theological analyses, Bérulle drew conclusions which were clearly very important. The first is that the prime object for the believer to study must be the living Christ, the real Christ as history describes him. 'The object of his insatiable curiosity,' writes P. Cochois, 'is the incarnate Word in each of his conditions, as he is in himself and in the new order of grace' (p.69). The second is that the apostle must have a major preoccupation: not so much that of making known God, as of making known Jesus Christ, of showing 'the unfathomable riches of the mystery of the incarnate Word'. He has been given the well-deserved title 'apostle of the incarnate Word'. These positions are immediately striking for their innovative quality (the commentaries of the period show this), and some people were even disturbed by their rashness. Thus we see Bérulle use formulas which at other times were reserved for language intended to describe God as the supreme being (and not the humanity of Jesus). For example, he expresses his reverence for 'Jesus, the true sun and the true centre of the world',[20] and he recognizes him as 'the saviour, the principle, and the father of the future age',[21] and so on.

Of course this did not prevent Bérulle from directing his thought intensively towards the thrice-holy God. However, we can see the approach he felt justified in making: it is because Christ has revealed to us the Father who is in heaven that we believe in him and can revere him. It was only at a second stage – the time of rediscovery comes after the time of search – that Bérulle sought to relate all the attention, the fervour and the love at the disposal of human beings to this transcendent God. At that point Bérulle proclaimed more than anyone that all depends on God and all returns to him. Here – in the second stage of his spirituality – Bérulle turned out to be more theocentric than anyone before him. However, as others have recognized, this was an attitude which was arrived at and permitted only as a second stage. It was the adoption of an ontological position: God, once known, must be regarded as the first of beings, and will be 'the first to be served'. However, that does not alter the fact that to have access to him – in the heuristic phase, which for human beings is and will always remain the first – we must first go through Christ. Thus the Christ becomes the Alpha and Omega – rather than God himself. This is the meaning of the christocentricity which Bérulle initiated.

What consequences would stem from this shift in perspectives? The first would be of a theological kind, and would make themselves felt in Bérulle's own works and in his spiritual activity. An early modification was of a technical nature, if we may put it that way. It appears in a discussion of the ideas one might have of the hierarchy of beings in relation to God: the relationship of the angels to Christ is modified. Whereas Dionysius the Areopagite puts the angels 'around the throne of God' and therefore above the humanity of Jesus, Bérulle puts Jesus above the angels. Orcibal notes: from 22 July 1614, Bérulle announces the institution of the solemnity of Jesus and, against Dionysius, proclaims that 'all the angels worship the God-Man, thus beginning a complete "reversal of hierarchies" '; and he adds that 'this is a crucial point in his conversion to theocentricity'.[22]

However, other much more important consequences can already be detected. In the first place is the appearance of historicity – in advance of historicism – in religious thought. This is a crucial event, and its consequences are immense. It orients Christian thought, and particularly Catholic thought, on the consideration of the historical aspect of revelation, and as a result, favours the historicization of this revelation and thus the faith that feeds on it. However, we must not anticipate. The importance of this change in perspective has been noted by most commentators. For example, P. Cochois remarks: Bérullianism 'presented a marked historic character. The incarnation is first and foremost a historical event, or even, more precisely, it is the centre of the history of the world . . . ; it gives the world a new centre'; and the author makes this portentous observation: because its metaphysical, and therefore strictly theological, connotations are considerable, 'it establishes a new principle in nature'.[23] He returns to saying that from Bérulle on – though Bérulle himself could not assess the consequences – the principle of faith, faith in God and his will, is no longer to be sought in nature but in history, in human development and not in the mystery of the world. Here is a 'decentralization' of religious thought with incalculable consequences: all modern christocentricity, which I shall study in the last chapters, and which goes so far as the adoption of a Christianity without God, an atheistic Christianity, is contained in nucleus in these methodological stances. We shall see how these developments take place in due course.

These deeply meaningful critical observations can be made retrospectively by us, twentieth-century witnesses. But it is interesting to note that some perspicacious figures were already able to make them, in one way or another, during the lifetime of Bérulle. Critics in fact not only perceived the revolutionary character of his conceptions ('the Copernican revolution') but guessed at the risks and the dangers that would threaten the integrity of the Catholic faith itself. In fact he was accused during his lifetime of idolatry. He was charged with having so magnified the person of Christ, of having so identified Christ's human nature with his divine nature, that he was leading believers to practise a real cult of *latreia* towards this human nature. The thoughts of Christ were directly divine thoughts; the actions of Christ were directly divine actions; that is why for Bérulle the worship due to Christ the man had to become a truly divine worship. Hence the accusation that would be made against him of favouring an 'idolatry' of Christ.[24]

Bérulle was led to make two responses to this criticism. The first took the form of an excuse. It consisted in saying that human weakness was at fault here. If man's thought were stronger, he could think directly of God; if he has need of Christ to think of him, that is because of his weakness. J. Orcibal notes: 'Accused of idolatry, Bérulle begins by presenting the current response: recourse to the senses is made necessary by our weakness, "God stammers to his children." '[25] However, in contrast, the second response is simply a confirmation of his basic position. It is necessary to take our side, he says: our way of thinking about the problem of God is wrong (the error has been made since Abraham, and in fact since the Greek thinkers). We must not seek to discern this supreme reality through nature and our conscience; from now on we must learn to reflect on it through history, through historical facts, and above all through a particular historical fact, the incarnation which came about in Jesus of Nazareth. Here, too, J. Orcibal gives a good description of his reaction. 'With more originality, Bérulle then showed a consequence of the Incarnation of the one who had been pleased to embody himself, not for a time, but for ever, in human nature . . . He wanted to establish a new religion in this world, based on the belief in and adoration of this mystery, and divine and corporeal religion all together.'[26] Thus according to Bérulle the first true religion was born only with Christ (so that all the others should be banished), and with it came the first valid way of thinking about the problem of God. Outside Christ there is no salvation. As we can see, the 'revolution' was important, even if its author clearly did not see its immense consequences at the time. The very foundations of Christianity, and in particular of Catholicism, were put in question. From then on Christianity would present itself essentially as belief in Christ. And this was the faith which from then on was expected to provide the believer with all the necessary facts and, among other things, faith in a transcendent God. Faith in God depends on faith in Jesus Christ. In this way modern christocentricity was born; and it was born with one particular characteristic that it did not have in the first centuries, when it formed a pendant to theocentricity: it laid claim to being exclusive. Faith in Christ had to be sufficient to meet all man's religious needs. It was enough to 'proclaim Jesus Christ' for religious life to regain strength and vigour.

The influence of Bérulle was exercised less by his writings than by his institutions and his works: we should not forget that his thought gave rise to the seminaries, so that every level of the Catholic church would be subject to his influence. It is interesting to see how this influence gradually spread, until we come down to our own day.

2. The development of an autonomous christocentricity

The influence of Bérulle on the evolution of the Catholic church was considerable: it was perhaps one of the most important influences that can be discerned. In the first place, of course, this was due to the profundity of his analyses (it has been said of him that he was the greatest spiritual theologian since Thomas Aquinas). As we have seen, they affected the psychological and social foundations of Catholicism (though of course without touching on its doctrine). However, that is also connected with the fact that his influence was felt through an extraordinary network of actions, the depth and variety of which have scarcely been equalled. Let me discuss for a while the profundity and efficiency of the psychological and social networks by which his teaching was diffused (and which functioned in full conformity with what we know now to be the laws of social psychology).

(a) The spiritual legacy of Bérulle

The first influential network was formed by the religious society which Bérulle founded in 1611, the Oratory of France (or as he called it, The Oratory of Jesus and Mary Immaculate), conceived of along the lines of St Philip Neri's Italian Oratory. There he found disciples dedicated to his ideas: Louis Thomassin (who died in 1695), Massillon (died in 1742) and above all the philosopher Malebranche (whose activity would extend up to 1715). The philosophy of the last-mentioned echoes Bérullian themes – when it ventures into the religious sphere, which is often, not to say constant. In Malebranche, everything is concentrated on Christ: he is the incarnation of the truth, of all truths. It is to Christ that we owe our knowledge of both mathematical truths and metaphysical truths.[27] One can say without exaggeration that his philosophy is 'christocentric'. Furthermore, when Bérulle was made Cardinal in 1627, his personal prestige, in the glow of pontifical favour, could only grow, and must have indirectly strengthened the authority of his disciples.

The second network of influence was formed by the structures of the Church of France (which were quite homogeneous: we are already in a very Gallican ambiance). Concerned for a spiritual renaissance which had become urgent, and which the Council of Trent had just set in motion, at that time this church was trying to strengthen its structures; in this connection it undertook the most urgent task, the reform of the clergy. To make sure that clergy were trained properly, very structured institutions were created, which were called seminaries. This formula was to extend in subsequent centuries throughout the whole of the Catholic church, and the original organization was retained right down to recent years. And who created and organized these first seminaries, gave them their atmosphere, their methods of work and education? The pupils of Bérulle. It was Jean-Jacques Olier (1608–1657) who began the institution, in the shadow of the modern church of St Sulpice (at that time still under construction).[28] To provide staff for these seminaries, he created a society of priests, the Messieurs de Saint Sulpice (or Sulpicians). It was under their direction that the new priests would receive their training (and prepare for the spiritual renaissance of the seventeenth century). A friend and disciple in the theological order of Bérulle, the great apostle Vincent de Paul, also created a similar group: the Congregation of the Priests of Mission, whose centre was the parish of St Lazare (hence their name of Lazarists); these model priests were also involved in the training of clergy in the seminaries. Now all these teachers of the young clergy, Sulpicians and Lazarists, were influenced by the teaching of Bérulle (resistance would come later). Thus all of them were more or less consciously active agents in spreading the Bérullian doctrine of christocentricity. Their influence was profound. The proof of this is that eminent priests soon began to emerge from these seminaries, some of which became saints. One might mention St Jean Baptiste de la Salle

(1651–1719), who in turn founded a teaching institution which was to exercise great influence, this time in civil society, the Frères des Écoles Chrétiennes; St Grignon de Montfort (1673–1716), who also created congregations which were destined to exercise considerable influence on religious opinion: the Missionaries of Mary and then the Daughters of Wisdom. Bérullian doctrine was spread through all these channels: in this way, little by little, for the moment it won over the whole world of religious thought in France. By the end of the century, the intellectual élite had been won over to Bérullian christocentricity. As we shall see, in the century following, its influence would simply spread wider and end up by leaving its stamp on the whole thought of the French church. Thus in creating the Oblates of Mary Immaculate, Monsignor de Mazenod (1782–1861) in turn gave a new force to Bérullian christocentricity. It was the same with the venerable Libermann (1802–1852), who restored the Congregation of the Fathers of the Holy Spirit, and who also took the side of Bérullian christocentricity. As the historian J. Orcibal remarked: 'For three centuries these various congregations have trained virtually all French clergy in the seminaries, and through them – *sacerdos forma cleri* – have shaped the religious sensibility of our country.'[29] Now all these congregations, following their founders, disseminated christocentric interpretations. Their members concentrated the fervour of their faith and their love on Christ: it was from him that they expected sole access to God.

Finally, this influence of Bérullian thought – after a passing eclipse at the end of the eighteenth century – would undergo yet further developments in France in the nineteenth century with some great spiritual figures like Père Gratry, who restored the French Oratory; Abbé Huvelin; Mgr Gay; and among the monks, Dom Marmion (whose works were very christocentric, cf. *Le Christ vie de l'âme*). One could include in this line of influence the action of Abbé Migne, who, by producing his famous *Patrology*, sought to give a more historical dimension to the foundations of the faith, thus acting in conformity to the wishes of Bérulle; in doing this he also contributed towards orienting thought in the direction of christocentricity. Little by little this influence of French theological thought – which continued to be exercised through the medium of Sulpician and Lazarist seminaries, now spread throughout the world – won over large realms of Catholicism. However, resistance would soon appear which would mean opposition to the excessive pretensions of the christocentricity inspired by Bérulle.

(b) Resistance to christocentricity

It seems that this resistance took on either a passive or an active shape, depending on circumstances. The passive resistance was of the type that the social psychologist would call hostility to innovation: every innovation comes up against the inertia of structures. This is what happened with some theocentricity. Thus the whole of the institutional church remained clearly theocentric: the Roman authorities of course maintained the traditional position in their declarations and their official positions, simply because it had the advantage of having been there first. We may note, for example, that the christocentric theses inspired by Bérulle could not breach the defences of the First Vatican Council. As one observer put it, 'The Fathers of the First Vatican Council did not dare to say that the church is the mystical body of Christ.'[30] For their part, the great monastic institutions remained strangers to the movement. The Carthusians maintained their theocentric course. There was a certain struggle between the two currents among the White Friars and Carmelites, at least in France (elsewhere, theocentricity continued quietly to occupy its ground). After the seventeenth century, the theocentric current was championed by Pères Duval and Gallimant. But Bérulle intervened personally.

He attempted a kind of seizure of certain Carmels from 1615 to 1620, imposing on the monks a curious practice, that of a 'vow of slavery' to Jesus and Mary. The religious authorities censured this practice a little later, as being 'excessive'.[31] There was a setback, and Bérullian christocentricity was kept under restraint in the chief Carmels of France, and then in the Carmels abroad. Consequently all the contemplative orders imperturbably maintained their faithfulness to theocentricity (as one can in fact confirm even today).

A degree of active resistance was also organized, in the immediate entourage of Bérulle. For example, at the Oratory, a great figure like Condren (1580–1641), close to Bérulle, since he was to be his successor as head of the Oratory, presented a spiritual doctrine of the incarnation which was completely opposed to that of Bérulle. For Bérulle, as I have said, the incarnation is as it were the 'accomplishment' of God (see above). Now with Condren the incarnation again becomes a 'humiliation' of God, to such a degree does he have an elevated idea of the divine majesty. 'God is so great,' he writes, 'so pure, so withdrawn into himself, so remote from creatures, that to bear witness to him the humanity of Christ is *destroyed* and consumed in his presence.'

The incarnation can only be represented as consumption, the destruction of a human nature. L. Cognet, one of his commentators, notes: 'The Word only assumes his humanity to have something to annihilate, which ends up in a strange nihilism of the incarnation.'[32] Thus Condren takes up positions diametrically opposed to those of Bérulle: we cannot know anything of God in Christ, since the nature of Christ is 'nothing', because it is radical annihilation. These views were in turn contested by P. Bourgoing (1585–1662), who shortly after Condren succeeded as head of the Oratory, and who defended the christocentric theses of Bérulle to the end.

St Francis de Sales (1567–1622) presents an interesting case. He was aware of Bérullian christocentricity: one even feels that he was sensitive to it for some time. Subsequently, however, his reaction was very vigorous. Perhaps he felt its latent perils. L. Cognet, whose analysis I have adopted, shows very well the reaction in the direction of theocentricity which St Francis de Sales adopted. 'Devotion predominantly to God, with its rejection of imaginative and conceptual approaches, always made him afraid . . . However, his own work also shows a very marked tendency to consider God in his philosophical entity rather than in his concrete historical manifestations, and in the last analysis it is towards the divine essence that he guides the soul of his disciple. Strictly speaking, in this approach, Christ does not play a primary role, and he is hardly envisaged as the Word incarnate: when there is some question of him, it is more to use him as an example than to seek him as a mediator. In this connection his spirit is clearly that of the Middle Ages, and it will be useless to look for Bérullianism there.'[33]

We can imagine how reactions will be even more vigorous from the Jansenist side. This can be seen in Saint-Cyran and Nicole.[34] The attitude of Saint-Cyran is interesting. As his biographer J. Orcibal shows, to begin with he was quite sensitive to views that Bérulle might put forward, in particular on the incarnation, but later he made a marked return towards theocentricity, perhaps following personal meditations on the human condition, on its wretchedness, and on the need for penitence (as I have said, an eminently theocentric virtue). Finally, the whole of the Jansenist movement remained very firmly attached to theocentricity: God is the centre of all thought, all action, all love. Similar reactions can be seen in the same period in non-Catholic Christianity. The churches of the Reformation were not influenced by Bérulle's views, nor were the Orthodox churches.The mystical sects of the period (like those arising from Swedenborg's visions) also remained eminently theocentric.

Thus Bérullian christocentricity generated a powerful wave. As we shall see, its effect has made itself felt down to our days. But we should not suppose, for all that, that it was exclusive. Solid positions remained, and were held by theocentricity. Many thoughtful figures remained distrustful of what Orcibal dares to call the 'theological clumsiness' of Bérulle.

(c) Reactions from the world of culture

The problem I am discussing is a strictly theological one. However, it inevitably had cultural, i.e. philosophical and scientific, consequences, because in this century religious preoccupations were inseparable from secular preoccupations. What positions were taken up? We can answer straight away: philosophical thought, like scientific thought in the seventeenth and eighteenth centuries, remained very strictly theocentric. All in all, the thinkers of this century were believers, and they centred all their specialist speculations on faith in God. Certainly there was little chance of their calling themselves christocentric: we cannot see what place a philospher, *qua* philosopher, and *a priori* a physician or an astronomer, could accord to Christ in their speculations (as I have said, an exception must be made in the case of Malebranche, who introduced Christ into his theories of knowledge, but I shall have to return to that). Thus, as I have said, Descartes is fundamentally theocentric: God is the key to his system. It is God who guarantees our evidence; it is God who creates the eternal truths; it is God who, by his initial 'flick', gives movement and life to the world. He pays minimal attention to Christ, at least as a philosopher; at any rate, historicity (and therefore that of Christ) has little credit in his eyes. It will be the same thing with Spinoza, whose God-substance is the absolute term of reference for his whole system. Certainly he accords a greater importance than Descartes – after his conversion – to Christ and his mission, but he puts it in the moral rather than the metaphysical order. Leibniz, too, is fundamentally theocentric; all the monads are in relation – according to a harmony established from all eternity – with the supreme monad which is seated at the summit of the hierarchy of monads, beyond the angelic monads. Christ figures in the hierarchy of beings, near to the summit, but of course he is subordinate to God; and as a Protestant Christian, Leibniz he shares the theocentric views of Luther (which he contrasts with those of the Catholic Bossuet who, as a distant disciple of Bérulle, had some leanings towards christocentricity). But in this philosophical sphere we must make one strange exception, for Malebranche. As I have said, he rejoined the Oratory, and in doing so came fatally under the influence of Bérulle. He read Bérulle piously and attentively. He nurtured his spiritual life on meditations on the states of Jesus, and in theological matters he continually thought with reference to Christ. He believed that it was by Christ and Christ alone that we can have 'access to the Father'. Now it is strange to note that we shall rediscover the projection of this theory in his philosophy. I have already pointed to this. However, I must stress once again that in his case both the pure philosopher and the scientist (Malebranche was a member of the Academy of Sciences) proved to be as christocentric as the theologian. His philosophy invites us to the contemplation of all things in God; we only obtain authentic knowledge in a vision of God (see *Les Recherches de la Vérité*). However, this 'vision of God' is not easy in itself. It is therefore fortunate that Christ came to help us to have it. Revealing himself by and in Christ, God gives us access to his secrets, and thus to true knowledge. So it is thanks to the intercession of Christ, and by his mediation, that we can have an assured access to whatever truths there may be: mathematical truths, physical truths, truths about man. Thus the philosophy of Malebranche is in perfect harmony with his theology – which is rare enough in the history of ideas. In the end, one could say that the two are one. This could be admirable, but it would nevertheless lead to some strange consequences. If it is true that for Descartes, an atheist cannot be a geometrician (he granted that the atheistic geometrician could not find any guarantee that his reasoning is valid), Malebranche is led to go even further: to be a good geometrician, to be a good physician, it is certainly necessary to believe in God, but it is still better to believe in Christ (a Jew and a Moslem would have more difficulty in proving their propositions; and he thanks God for having given him faith in Christ). All the same, this welcome accorded to christocentricity by Malebranche, philosopher and scientist, is curious.

All in all, the thinkers of the seventeenth century were theocentric. So too were almost all the thinkers of the eighteenth century. Kant based all his philosophy on belief in a God, a moral personage, supreme judge of consciences. He is the foundation of duty, the source and guarantor of all noumenal realities, that is to say, true realities. For their part, the great literary authors of the seventeenth and eighteenth centuries remained profoundly theocentric: here the influence of Bérulle was minimal. Racine is theocentric (to be persuaded of this, it is enough to reread his plays with a religious dimension, like *Esther* and, above all, *Atha-*

lie). In the eighteenth century, Voltaire was theocentric in his own way: he could not escape the Great Watchmaker. Rousseau was theocentric: his Savoyard curate worships God, creator and ordainer of the worlds and the beauties of nature. In his pantheistic paganism, Goethe is also theocentric: Doctor Faustus trembles before God (and engages in dialogue with his adversary Mephistopheles); there is little reference to Christ, even on the eve of a paschal resurrection which sees the doubtful salvation of Marguerite. So we can say that in the seventeenth and eighteenth centuries, the whole of the cultural world remained massively faithful to theocentricity. The influence of christocentricity had not yet penetrated – for the moment, at any rate. By contrast, this influence would gradually infiltrate, little by little, into the life of the Catholic church – according to the laws of social psychology.

3. The penetration of christocentricity into the church

In the course of the seventeenth and eighteenth centuries, christocentricity penetrated slowly but surely into the church – I am speaking of the institutional church – following the networks (or if one prefers, the channels) which any society offers to an expansion in the realm of social psychology, namely, its administrative structures, its rites, its patterns of expansion and its vital nerves. First christocentricity won over the social structures, that is to say, the institutions which safeguard the perpetuity of the social body of the church. Granted, the Papacy, guardian of the faith, did not modify its doctrinal positions in any way. No one felt the need to convene a council during these two centuries: from both a practical and a dogmatic point of view they lived on the momentum of the Council of Trent. As a result, the initial equilibrium between theocentricity and christocentricity adopted by the first councils (at least through the virtue of prudence) was maintained and conserved. As for the Papacy itself, in its way of living and acting, of governing the church and promoting the faith, it remained strictly faithful to the predominant and vigorous theocentricity which had prevailed from the beginning of the age of Constantine. The Pope governs, as common father of pastors and the faithful. He exercises his authority in accordance with the social model of the father which I described earlier. For their part, the faithful offer the Pope deferential and submissive obedience. The society of the church remains an integrally hierarchical society (despite the continual criticism of the Protestant world). However, if the social status of the Pope, and also of the bishops, remains unchanged, that is not the case with priests. Under the influence of

Bérullian christocentricity the status of the priest changed in a profound way (as we shall see, this was perhaps one of the most important factors in the general evolution of the church towards christocentricity which took place in the twentieth century). This is connected with the fact that the influence of Bérullianism was exercised above all through the medium of the seminaries, where future priests were trained. We know the immense interest that Bérulle had in the priesthood. His writings on the subject are innumerable. It was the same with his disciples. Here are some of the important changes which he introduced. Before him, in fact, the model of the priest in the Catholic church was inspired by the priest in the temple of Jerusalem. This was a very theocentric conception. The priest was above all the man of God. He was the man, among other men, called by God himself (through a vocation analogous to that of Samuel), set apart (*segregatus*, as the ancient texts put it), and charged with a sacred mission, that of interceding for his people with God. '*Plorebunt sacerdotes inter vestibulum et altare*.'

Bérulle would change all that. He proposed a directly christocentric model: the priest must be 'another Christ'. '*Sacerdos alter Christus*', people said after him, using a formula from the seventeenth century which, we should note, does not appear in scripture. And when one is aware of the characteristic role that he assigned to Christ – which I have tried to demonstrate above – we can see the revolution in social psychology that would take place. To be precise: if for Bérulle Christ is the presence of God among men, his only attributable and meaningful presence, and if we consider that the priest is another Christ, that amounts to saying that he, too, is the 'sign' of the presence of God among men. This brings about a complete reversal of the role of the priest; instead of being the presence of man to God, he becomes the presence of God to man. The biblical priest brings men's prayers to God; the Catholic priest brings down the grace of God on men. From that point he exercises a 'sacerdotal' role: he is charged with distributing sacred things to men. Granted, this conception is not entirely new: spiritual writers had already put it forward. But it was proposed as representing the second mission of the priest; he was considered above all to be the ambassador of men to God. Bérulle brought about a reversal of relationships between these two functions. The second mission became the first. For the priest himself, living out his priestly ministry in person, this change of relationship appeared to be of little importance, but in social life, where the laws of influence remained bound to inexorable logical consequences, over a spread of more than two centuries, very important consequences would ensure. The effects of this 'reversal' made themselves felt in the various forms of activity which the priest exercised in religious society itself, and from there in secular society. No longer feeling himself essentially the representative of men before God, but rather that of God before men, the priest would be led to modify his ministerial attitude; he no longer regarded himself as the worshipper of God, but as the good shepherd, seeking to draw souls towards God. This conception is virtually non-existent in the Old Testament. It is typically christocentric ('I am the Good Shepherd'). We can see it spreading in the seminaries, and soon in the parishes. Consequently a new model of the priest developed which had not been known hitherto: the priest as pastor of souls. He was less preoccupied with God than with his faithful (later, even the altar was turned round in church to make this idea concrete). He, above all, had a cure of souls. This model underwent a great development (at least in the Catholic church, because it is unknown in Protestantism and even in Orthodoxy). It spread, little by little, during the second half of the seventeenth century and during the eighteenth (when there were so many 'good pastors', even if the élite was anti-clerical). Thus this model of the priest would extend to the whole of the Catholic church; so much so that many people imagined it to be the only one possible, though it is barely three centuries old (the type of the 'curé' of the parish is unknown in the primitive church, and even in the Middle Ages and the Renaissance; it is what one might call a Bérullian product). The influence of this kind of priest was considerable. And even those who are not sociologists may suppose that he was the one who for the most part gave its original appearance (in contrast to that of other churches) to the Catholic church in the course of these last centuries. So it was through the grass-roots that Bérulle's contribution in favour of christocentricity was made in the church.

The penetration of Bérullian christocentricity also made itself felt in a development of liturgical rites. In the first place, we may note the introduction of religious feasts devoted to Christ as man. Among the innovations dating from the seventeenth century and made on the impetus of Bérulle and his disciples we may note the feasts of the Transfiguration, of the Precious Blood, of the Holy Name of Jesus: later, we see the appearance of the Sacred Heart and the Five Wounds of Christ. Some of these festivals did not last very long, like the feast of the Lance and the Nails; of St Suaire; or that of the Sacred Head of Christ, which was to complete the feast of the Sacred Heart of Christ. The last introduction of one of the feasts inspired by christocentricity was that of Christ the King in the twentieth century. Saint Jean Eudes, whose spirituality is of Bérullian inspiration, and therefore christocentric, did a great deal to develop the cult of the Sacred Heart. He even proposed that each year a great feast should be celebrated in honour of the historic humanity of Christ, which he called the 'Feast of Jesus'. This initiative was approved in Rome in 1623, but it fell into disuse. This penetration of christocentricity into liturgical life is also represented by the considerable development undergone by certain devotions. One of them is that of the cult of the Heart of Christ, celebrated for the first time in 1672. This celebration was strengthened by the appearances of the Sacred Heart at Paray le Monial, which took place the following year, in 1673. People also tried to arouse devotion to the Heart of Mary, but the initiative did not have any results (St Jean Eudes had produced an office of the Heart of Mary). Furthermore, devotion to Christ under the form of the eucharistic presence also underwent a great development. At that time a special celebration, with the exposition and benediction of the Holy Sacrament, was started. It was called 'Salut du Saint-Sacrement', and was to enjoy great success among the faithful (right down to our days, or almost so). The practice of 'visits to the Holy Sacrament' was also commended.[35] M. Olier, appointed vicar of the new church of Saint Sulpice, brought this last practice into fashion, from 1642 on. The priest is invited to order his life around eucharistic piety: he is advised to celebrate the mass every day. It is from this custom that we can date the popular habit of regarding the priest as the one who says mass (a very widespread formula in France, in particular). To these devotions may be added practices which indirectly reflect a very marked tendency towards christocentricity, like devotions to Mary. At that time they enjoyed a great boom. Olier commended devotion to the childhood of Our Lady; he laid great stress on the feast of the Presentation of Mary in the Temple (21 November), which became the major feast of the Company of St Sulpice. It was the same with the festival of the Holy Family. Another Bérullian, St Grignon de Montfort, multiplied centres of devotion to Mary, especially in the Vendée.

The influence of christocentricity in this period also spread to the realms of action and the apostolate. The missionaries who went on long journeys, in the footsteps of the great explorers of America and Africa in the previous century, set out not so much to reveal to these pagan populations the existence of the true God, but, in accordance with the task entrusted to them, to proclaim Jesus Christ directly. We may recall the numberless engravings, windows or bas-reliefs depicting the missionary disembarking in some distant land and beginning by brandishing the crucifix (and in principle the natives were converted on the spot). This is the way in which people portrayed the arrival of St Francis Xavier in India, for example (he had been active in the previous century, and no doubt in a more subtle way; but the engravings in this style appeared in the middle of the seventeenth century). The great missionary movement of the seventeenth and eighteenth centuries was strongly marked by the dominant christocentricity, at least in France and in neighbouring missionary countries. Within France, apostles were also active struggling against the impiety prevalent in many European countries, and in France in particular. The methods of the apostolate were similar among these populations. They preached directly a 'Christ crucified who died for our sins', and tried to move the recalcitrant to pity. So it is that the Lazarist 'missions' were active in the country, as were the Redemptorists (a congregation created by St Alphonse de Liguori in Italy, which was also very christocentric in inspiration).

Little by little, the whole spiritual life of the church was impregnated by Bérullian christocentricity. Certainly the great classical congregations and their spiritual descendants remained faithful to the theocentricity which had become traditional. This was the case with the contemplatives in their cloisters, like the Carthusians, the White Friars and Carmelite nuns, and all the Benedictines. They remained faithful to their mission of being worshippers of God Most High. They lived in penitence and prayer, fulfilling their exalted task of singing the glory of God: continuity was maintained with the great solitaries of Mount Carmel at the time of Elijah. As a result, it should be said in advance, christocentricity could not flourish among the great contemplative orders; they remained faithful to theocentricity. However, during this time, christocentricity gained in influence among the whole of the Christian population: the part that it assigned to sensitivity certainly favoured its expansion. Popular traditions with religious orientations developed; they all favoured christocentricity. Thus, for example, in its devotions and practices the Christian people attached increasing importance to times as christocentric as Advent (we know the interest in it which Bérulle, Olier and the French School had; it was in this context that *Rorate coeli desuper*, a characteristic hymn of the time, was composed). Numerous popular songs were in circulation which evoked the love of Christ, his power and the saving virtue of his sacrifice. One brilliant writer composed *Jesu dulcis memoria*. Consequently popular piety tended to place the whole of life under the sign of Christ. Taking account of the practices of this period, one historian, M. Gautier, entitled one of his writings *Toute la vie en Jesus Christ* (All life in Jesus Christ). One kind of sanctification was proposed which aroused some interest. It must be said that all this time the good people, those who lived close to nature, remained quite spontaneously theocentric (for the reasons that I mentioned earlier). They remained faithful to the daily prayer consisting in praise of God and petition to him. They continued to mark the great rhythms of life by theocentric observances: they were born under the sign of God with baptism, married with the support of the divine grace 'in church', and buried with the divine blessing. 'Life with Christ' was not their lot. Doubtless that seemed to them to be too elaborate, and it already presupposed a degree of culture. Some christocentric practices certainly had an effect on the people, as for instance the practice of the *Angelus*, rung three times a day on the village bell. It was accepted as a rite, if not as a conscious devotion, from the seventeenth century on (having been inaugurated in the previous century, after the victory of Lepanto), not for its mystical meaning but doubtless because it made its mark on the rhythms of daily life, at least in the rural world.

The activities of charity also took on a christocentric stamp, above all under the influence of St Vincent de Paul, a great admirer of Bérulle. He conceived of charity not after the manner of St Thomas, as a diffusive extension of the divine love, but as participation in the love of Jesus Christ. First of all he tried to show the poor as 'brothers in Jesus Christ', and the sick as 'suffering members of Jesus Christ', a new approach, born completely of Bérullian christocentricity.

In short, we feel that christocentricity is on the march through the seventeenth and eighteenth centuries. Each day it gains ground. It certainly encountered resistance in the 'spiritual élite' and among the church authorities. But it developed among the mass of faithful. Little by little it penetrated the very foundation of Christianity. And starting from the grass roots, as we shall see, little by little it reached the summits.

V

The Growing Predominance of Christocentricity
(Nineteenth and Early Twentieth Centuries)

On the threshold of the nineteenth century (from the point of view of social psychology), two logics cross and finally enter into competition in the inner sphere of the Catholic church: a logic which stems from theocentricity and one which stems from christocentricity.

The logic of theocentricity follows from an assured faith in God, in his transcendence over history, and calls for attitudes and practices which lead to deference and submission. The logic of christocentricity derives from faith in Christ, the presence of God immanent in history, and inspires attitudes and practices which provoke changes in society and action for reform. The two currents have almost equal force at the beginning of the century.[1] Subsequently, the christocentric current makes itself increasingly felt and soon supplants the earlier theocentricity. One might say that this evolution takes place in two stages: first of all we see, outside the Catholic church, and then within it, a progressive weakening of theocentricity; and concurrently, in a particular way which I shall outline, we see a progressive strengthening of christocentricity, to such a degree that on the threshold of the modern era (from the beginning of the twentieth century on), we end up with a real triumph of theocentricity, which finally even takes an exclusive form. Each of these stages must be noted if we are to understand the present situation in the Catholic church.[2]

1. First stage: progressive weakening of theocentricity

The very foundations of theocentricity are shaken, in that belief in God goes into serious eclipse, in both the philosophical and the historical spheres (and therefore also in theology).

(a) Shaking of faith in the 'God of philosophers and wise men'

I have shown how from the start this philosophical and scientific foundation was thought to be the indispensable support for religious faith (see chapters I and II). The faith of the Gospels, of the apostles and the first Christians, presupposes an assured belief on the part of human reason in the existence of a supreme reality (even if there are ambiguities over the exact content of this faith). As I have said, there is no place for atheists in the Gospels.[3] Everyone more or less believed in the existence of a supreme reality: the Jews, the Greeks and even (in a way) the Romans, with their mythology. For example, in his Epistle to the Romans St Paul appeals to this faith which derives from natural reason (Rom. 1.15–20) in speaking of God revealed in Jesus Christ. He sets out merely to confirm natural faith by introducing supernatural faith. 'I will reveal to you this unknown God whom you seek to know,' is the substance of what he says to the sages of the Areopagus. This sort of metaphysical security was assured to Christianity, come what may, over all the following centuries, from antiquity to the Middle Ages, and down to so-called 'modern' times. Now this security was suddenly shattered in the nineteenth century. For the first time in the history of humanity, men and women from very different backgrounds would declare publicly that in their eyes there was no supreme reality of any kind; there was nothing above man. The heavens were empty. This was modern atheism, and this atheism was not only proclaimed in the realm of ideas, but lived out in individual and social life. People showed that it was possible to live quite happily – that is to say, in order and peace – even if one admitted that there is no God above men. This mild atheism began during the nineteenth century: first of all in certain intellectual spheres and then in a particular élite, and from there it went on gradually to influence lower strata of the populace (now one can even find atheist children, of eight to ten years old). This must be noted carefully: for the first time in its history Christianity had come up against atheism. That is not always remembered, but it is a historical fact. It might perhaps be said that there was one period – albeit brief – when Christianity nevertheless found itself confronted with a degree of atheism that claimed attention, which certain brave spirits had dared to commend openly at the Renaissance, appealing to growing science and to philosophy: one thinks, for example, of Giordano Bruno and Campanella. However, it is clear that the church dealt with the problem fairly quickly: the 'hellhounds' were burnt. There was no dialogue. This impious sect was rapidly decimated. And for a while the church found itself back in a state of 'tranquil possession': belief in a God who ordered the world again became the common metaphysical basis of human consciousness to which Christianity addressed itself. However, times were to change.

(b) Remote causes of the crisis

This crisis over theocentricity was provoked by a challenge to its very basis, belief in the existence of a God. It seems that the very first murmurs in this direction can be found in Descartes. As I have said, Descartes believed in God with all his heart. However, to arrive at God, he no longer followed the approaches indicated by Descartes, the famous five ways (by movement, causes, contingency, the perfections and the order of the world). His method forbade this: one cannot doubt experience and then rely on it to get to God. He favoured an approach which, starting from man, must lead us to a human idea of God, since he took pains to show us that this human idea has a 'superhuman' orientation which will take us to real divinity (this is his famous 'ontological' argument). Does it succeed or not? After Kant, there is agreement that this is impossible. However, without entering into the debate we must affirm that the God to whom Descartes leads his contemporaries is in any case a voluntarist God. He is no longer the being subsisting in himself; he is a will which created all things, both truths and realities. This was to give an irrational corner-stone to the universe. The consequences must ultimately be first, agnosticism, and then, logically, absurdity.[4] The 'patching up', proposed by the post-Cartesians, does not work out, either in Malebranche (who found intellectual compensation, as I have pointed out, in the christocentricity inspired by Bérulle), or in Leibniz or in Spinoza. In the last-mentioned we end up with a God without transcendence, who is identified with nature ('*Deus sive natura*'). All in all, people began to get used to the idea – in intellectual opinion, and three generations afterwards, in public opinion – that at all events any human thought of God is, and will always remain, human thought, and therefore relative.

Kant's criticism simply formulated as a law – by the critical analysis of reason – what perceptive spirits had already suspected. Whatever its efforts, human thought could never go beyond itself to arrive at a hypothetical Being-in-itself which could be put above its categories. Human thought cannot transcend itself. So it will remain expectant. Certainly Kant tried to find a more promising way out, by turning towards practical reason, towards the moral conscience and its dictates, which might perhaps lead us to the discovery of a sovereign judge, master of consciences. However, although this approach seems substantially to have sustained the thought of Kant himself, it left the majority of his successors incredulous; to such a degree that Kant's severe criticism only left relativism and criticism in its wake. From now on access to a transcendent God seemed barred to the human conscience. Man was on his own. Thus traditional theocentricity, which leant with all its weight on this belief in God, through speculative theology and moral theology, lost its secret complicity with human reason. This would be a crucial test for it, and we can still experience the harsh consequences.

At the beginning of the nineteenth century, a desperate effort was made by Hegel to try to save the natural reference to God. It is difficult, at least in a few words, to explain why. One has the feeling that at this point human consciousness experienced a kind of nostalgia for God (the great void). It looked for him obstinately and at the same time in confusion: it groped for him. Hegel's reaction in this connection is typical. If speculative reason can only lead to the solitude of the spirit, perhaps, he said, we can find more opportunity in the reactions of 'historical reason', in reason as it acts, as it transforms the world, as it builds history. And Hegel then analyses the action of reason through time, in historicity. He thinks he can see there the work of a reason immanent in the world and among men: it works secretly and sometimes cunningly for the arrival of better worlds, that is to say, ever better states of universal consciousness. It is in this arrival of immanent consciousness in the world that he sees the ultimate response to our questions. And since this is the ultimate response, why not conform to custom and give it the name God (though this abuse of trust gave rise to countless protests)? So it is that Hegel comes to talk of God, in season and out of season, as one might say. He sees God everywhere; he sees him in action everywhere. God brings the worlds into being and makes human activity fruitful. He is the force that makes the passage of time (which one might call History with a capital H) fruitful. It will be also possible to say of this God (with complete ambiguity): 'he who was and is and is to come', without making precise whether he is situated above these times which go past, or whether he is deployed through their course as a guiding force.[5] For a certain period, under the remarkably subtle influence of Hegel, we see the affirmation of a degree of faith in God restored to favour in the thoughts and the writings of notable men of the nineteenth century (above all in the second half). In French cultural circles, and to some degree also abroad, Renan made himself the spokesman of this new interpretation of belief in God. 'How can they accuse me of being an atheist, when I believe in all the religions?', he exclaimed. However, to believe in all the religions is to believe in all the gods; it is to believe in all beliefs, to hold that each of them has spiritual values, that each of them is an 'element in universal consciousness'. This was, in fact, to end up with a cultural pantheism. The very notion of transcendence no longer has a place in such an interpretation: the God of Abraham is the God who belongs culturally to Abraham, and the same is true of the God of Isaac and the God of Jacob; and ultimately for the God of Jesus Christ. The 'sweet dreamer of Galilee' (Renan) could only dream of a God of mercy. The idea of God is to be regarded as one of the greatest successes of human genius. God is the summit of human genius, but as Nietzsche will say, he is always 'human, too human'. It is not enough, then, to speak of God to provide an objective foundation for faith in God, the supreme being, transcendent to human thought. When Nietzsche intervened, proclaiming 'the death of God', he was only noting the evolution which had taken place in the course of the century, and forcing men of his time to reject the mask of hypocrisy which they still wore in talking of a God who was no longer God.

More honest would be the formal denials of the existence of God as formulated by Feuerbach, or Karl Marx ('I hate all gods'); radical negations, which led those who made them to draw from them all the logical consequences concerning man, and to make a new society with no reference to any deity (this was not easy, seeing that it came up against a tradition which had lasted for several millennia). Here the situation is clear: every reference to theocentricity has disappeared radically, and if a degree of religious feeling can be maintained – by concession to public opinion – it goes without saying that it will be cut off from any theocentric roots (we shall see, later, the conditions in which a degree of christocentricity could be maintained). With Nietzsche, too, the denial of God is radical; however, as I have said, for him it was above all a matter of making an assertion. Philosophical thought was exhausted; theological thought was emptied of substance; moral thought no longer had any proper basis (practical Kantianism was rejected). It was a question of saying clearly what all the world was thinking confusedly: God no longer exists for anyone. Nietzsche shouted this out with an almost morbid vehemence. 'God is dead; we have killed him.' All religions became impostures. Later, a generation after Nietzsche, Freud would say the same thing at the beginning of the twentieth century, basing his views on analyses of consciousness in depth. His psycho-analytical explorations do not come up against metaphysical problems, because they do not recognize them (speculations are defence systems, though that does not mean that they are valueless), and lead him to regard the reference to a deity as a last resort of the anguished conscience (as he says in his *Civilization and its Discontents*, 1930, and *Moses and Monotheism*, 1939). Certainly, when Freud analyses religious behaviour he sees in the worship of a good and omnipotent God reference to a Father God of the kind conceived of by theocentricity ('Our Father', as I pointed out above). But whereas this reference to the image of the Father is regarded by theocentricity as the inevitable 'reclothing' of images, the allegorical ornamentation with which one adorns a reality otherwise firmly based in reason, Freud, having put the rational reference in parenthesis – though without denying it – only regards this reference to the Father as a sublimation of original impulses emerging at the level of the super ego. In short, belief in a Father God is only an infantile reaction. This succeeds in emptying reference to God of all valid objective content. Finally, I should add that these philosophical denials of God come on top of the agnosticism (virtually equivalent to atheism) adopted by the scientific thought of the period, in the name of positivism.

In the face of these denials of the existence of God which emerged in philosophy, the efforts nevertheless made to attempt a justification of God did not bear fruit. Blondelism remained hesitant.[6] Neo-Thomism did not have sufficient impact on the scientific world. Bergsonism left people perplexed: did it lead to pantheism or to theism? At the beginning of the century, no one could say. People began to have some awareness of the themes of Kierkegaard, in favour of faith lived out existentially, but they were not yet appreciated as much as they should have been. The first work of Teilhard de Chardin did not show its promise. The result was that no matter in what direction one turned (German thought, French thought or Anglo Saxon thought), the philosophical thought at the beginning of the century seemed void of any serious reference to a deity, a reality superior to man, to whom he was invited to relate himself. 'The heavens are empty, we have put out the last stars', a politician (Viviani) of the times would say: a characteristic statement of the impression that might be had by anyone living in the last generation of the nineteenth century and the first of the twentieth. This great spiritual void is what the Catholic church had to face at the beginning of the century. What was its reaction?

(c) Shaking of faith in the 'God of Jesus Christ'

If one of the bases of theocentricity, its philosophical basis, was shattered ('the God of the philosophers and the wise men' seemed to have disappeared), the theological basis of theocentricity remained, its faith in the 'God of Jesus Christ' (again to use Pascal's terms). One of the first reactions of the Catholic church, confronted with modern atheism, was then to take refuge in this theological basis. That is the reason why during the first third of the century we see the emergence of a whole series of works devoted to positive theology, in which, to put it briefly, God is found in a historical context.

In fact an intellectual outburst of great promise took place in the church during this period. The authorities of the Catholic church said to themselves: 'Since philosophical and scientific thought has betrayed us, we shall show that, by contrast, historical thought strengthens us. We shall prove that the fact of the historical revelation of a transcendent God and saviour of men has never appeared more assured.' So historical works on the texts of scripture multiplied: texts of the Old Testament and then texts of the New, and to supplement them, new editions of Greek and Latin patrology. History would never be more held in honour in the church; that was where salvation was expected. The German theology of the nineteenth century had opened up the way. French theology followed. So between 1880 and 1930, over half a century, we see exegetical work multiplying. People undertook studies on the Pentateuch and the prophets, then works on the gospels. Lives of Jesus appeared, by Papini, Père Lagrange, Karl Adam. Men of letters like Mauriac and Daniel-Rops joined in the movement. In parallel, works on patrology, inaugurated, as is well known, by Abbé Migne with the republishing of hundreds of volumes of the fathers of the church who had been forgotten – again, with apologetic ends in view (in the face of increasing atheism in the nineteenth century) – gained new topicality and vigour. Collections were begun, aimed at restoring the status of 'Christian sources'. This was the great period of what is customarily called 'positive theology'. Everywhere, and in every way, people endeavoured to rest their faith on historicity. Since speculative reason had betrayed them (philosophy seemed to have become atheistic, and science equally so), the supreme hope was in history. This seemed to be the position of those in authority in the Catholic faith (a similar, though less exhaustive movement, also developed in the Reformed churches). Because history was in favour everywhere, there was the thought of killing two birds with one stone:

strengthening the bases of faith, and in addition gaining a new audience from intellectual spheres.

This approach in the context of positive theology had an undeniable success. It seems that we can put to its credit the twofold renaissance of faith which happened throughout the Christian world between 1900 and 1950: a renaissance of faith in the literary world, above all in France (the conversions of Brunetière, Claudel, Péguy, Psichari, Gabriel Marcel, and so on), and the renaissance of faith in popular circles with the appearance on the scene of what was called Catholic Action, after 1930. In my view these two movements certainly arose from this renaissance of positive theology. The only explanation of them, different as they are, is contact with the Bible rediscovered in its primitive authenticity, and contact with Christ rediscovered in his historic authenticity, the 'living Christ', as people said at that time. In both cases the return to historical sources brought about the revival. There is no question in this era of a return of philosophical or scientific thought towards God.[7] From all the evidence, it was the rediscovery of the historical Christ which played a role (which explains how a sudden development of christocentricity appeared immediately afterwards). What was rediscovered was truly 'the God of Jesus Christ'.

However, in fact this movement did not have a very prolonged effect. An event in the epistemological order in fact took place which would compromise everything. As I have said, this 'renaissance' was based on another renaissance, that of positive theology, which derived its authority from the trust which was placed in history. Now from the middle of this century, more and more resolutely, history itself ceased to enjoy this trust – and so did historicity. At any rate, it no longer had demonstrative value. This change of opinion about the value of historical methodology had the gravest consequences for the generation which followed, i.e. that to be found between 1950 and 1970: reference to the 'God of Jesus Christ' was in turn undermined. Here theocentricity lost its last foundation.

We must look at things rather more closely. What was in fact conveyed by 'history' at the middle of this century? First of all, history as a heuristic discipline changed its method, its objective and its aim. Its method changed: it no longer prided itself on the title of a positive and scientific discipline, as it did in the times of Seignobos and Lavisse. It recognized that it was only a conjectural discipline: it made reports on the past, but no longer claimed to establish causal links and provide objective explanations. It was well aware that the historian conditions the history he narrates.

According to the formula of Raymond Aron, 'The historian expresses himself and his universe in the past that he chooses.' The facts are selected and interpreted through personal options of the historian (which are often unconscious): cultural, geopolitical or religious options. One only sees an event through the refracted image which the historian's sensitivity sends back (in this connection, exegetes invoked the theory of form criticism). In the last resort, history in our day can do no more than make claims in the area of social psychology: it shows how the conscience of a society could react at a particular era, confronted with events . . . of which we have no knowledge. It can only have socio-psychological objectives. In this respect it can again have a cultural aim in the broadest sense of the term, namely, to contribute to the enriching of the cultural capital of a society: it can no longer lay claim to any kind of scientific objectivity. History, which had been built up as a synthetic discipline in the nineteenth century and presented as the new form in which wisdom was garbed, therefore found itself as completely 'demythified' as science is in our century. In that case, how was it possible from then on to rely on it to provide a basis for belief in God? Any historical contribution in this direction could only be regarded with suspicion. Thus people invoked the revelation made to Abraham, about thirty-seven centuries ago. But who can verify scientifically the authenticity of such an event? People also invoked the theophanies with which Moses was blessed on Horeb ('I am who I am') and on Mount Sinai ('the Decalogue'). But who can tell what is fiction and what is authentic in these stories? Of course some claimed that these theophanies are projections of the Hebrew consciousness. Finally, appeal was made to the witness of Christ himself: but, said others, who can provide a scientific basis for the value of such witness from more than twenty centuries ago?

The development of the mentality of young Christian generations is very typical in this connection. Whereas round about 1950 reference to history was regarded as the height of accreditation by the religious consciousness (one can remember the success at that time of books on Abraham, on the Old Testament prophets, and so on), quite suddenly disillusionment with historicity arose (also under the influence of structuralist analyses, which were all concerned to discredit history). The last generation has the feeling that history is 'loaded'. It mistrusts history. In these conditions the hope which those in authority in the Catholic church might have put in history as a basis for faith in God could only crumble away; one could no longer count on it to lead spirits to God. Besides, on the contrary, by reason of its relativity, history could only turn people from God: that was the clearest result. For all that, this reaction seemed quite justified. For if we analyse the use which some Catholic thought made of the historical method, we can see that this usage could only lead to impasses. In effect, the choice is one of two things: either one accords full value to historicity (to its methodology): in which case one ends up with a God inscribed in history, immanent in history; that is the trap of historicism. Or, one accords no value to history, and reduces the faith in God peculiar to a given society to an epiphenomenon of its cultural structures. Either way, historical methodology does not seem to offer adequate intellectual implements for tackling the problem under consideration. History cannot lead to transcendence. The fault is in the instrument itself. That, at least, is the feeling which seems to have divided Catholic thought after the 1950s, having been the infatuation of the 1920s and the years afterwards. From that point on people found themselves in a vacuum.

For many Christians, the ways forward are closed, and access to God has become impossible: rational access is prohibited by philosophical criticism, and historical access by historical criticism itself. So what is to be done if someone wants to remain attached to the community of believers with whom he feels psychologically connected with all his being? Can he maintain a Christianity which, from henceforth by-passing reference to God, can nevertheless retain the values peculiar to this religion? The temptation may be to found Christianity solely on faith in Christ, without faith in God. This gives rise to the audacious hypothesis of a 'Christianity without God', an atheistic Christianity. However, before ending up in this ultimate position, the movement towards christocentricity had to pass through more and more pronounced stages, which it is important to retrace here.

2. Second stage: christocentricity regarded as a 'lifeline'

Thus round about 1950 a new attitude can be detected. Since access to God is forbidden to us, let us try to seize hold of Christ. For many people, faith in Christ, total, mystical and almost blind faith, will be a lifeline in the face of modern atheism and the destructiveness which it piles up. Already in the nineteenth century, but even more in the twentieth, this produces a whole literature which on the one hand is doctrinal and pious, and on the other hand social and political, which concentrates on the person of Christ and only on the person of Christ (making no reference to the transcendent God), and which is concerned to show that by virtue of his character as a man of Galilee, who experienced the human condition to the full, in a particular time and place, Christ can serve as a support, by his very example, for the faith which is called on to nourish those who adhere to the Christian religion.

(a) The hope placed in christocentricity

So all philosophical speculation was banned. Historical research was abandoned. People put themselves before the figure of Christ as before a model in whom they could perceive all the spiritual truths which they needed. But – it may be objected – was this not again to appeal to history, since the Christ to whom reference was made lived almost twenty centuries ago? In fact, no. For those who adopted this attitude did not imagine Christ as a historic figure, whose image emerged from the mists of the past as critical studies improved their methods and the authenticity of his person appeared. They never thought of a historical Christ. This was a Christ like the one who appeared in the texts of the Gospels, supposing that these texts could be taken literally and read as timeless witnesses. People read the texts for the ideological stimulation that they received. They read the Gospels as they read the *Declaration of the Rights of Man* or the *Communist Party Manifesto*. The Gospel was a text to be brandished.

In these conditions the Christ is regarded as one of the great 'inspired' figures of human history (as Schuré put it). He was listened to as a prophet, revered as a master, followed as a leader. This way of understanding Christ was not new. The nineteenth century is full of interpretations of this kind. Hegel wrote a *Life of Jesus* on this model. Even Karl Marx, during the brief period when he was tempted to adopt Christianity (when he was eighteen or nineteen) wrote some fine pages on Christ (cf. his *Dissertation on Jesus*). The liberal Protestants read the Gospels in this way (Harnack and Strauss), and Renan took a similar attitude in his famous *Life of Jesus*. One may even recall the attempt by Bergson – with such lofty and rigorous honesty – in *Two Sources of Morality and Religion* (1932), which tends to present Christ from a purely human point of view. However, in the Catholic church itself – and from the most qualified of its representatives – we see the proliferation, after 1920, of publications on the human life of Christ. Once again let me recall the names of writers like Père de Grandmaison, Père Lagrange, Père Prat, Père Huby, in France; Karl Adam, Papini, Drews, Wellhausen, Middleton Murray abroad, without mentioning literary presentations, and sometimes novels, by writers like Mauriac, Graham Greene. It was at this period (in the middle of the twentieth century) that the work of Daniel-Rops, *Jesus in his Time*, enjoyed such astonishing success.

However, two reactions soon appeared in connection with the intentions which directed the authors of these presentations of the human life of Christ. Some continued to see it as a way of 'leading souls to God' (provided that it was used with a great deal of care and in as convincing a tone as possible): they wanted to draw people to Christ so as to go on to lead them to God. But we can also feel the development of quite a different tendency; some people began to present Christ for the interest he compels in himself (without seeking to make any reference to God): he was presented as the incomparable humanist, or more often the matchless philanthropist. In this period (1920–1940) such attempts were still timid and only appeared in certain articles, in particular in the journals of Catholic Action. What people sought to show was that Christ, in himself and by himself, can and should become the 'master of thought' and 'master of action'; that it is not so necessary to devote oneself to reflection on God (which is too speculative). Reflection on Christ must suffice. We must pause over this stage in the evolution of ideas. It will be decisive.

(b) Towards a systematic christocentricity (1930–1960)

From the 1930s onwards, Catholic thought continually allowed itself to be won over towards a christocentric attitude. The age moved it in that direction. Never in the political and social sphere had there been so much of a cult of Man (with a capital M). The great totalitarian movements of the era, Fascism, Nazism, Stalinist Communism, devoted all their efforts to an exaltation of human power: the personality cult of leaders, exaltation of human prowess in every sphere: sport, the military, production. It was felt to be a Promethean, or if one prefers, a Nietzschean era, in which man and even superman was exalted. It was clearly tempting for the Christians of the period to respond in turn to this challenge over man by the exaltation of a superman, by presenting Christ as this superman whom humanity was confusedly looking for. I am not saying that this was a carefully elaborated tactic. It was more an unconscious reaction. Christians, and above all young people, felt more or less consciously the need to contrast their faith in a person whom they felt to be infinitely superior to the others, that of Jesus Christ, with these supermen whom the Hitler Youth saluted in their Führer, the Fascist balillas in their Duce, and the komsomols and Red Falcons in the brilliant Father of Peoples, Stalin. They wanted to contrast faith in a divine person with the personal adulation which was raging at the time: this was not the moment to invoke a doctrinal faith founded on a serene reflection which could lead to an invisible God. What was needed was a faith in a person, living and inscribed in history; and people thought of Jesus Christ. This was the profound cry of the Jocistes, for example in their 1937 Congress in Paris. 'We too have a leader – and he is superior to all others – it is Jesus Christ.' That was the cry which came from the bottom of their hearts. A social psychologist can understand this kind of reaction. It conforms with social logic. The influence of the political climate of the time is undeniable here, at least in Europe (it was quite different in North and South America). Now this need to resort to a person to inspire faith came to add itself to the intellectual needs described above. All these influences taken together were to lead to the progressive and systematic elaboration of a christocentricity which soon became exclusive. It is easy to discern its features.

From the 1930s onwards, first of all apologetic – or if one prefers the term, catechesis – took on a resolutely christocentric form. Works devoted to this kind of research began to have significant titles: 'Towards Christ'; 'Christ, light of men'; 'My life with Christ', and so on. Anyone who thumbs through these works can see that they are largely devoted to the human figure of Christ, his goodness, his clairvoyance, his moral strength, his humanitarian concerns. An impartial observer – for example, belonging to another religion – could note that they are very little concerned with God himself, the virtues which lead to contemplation, his sovereign greatness, the moral disciplines which favour the recognition of his dominion over men and the world. One senses a desire to direct human awareness – and above all the minds of children – towards the recognition of a human Lordship of Jesus which can captivate people more than all the other 'Lordships' in vogue at the time. A malicious critic would see here an exercise in social seduction, aimed at presenting a challenge, or making a rival withdraw. Read again, for example, the words of the hymn then in vogue among the Jocistes: 'We want to conquer the world, to win it for Jesus Christ.' People seek to 'conquer', to 'win': the language is unmistakably that of challenge. There is a concern to gain the victory of a Person.

A similar development, though more profound, also took place in this period (1930–1950), in the sphere of theological and even dogmatic research. The major preoccupation of researchers would be to base the whole edifice of the Catholic faith on personal adherence to Jesus Christ (with the idea that 'the rest will be given as well'; the rest being faith in a transcendent God and in the order of grace). Numerous theologians, Germans in particular (who above all had had to endure the appeal to another superman), came to orient the whole of their theology on faith in the Christ-man alone. Let me quote just one example for the moment, that of a theologian – a Protestant, though his views were welcomed avidly by some Catholic theology – who died as a martyr for his faith in Jesus Christ, Dietrich Bonhoeffer. For him, the 'historical' life and death of Jesus form an 'intra-historical' event which overturns the intrinsic evolution of the history of the world. Everything takes place within history and for the historicity of mankind. The death of Christ in particular creates a 'vacuum' which sucks in man and involves him in a totally immanent redemptive adventure. We find similar reactions – though in a different key – in authors like Hans Küng (from this time on, but above all in the 1970s, as we shall see); and similarly in Schoonenberg and Hulbosch. Along this line, but taking christocentricity to the point of the radical negation of all transcendence, we soon find Bultmann, who redoubles his efforts to arrive at a total demythologization of the figure of Christ. We can discern similar tendencies in the first researches made in this direction in the Latin countries; in France, for example, with C. Duquoc, and equally in Spain.[8] Of course that is not to disguise the direction taken by the works of other theologians, like Karl Barth, Karl Rahner, Ratzinger and Hans Urs von Balthasar, who also concentrated their attention on Christ, but did not fail to bring out the transcendent character of his mission. It nevertheless remains that the orientation of the first-mentioned would appear more significant to the observer. One can see an underlying tendency which the social psychologist has to bring out, as being the consequence of an evolution the logic of which can be found in the earlier options.

Within Catholicism, moral theology also begins to take a christocentric direction. The traditional morality accepted up to that point in Catholicism was inspired essentially by Thomas Aquinas, and had been carried on by figures marked by the same spirit, in particular St Alphonse de Liguori. It was fundamentally theocentric, and aimed at developing within the Christian soul attitudes which would allow it, as easily as possible, to arrive at the contemplation of God, and to enjoy the resultant felicity. From the 1950s onwards we see the development within Catholicism, above all in France and Germany, of a new conception of morality, which seeks to be detached from all reference to traditionally theocentric moral philosophy, and which takes a resolutely christocentric form. The aim of Christian moral life changes: it is no longer a question of rising towards the contemplation of God but of leading people towards an imitation of the life of Christ, which is taken in itself as the ultimate norm. To live morally is to live 'as Christ'. This morality spread around the Catholic universities through oral teaching, but it also inspired numerous magazine articles and was transmitted through countless so-called 'retraining' sessions. There was no longer an appeal to the judicative moral conscience, demanding of it an outline of the features of a moral order governed by the practice of the cardinal virtues (prudence, fortitude, temperance and justice), and completed with an appeal to the theological virtues (faith, hope and charity). There was an appeal to spontaneity, so that faced with any given situation (situation ethics) one could have the reaction which (as far as we are able to divine) would have been that of Christ Jesus himself. There was an invitation to a kind of 'mystical spontaneity'. This practice would give rise to what from the 1950s onwards people began to call 'involvement'; this was thought to represent the inspiration which anyone who became 'involved' could have felt in his 'personal encounter' with the Christ of the gospels. This form of reaction henceforth justified collaboration with all the social movements which arose, even with those which claimed to be basically irreligious (that could be with Marxism in some countries, or neo-Fascism in others). Because of the more or less veiled historicism of which it was the vehicle, christocentricity applied to morality allowed the most unexpected involvements, which could be justified by the historical circumstances. There was no longer any 'defence' of a 'moral order', nor did people seek to restore one if danger threatened. They simply tried to 'inject' a degree of Christianity into the political and social 'situations' which presented themselves, whether on an individual or a collective level. What the early moralist approved of and commended as a second best became the habitual rule; in fact, taking up the technical language used by the moralists of previous centuries, one could say that from then on the 'hypothesis' became the 'thesis'.[9]

This seems to be the predominant orientation which governed Catholic thinking towards the middle of the twentieth century. That should not allow us to forget that as far as both apologetic and dogmatic and moral theology are concerned, theocentric inspiration continued in important areas of the Catholic church. As one might expect, one can see it preserved in centres of contemplative life, and among the church authorities, i.e. in administrative circles. Belief in the transcendent God and the vocation to adoration continued in the great monasteries. That was the case with the great orders like the Benedictines, the Carthusians, the Trappists. It was the same with the Carmelites.[10] The schools of thought also maintained this current in the intellectual sphere, above all in the Roman universities (for example, those around Père Garrigou-Lagrange and his successors). Furthermore, in this same period certain prestigious writers made it a point of honour to maintain faith under its theocentric form. One might mention names like those of Bernanos, Gabriel Marcel, T. S. Eliot, and, in his own way, Samuel Beckett. One or the other kept alive in the hearts of their contemporaries the sense of 'waiting on God', to use the phrase of Simone Weil, herself witness to a demanding theocentricity. They kept the flame alight. However, the neutral observer – the social psychologist who wants to note without judging – must recognize that their influence in the general evolution of the Catholic in the middle of this century remains very much subordinated to that of the adherents of christocentricity. These are present in the most active areas of the Catholic church: they form its 'leading edge'.

3. A decisive turning point: the launching of Catholic Action (1930–1960)

The Catholic church was seized with one major preoccupation in the 1930s, that of apostolic action, which was to be carried on within the social perimeter of what had hitherto been regarded as Christian society. Until now people had thought only of sending missions abroad, to distant lands; now they dreamed of inner missions. In fact the church had been seized with a new awareness. It had noted that it was being emptied of its inner substance: 'paganism' was not at a distance, but in the interior of Christianity. There were real 'mission areas'.[11] Certainly people knew that the task of Christianization had always to be begun all over again; from the seventeenth century they had inherited the techniques of internal re-Christianization, as practised in particular by the Lazarists and the Redemptorists. This time, however, it was discovered that entire sectors of ancient Christendom had to be 'reconquered for Christ'; sectors of the working-class world, the peasant world, the intellectual world. Given the size of the task and the small number of the clergy, it seemed insufficient to appeal to them, i.e. to the 'professionals'; they seemed inadequate, moreover, given their lack of adaptation to the different milieux which needed to be evangelized. A new method of apostolicity was launched – this was an original idea of Pope Pius XI: the apostolate of the milieu by the milieu. Thus workers who had remained Christian were asked to evangelize those who were no longer Christian, and similarly those who lived in the country, students, and so on. However, energy had to be mobilized for that to be done. It was necessary to create a mysticism of action: the time was relatively favourable for that. In fact, this type of mysticism was 'in the air'. After the debilitating period dominated by 'dilettantism', the 1900s and the 'belle epoque', people had rediscovered a taste for action, its fruitfulness, its excitements. The philosopher Blondel had opened the way with his thesis on *Action* in 1893. This theme was taken up in politics by the monarchists with their appeal to *Action française*, at the beginning of the century. Subsequently the theme of action aroused real excitement with Georges Sorel, Benito Mussolini and his blackshirts, Malraux and his heroic figures, in *La Condition humaine*. In the 1930s this theme of action spread right across Europe (and partly through America with the appeal to pragmatism fostered by James and Dewey). Under a variety of forms, action was glorified among the young, to fight also against the apathy of a generation of adults who had become easy-going after the pressures of 1914–1918. With clear-sightedness, Pope Pius XI was able to sense this taste of a generation for action, and he thought that the moment had also come for the Catholic church to renew itself from within, in turn launching out on a form of action which was to be called *Catholic Action*. It was an immediate success; and its effects were beneficial during the 1930s for the Catholic church (the other churches, Protestant and Orthodox, did not take this course). Only later did the church discover the serious dangers that could arise from this appeal to action – that took thirty years. I shall now try to analyse the effects of this clearly ill-considered call to action, and all the consequences deriving from it – with the objectivity of the observer who devotes himself to a study of social psychology.

(a) The appeal to apostolic action

First of all, let us remember that any call to action, above all on the part of a human group which is in fact organized for contemplation, carries with it inevitable dangers. Classical philosophy has long since denounced them. It has shown that fruitful action can only stem from contemplation. To act is to embody an idea. If one wants to act in a fruitful way, it is necessary first of all to have 'some idea' of the object towards which the action is directed, and to think it through thoroughly; creative inspiration will stem from this thought.[12] That is specially true for spiritual action, as is the case here. Those who 'thought' at the beginning of Catholic Action were perfectly aware of this, at least in the ranks of the church authorities. Thus, for example, a small book which gave a clear indication of the direction to be taken was commended to all who were planning to involve themselves in this action. This small book, of which thousands of copies were printed, was thought up by the first apostles of this new crusade: it was the book by Dom Chautard, Abbé of la Trappe de Sept-Fons, *L'Ame de tout apostolat*. It had been written in 1915, but it was republished on behalf of the initiators of Catholic Action: more than 220,000 copies were printed after 1930. It was presented as a breviary for all the militants of Catholic Action. The text began with an invocation to the Holy Trinity (so the basis was very theocentric). Action had to proceed from the rays which emanated from the Trinity itself. 'You alone, worshipful Trinity, are the perfect inner life, abundant and infinite. Goodness without limit, your will to be extended outside your inner life.' Subsequently the text indicates that action must be maintained within a hierarchical conception. The impulse must come from the hierarchy. 'The first place in this apostolate is taken by the clergy, whose hierarchy forms the cadre of the army of Christ; the clergy represented by both bishops and holy and zealous priests . . . Alongside the clergy, from the beginning of Christianity, there have appeared companies of volunteers' (p.5). The text makes this more precise. 'At every epoch of its history the church has encountered valuable helpers among the simple faithful . . . ' (p.6). Then the author indicates the dangers which threaten the man of action. They can be summed up in a formula: 'the risk of externalization by works' (p.7). The author follows Mgr Mermillod in denouncing the 'heresy of works' (p.12). He recalls that Leo XIII had warned against the dangers of activism, denounced under the name of 'Americanism', in his famous letter addressed to Cardinal Gibbons, Archbishop of Baltimore. Then he puts forward as a model of true Christian men of action figures like Père Chevrier, Dom Bosco, Timon-David, the Curé d'Ars, Père Lallement (all clergy). And the analysis is taken up again in this condensed formula: 'Active life must proceed from contemplative life, represent it and continue it outside, while detaching itself as little as possible from it' (p.54). In brief, the book is a commentary on this statement. It gives a good indication of the basis on which Catholic Action was founded towards the 1930s.

All the directives given to those who began to be called 'militants' were from the start inspired by this spirit. A strong inner life was warmly commended to the militants. They were reminded that above all they were called to bear witness: witness to the presence of God. They were then given a method which was inspired by the basic principles. The orders could be summed up in three words: 'see, judge, act'. Indubitably priority was given to contemplation; we can see this on the level of the first two attitudes: 'see and judge'. One can only see with the help of a certain light, that of contemplation; one can only judge well when illuminated by that same light. All in all, these rules were fairly well followed in the main countries where Catholic Action was launched between 1930 and 1940. And we have to recognize that the results were very beneficial to the church. The churches were crowded once again (as was the JOC Congress in Paris in 1937). The seminaries filled up: new buildings were put up everywhere because the vocations had increased so much. Cardinal Verdier, then Archbishop of Paris, forecast a complete re-Christianization of France in less than ten years.

(b) The first ambiguities

These arose in 1950. During the war years, despite the difficulties, the impetus of Catholic Action was maintained: among combatants, prisoners, the civil population, often compelled to do forced labour in occupied countries, and even in the countryside. However, in the post-war years a marked development took place. Little by little, people began to abandon the firm rules which had been adopted initially and fell into the traps of action which the spiritual guides of the 1930s had denounced. The link between contemplation and action was stretched. The first ambiguities arose at the level of the first operation, 'see'. It had been understood that 'see' meant to look in accordance with 'God's view'; that is to say, to see beings and things in the perspective which the creator had on them; to see men themselves as God's creatures; institutions as modes of the common good; work as a collaboration in the work of God, and production as an enrichment of creation (the Jociste hymn had this very theocentric profession of faith . . . : 'Be proud to be a worker, your work is fruitful; without you, what will become of the world?'). But things changed: instead of seeing the world through God's eyes, people began to see it simply through man's eyes; the vision became immanentist and historicist. The militant gradually felt himself to be an 'agent' among other agents, immersed in the flood of natural forces. He took his bearings from a vision of men and things which was no longer contemplative but practical. It was just the same with the second operation, 'judge'. People did not judge so much in the light of the spiritual and transcendent ends of human life; they judged in the light of purely terrestrial objectives: the liberation of men or peoples, the increase of prosperity, raising living standards, and so on. There was always a reference to

Christ, but to the degree that his teaching could be found to contain elements which could come to the support of the social theories which were being defended. All this led to a form of action – the third term in the slogan was 'act' – which took on all the appearances of a praxis pursued as an end in itself. No longer being illuminated by a contemplation which established the end and therefore the means, action developed according to its own dictates. It then evolved towards a perpetual shift in society, which is undeniable, and on to a revolutionary process. In the implementation of this practice, the reference to Christ, which was resolutely maintained, served only to justify the claim of belonging to the church; it served as a cover. A ready choice of formulas borrowed from the gospels made it possible to dress in Christian garb the revolutionary practice which was maintained. Here, of course, the push towards christocentricity was particularly marked. One could even say that this christocentricity became increasingly exclusive; all trace of reference to a transcendent God virtually disappeared. This is a radical christocentricity. By way of practice we arrive at an integral christocentricity, the signs of which have been evident on the horizon in the Catholic church for several decades. However, in one sense, Catholic Action anticipated the evolution that we now see in theological thought, strictly speaking. That is the development which I shall now trace. It only affected a small part of Catholic thought, but it was the thought of an active minority which was to exercise a predominant influence on the church from the 1960s onwards.

VI

The Triumph of Christocentricity
(Second Half of the Twentieth Century)

I have just said that from the 1930s onwards, Catholic Action was oriented on a resolute christocentricity (expecting that it would become exclusive). In this case action preceded reflection, hence the anomalies of every kind which ensued in the church. However, theological reflection, treading in the footsteps of action – which *a priori* is unhealthy – in turn deliberately adopted the christocentric orientation a little later, with a time lag of about twenty years. So-called 'avant-garde' theology adopted this orientation between 1950 and 1970. Vatican II also exercised a certain influence in this respect, at least indirectly, from 1964 on.

1. Towards a radically christocentric theology

One general theme which developed during these years was that all theological thought must be concentrated on the person of Christ. Reference to God is not absent (at least, not yet), but it only appears as a consequence of faith in Christ. The pattern is simple: it is necessary to believe in Christ, and, following that, to believe in all that he believed, i.e. in God, possibly in angels, in the beyond, and so on. Whereas it was once said, 'Outside the church there is no salvation', people now began to say, 'Outside Christ there is no salvation' (which – quite apart from other inconveniences – would create difficulties in relations with non-Christian religions which are nevertheless monotheistic: I shall return to this point later). Thus christocentricity tended to become exclusive. The exclusiveness made its mark progressively at different levels: it was exercised with regard to Christ himself, then with regard to the situation of the Catholic church in the world: soon it touched the very doctrinal content of Christianity or, more precisely, of Catholicism (though Protestant was equally affected, albeit to a lesser degree). Finally, it even extended to ways of living and acting.

(a) Christ regarded as the absolute master of thought

The concentration of the attention of writers on the human presence of Christ, which, as I have already said, took on an increasingly heightened form from the beginning of the century, was intensified even further. It is enough to look at a list of books published to see this. There was a proliferation of writings on the person of Christ, and even more often, there were reissues of earlier works. The success of a work like *Jesus in His Time*, by Daniel-Rops, published in 1945, which went through dozens of editions, is typical in this respect. The stage of erudite investigations (e.g. Lagrange and de Grandmaison), which I mentioned earlier, was therefore over. People worked on studies which were capable of as great popularization as possible: clearly, they had an apologetic end in view. It was not just a matter of informing, but also of convincing. So we see the spread of reissues of numerous writings on Jesus: by Goyau, Prat and Lebreton; by Ricciotti (of Milan); by the Hungarian writer Tihamer Toth; by the German theologian Karl Adam; by Abbés Klein, Huby and Steinmann. One could quote dozens, not to say hundreds, of authors here. Soon audio-visual media were called into use. Films on Jesus multiplied, as did radio and television broadcasts. Furthermore, a kind of craze developed in favour of pilgrimages to the Holy Land ('in the steps of Jesus'), at least among Catholics (for Protestants remained very reserved towards this kind of curiosity about 'holy places', suspecting, after Luther, a tendency towards idolatrous religiosity). Various magazines set out to exalt the human presence of Christ, magazines aimed at the working-class public (in France the *Masses ouvrières* editions), the country public and sometimes even a certain intellectual public. The themes discussed varied, depending on the audience addressed: workers were introduced to Christ as an idealized worker (though he had never been a worker – and had never had a boss); or he was shown to be concerned for the 'liberation' of the working-class masses, for the dignity of workers; his feeling for man's hardship was stressed. Hence it was easy to pass on to the theme of a Christ preaching the struggle against social oppression; a Christ who sowed in the souls of the humble a ferment of revolt (that required a great deal of imagination, because in fact Christ had always preached submission: 'Slaves, obey your masters, as Christ,' says St Paul in his name). The portrait of a social, humanitarian Christ, the liberator of the oppressed, came into being (in these magazines we can find many themes – and sometimes formulas – resembling those developed a century earlier by Lamennais in his famous work *Paroles d'un croyant*). Readers in the rural world were shown Christ as defender of the lesser (landowners) against the great; of servants against masters (all this with more imagination than historical fidelity). Thus the myth of a revolutionary Christ tended to take shape and spread: in certain Catholic countries this allowed the establishment of connections with Marxist revolutionary movements. In so-called 'intellectual' circles, the arguments developed in some publications of the time tend to show Christ as the liberator of human consciousness from all 'alienations' (to take up a formula deriving from Marxism). This was the argument which people sought to justify above all in student circles during the troubles which affected various countries in 1968. The theme of Christ the 'liberator' reappears constantly in the literature of the time (with formulas equally close to Lamennais). The analyses remain rather vague when it comes to stating precisely what the alienations are from which Christ is thought to liberate man: they range from the tutelage of the 'powers' to pollution, going through economic servitude and cultural and linguistic 'domination'.

Another theme developed in this period is that of the place of Christ in human history. Starting from the postulate that there is a 'meaning in history', people tried to show that the whole of human history revolves round a pole marked by the coming of Christ on earth. During the millennia which preceded his coming (people only talked in terms of millennia because they did not dare to follow human palaeontology in talking of the two million years which are assigned to this stage in the human adventure, since these facts make the mind boggle), during this long period people were 'waiting for Christ'; then for a generation, almost two thousand years ago, they experienced *the* event, the coming of Christ, and from then on they have experienced the consequences of this event. The actions and deeds of men at every level, whether in politics, economics, culture or society, are to be 'read' with reference to this coming of Christ, even in the case of the history of non-Christian peoples. These themes were developed primarily, not to say exclusively, by authors who in this period evidently accepted the postulate of the coherence of historicity (for others the problem did not arise). Thus we find this thesis in writers like Père Chenu, Père de Lubac (see certain passages of his book *Catholicism*), Père Congar, and Père Daniélou (see his *Essay on the Mystery of History*, 1953) in France; in German theology similar themes are developed by Hans Urs von Balthasar in his *Theology of History*. In the Anglo-Saxon world, people could read the works by Rust, *The Christian Understanding of History*, London 1947, or Reinhold Niebuhr, *Faith and History*, New York 1949. In one way or another, all these authors wanted to try to create St Augustine's *City of God* (with all the risks which, as we know, this enterprise involves). Common to all these writers is above all a preoccupation with what one could call here a 'historical christocentricity'. Their favourite theme is that Christ alone holds the 'key to history': from *sinanthropus* to present-day man the whole human adventure can only be understood as a function of Christ, whether this is his political adventure or his cultural and scientific adventure.

Let me try to analyse rather more closely the direction of this effort of thought attempted by Catholic theologians between 1950 and 1970. Two postulates underlie their researches: that of the coherence of history, and that of the radical excellence of Catholicism in relation to other monotheistic religions. In fact, all have in common (and this will make the specialists from the 1960s and 1970s smile) a total faith in the possibility of giving a coherent representation of human history considered in its totality (i.e. over two million years); in other words, they believe in the possibility of a 'philosophy of history'. Furthermore, in principle they argue that Christians alone, and Catholics in particular, can hold the key of this philosophy of history, doing so in relation to Christ. Explicitly or implicitly, these two postulates were assumed, everywhere (which inevitably widened still further the gulf between Christians and the adherents of non-Christian religions).[1] This was an audacious attitude.[2] It was to receive unexpected reinforcement from scientific thought after the late spread (after 1955, because of posthumous publication) of the theories of Pierre Teilhard de Chardin. He set out to show in a rigorously scientific way that a careful application of extrapolation could allow one to think that the whole evolution of the cosmos, from the mineral world to the world of plants, from the world of plants to the human world, over a total of almost three thousand million years, had to lead – at least on our planet Earth (though there is the implicit assumption that it is the 'centre of the world') – to the recapitulation of all humanity in the mystical person of Christ, regarded as the Omega-point towards which the evolution of the cosmos is converging. Here christocentricity plays an even larger role than before: it is literally a question of a cosmic christocentricity (sometimes Teilhard speaks of a cosmochristocentricity). The success of the theories of Teilhard – whose posthumous works appeared in a single series of publications – was considerable between 1955 and 1965; then it diminished rapidly.

Thus the development of christocentricity went on with exceptional vigour during this decade, a vigour which astonishes the observer, whether he be historian or social psychologist. It was essentially due to the convergence of several very different currents of thought for a short period: the need for Catholic Action to provide itself with a consistent 'ideology'; the seductions of an increasingly imperious historicism; an acute need for the personalization of belief, all merging with the themes of Teilhard. We can also see this accentuation of christocentricity represented in the practical life of Catholicism, particularly in its liturgy and its inner dynamic.[3]

Liturgy between 1950 and 1970 in fact adopted a christocentric position with constant fidelity. Thus the rite of the mass was definitively regarded by the avant-garde reformers as a communal meeting where, on the occasion of a celebration of an agape in which bread and wine were consumed, people shared the same faith in Christ and exchanged the same gestures of charity. The desacralization (chastely called the demythologization) of the sacramental rites was carried on from that point: the idea was introduced that in each case it was a celebration and not a rite which automatically produced spiritual states (a conception denounced as being stamped with residual magic). Thus baptism was presented as a celebration intended to mark entry into the church (and no longer a change of condition from being 'a child of the world' – much less of Satan – into a 'child of God', a conception which was held to be too loaded with theocentricity). Confirmation changed its significance: it was no longer seen as the occasion for the descent of the Holy Spirit into the soul (a theocentric conception) during the course of a ceremony marked with as much 'sacralism' as possible, usually with the intervention of the bishop. Rather, it was proposed that this should be seen as entry into the Catholic church, the church 'militant' of Christ (another christocentric conception), a celebration which did not need a dignitary, a pontiff to intervene; on the contrary, the welcome into the active community was made by representative members of this community. The interpretation has changed direction (to use the language of this period, one could say that 'verticality' had to yield to 'horizontality'). The eucharist was no longer regarded as an intimate encounter with the real presence of God, conceived of along the lines of the great tradition of communion with the sacred, revered by the most ancient religions: people prepared to see here the symbolism of a meal which brought them near to Christ. The tabernacles were detached from the altars, where their appearance recalled the sacrificial signification of the Real Presence, and found a refuge on peripheral credences, removed from the altar, where they took on the guise of 'reserved' sacraments for possible use later (without there being full awareness of the precise use for which this reservation was made). Confession tended to lose its significance as the transmission of God's forgiveness by an accredited priest, and took on that of a psychological operation of 'reconciliation' by which the soul, anxious at the thought of its imperfections, sees itself reintegrated in the Church of Christ, and rediscovers its tie of spiritual friendship with Christ. The other sacraments underwent similar evolution. Ordination, it was said, made the new priest the mandated delegate of the community of believers in Christ (the reference to the priesthood of Melchizedek, to the sacred mission of conferring the gifts of God, was definitively abandoned). Marriage became a 'celebration' where the future couple swear faithfulness to each other and a common faithfulness to Christ. Extreme unction, which had become the 'sacrament of the sick', was not understood, as it had been over the centuries (rightly or wrongly), as the rite of immediate preparation for death and therefore for appearing before God; it became a spiritual help to allow the sick Christian to associate his suffering and anguish with that of the suffering Christ. Thus all these religious rites of the church were conceived of – at least among the authors who were more 'involved' in the evolution of ideas – as 'celebrations' tending to bring people nearer to Christ, to unite them with Christ, to enable them to live in Christ. Finally, we should note that the texts of the new liturgy of the Roman mass show a clear development in the direction of christocentricity (I am thinking particularly of Canons III and IV). This is, of course, an evolution in a particular direction and not the abandonment of earlier positions.[4] Some people here talk in terms of 'restoring a balance'.

In its inner dynamics, that is to say, in its way of seeing its place in the human world, and its conception of the future, during these twenty years (from 1950 to 1970) Catholicism also adopted attitudes more and more in line with christocentricity. The problem was to know where these events would take Catholicism. It was important to find new ways, people said, because it was accepted that Catholicism was 'in a period of change', according to the formula then in vogue.

But how was it possible to discover which direction to take? A theory now took shape: the traditional appeal to the virtue of prudence was replaced by 'listening' to invitations of a 'mystical' kind. This 'listening' was directed towards two phenomena: the rise of 'prophetic actions' and a reading of 'signs of the times'. The theory of 'prophetic actions', which was formulated above all from 1955 on, can be understood in the following way: first of all, one accepts that history has a meaning (this is the basic postulate); secondly, that this history develops through a series of successive innovations; and thirdly, that it is the innovative character of these actions which ensures their fruitfulness (this is another postulate – which supplements the first in a very precise way – that everything new is good simply because it is the opposite of what went before: here we can recognize the appeal to a dialectical pattern). Every innovative gesture which 'opens up new ways', according to the formula in vogue, has to be taken into consideration, since the new is identified with the good. So it is right to see these innovative actions as fruitful options for the future: that is why they are called 'prophetic actions'. From a methodological point of view, the theory of 'signs of the times' is quite close to the previous one. The formula appears in the gospels, though only rarely; then it has an eschatological significance: these are signs written in the heavens which announce an imminent end to time. This formula was taken up by representatives of Catholic thought, especially from 1955–1960 on, in quite a different sense. 'Signs of the times' denoted events the meaning of which could be seen as a sign of hope: instead of being transcendentalist, the meaning had now become immanentist. People were invited to accept a certain interpretation of history (and not of eschatology), an interpretation which – again on the postulate according to which history has a meaning – could indicate the directions to be taken. Who was qualified to make these interpretations? No one knew, because no existing authority had been accredited for this. In fact the only possible credential, which people sought to stress, was 'subjective ardour' (that is, something very subjective). More precisely, there was a desire to legitimate the idea that these 'prophetic actions' and this reading of 'signs of the times' would produce a kind of mysterious communion with the vocation of Christ in his historic mission. So this was a projection in the 'noetic' sphere, if one could put it that way, of the historical christocentricity which was developing at this time. At any rate, that is the historicist postulate which always lay beneath these different interpretations.

(b) Christianity regarded as the exclusive mode of wisdom

From 1950 onwards, even some Catholic avant-garde thought could be seen to be going even further along the line of christocentricity. Not only was it said that Christ had to be regarded as the sole master of thought who had to be the inspiration for thought, action and creation, but in their exclusiveness some thinkers went so far as to claim that Christianity, this time conceived of as a body of doctrine, was itself capable of conveying all truth to man and that in itself Christianity constitutes a self-sufficient body of doctrine, and therefore that it is legitimate to eliminate, or at least to set aside, all other forms of thought, philosophical as well as moral, cultural and even scientific. This was certainly a well-known thesis. We can find a version of it in Blondel at the beginning of the century, and even more in Laberthonnière. The reasoning is as follows: if Christianity contains the whole truth, it is useless to look elsewhere for other truths. So Christianity must have the status of unique wisdom: it must be considered not only as a religion (contributing its part of truth, which is from the supernatural order), but also as a philosophy in the full sense of the term. Christianity is a philosophy, indeed a philosophy with a better base than others, since its founder, Jesus Christ, spoke in the very name of the 'Father who is in heaven'. So from that point on people followed Laberthonnière in speaking of a 'Christian philosophy', that is to say, the philosophy of Christ (in the same way as one talks of 'Cartesian philosophy' to designate that of Descartes).[5]

This theory had been discussed a good deal even at the beginning of the century. It was denounced as a confusion of genres. The Thomists in particular (with Maritain at their head) had pleaded for the autonomy of philosophy as a discipline with its own standing, which conformed to the most authentic thought of St Thomas himself. Others had discovered here a marked propensity to fideism; yet others saw the danger of cutting off all possible philosophical relations with other non-Christians. If Christianity absorbs all human wisdom into itself, we must conclude that outside it there is only error and darkness ('Outside Christianity, no salvation').[6] These objections had provided food for thought. So it is all the more curious to note that among the Catholic thinkers with a reputation for boldness we can find a renaissance of this kind of thought, above all after the 1960s, and up until recently.

One could cite numerous examples of this Catholic 'absolutism'. Under the pretext of raising faith in Christ to its utmost purity, people ended up by imprisoning themselves in purism. This is the direction in which the thought of a Catholic thinker like Maurice Clavel is oriented. For him, to look for the truth outside the message of Christ is to go astray. The only metaphysic is that of Jesus Christ. To seek to make metaphysics an autonomous science, as the great philosophers do, is to commit sacrilege, apostasy; and Heidegger is cheerfully denounced as a fiend of Satan.

We can see the same phenomenon in strictly theological thought about God – because this is still evident in these last years, despite the retreat of theocentricity. There can be no thought of God without thought of Christ. A curious instance is that of Père Varillon, in his book *L'Humilité de Dieu*, 1974.[7] Commenting on this volume, E. Borne writes: 'Henceforth christology is the centre and the crux of all theology, and there is no other God for Christian theology than he of whom Christ is the image to the point of identity.' Going further, the theologian here allows himself to take up positions on strictly philosophical problems, like that of creation, for example, still regarded from a purely christocentric point of view. This gives the following result (here I am again taking up the summary given by E. Borne): 'The incarnation appears as the *raison d'être* of creation, which the Word has the task of reconciling to God, and without which there would not be the Word . . . God is God to the degree that he makes himself Trinity, creates and becomes incarnate in a single movement.' These are strange statements, but specialists will find no difficulty in recognizing in them theses already put forward in the sixteenth century, by the Rhenish mystics, by Meister Eckhart, and above all by Nicolas of Cusa (who, as is well known, ran into difficulty with the Roman authorities). Philosophical positions are taken up under the cover of theology (it is a good thing that scientific positions are not taken up as well . . .).

A similar reaction is evident in the sphere of morality. Attempts are made to put forward a morality which is 'purely' and 'exclusively' christocentric. However, morality is as old as the world. It is one of the prerogatives of philosophical thought. However, theologians from the 1960s, and above all after 1970, tried to 'finesse' twenty centuries of efforts by 'practical reason' and lay down the principles of a morality which would owe everything to Jesus Christ and only to him. They despised the teaching of the Stoics, the morals of Aristotle (though these had enlightened millions of men) and the morals of India. The attempts of St Thomas Aquinas to build up a natural morality which could be presented to all men were regarded as a dead letter. The cardinal virtues of prudence, fortitude, temperance and justice were ignored, and the theological virtues forgotten. What was proposed was a morality drawn entirely from the thought of Jesus Christ. This was to construct a form of 'purism' (I was going to say of 'catharism'). Only the supernatural virtues were to be practised. So the virtue *par excellence* was charity, a charity without norms and without limits, a charity which makes a mock of prudence and temperance, a charity which 'excuses all things' and does not 'calculate' (St Paul). Henceforth the preference was for a kind of caritativism without rules and without intentions, a diffusive caritativism (alongside which that of Tolstoy appeared quite rigorous . . .). 'Love and do what you will,' people repeated after St Augustine. All the traditional moral 'rules' – which, as I have said above, were theocentric in inspiration, were abandoned in favour of a spontaneity based on love and human charity. Furthermore, the influence of historicism led some moral theologians in this period to formulate the conception of so-called 'situation ethics': one can only pass a moral judgment in connection with a particular concrete situation.[8] 'Historical conditioning' provides all the elements of valuation: in the end, historicity is the basis of normality (that is to say, its integral relativity, and even its simple positivity). Starting from this interpretation, Catholic moralists – having thus removed every reference of a theocentric kind – found themselves led to formulate a kind of 'non-directive' morality, where the subject was simply invited to follow the appeals of a conscience which was said to be inspired by 'the spirit of Christ'. A kind of gospel spontaneity seemed to develop: faced with each particular cicumstance, it was a question of discovering the attitude that the historical Christ would have taken. What would Jesus have done in this case or that? As no objective reply could be given to this question (what do we know?), the only thing was to follow the personal interpretation that could be given of intentions hypothetically attributed to the historical Christ. The radically christocentric (and therefore historicist) morality which tended to be current about the 1960s ended up in this subjectivity.

The expansion of christocentricity also won over other spheres. So it began to determine a new attitude with regard to science itself. Of course, as a background to this development we find the remains of the great confrontations of the nineteenth century. The scientism of the nineteenth century claimed to be able to eliminate religious thought and 'put out the last stars in the sky'. People resigned themselves to the idea of a definitive hiatus between religion and science. What was new in the middle of the twentieth century, however, was that this time religion rejected science – and again through christocentric purism. This is in fact what happened. It was found that modern science had first of all evolved in its methodological positions. It did not favour a determinism as rigorous as that of the nineteenth century. It presented its statements on the world (laws or theories) as 'approximate views'. Consequently it no longer denied that outside its views there was only ignorance or fantasy; it left room for mystery, and therefore, felt called to respect intellectual disciplines which sought to explore this mystery outside its own approach. It no longer contested them; it even respected them. In these conditions, metaphysics once again became possible in the eyes of science; and equally moralism, aesthetics and – why not? – the religious quest. The methodological conflict between scientific and theological thought had been removed.[9]

Subsequently matters developed in an even more astonishing way. Not only was science no longer in conflict with faith, but in one way it seemed to have joined forces with it again. The most advanced scientific thought – that of the last fifteen years – slowly moved towards the rediscovery of a supra-rationality of the world. The scientists themselves began to recognize the presence of a Logos, pre-existing the world, and communicating to it part of its rationality (which made it possible for it to make itself at least partially 'intelligible' to feeble human intelligence). A faithful echo of these theories has been brilliantly presented to us by the French philosopher R. Ruyer in his book *La Gnose de Princeton*, 1974,[10] in which he describes the astonishing spiritual development among the great American researchers in connection with this problem of the ultimate explanation of the world. Granted, the Logos with which these great researchers end up is not perhaps the God of traditional reason and faith, but from our point of view – that of the social psychologist – it is important to note a marked evolution of science in the direction of belief in God. In other words, the most advanced modern science has to some degree rediscovered the way to theocentricity (as I defined it earlier). That is the situation.

Now, as I have said, it was precisely at this moment that some advanced theological thought chose to renounce theocentricity and imprison itself in an increasingly exclusive christocentricity. The beginnings of a reconciliation with science began in the 1950s, following the publication of the writings of Teilhard. What we have, however, is a divorce from the 1960s on, paradoxically pronounced, as we should note, by the theologians. An attitude was spreading. Let science, they said, develop in its order, and theology develop in its; they cannot meet. Religious faith cannot have anything to do with scientific rationality. Since in essentials religious faith is here being reduced to faith in Christ, there can be no question of a scientist looking for any possible reconciliation between science and the gospel (put in these terms, the problem in fact seemed insoluble). If the scientist wanted to be a Christian, there was only one possible attitude to adopt: pure faith, that is to say, irrational adherence to Christ as a religious guide (such an attitude has been described as fideism).[11] These were the reasons for the divorce 'proclaimed' in the 1960s between theology and scientific thought. In this way we can see the extremity to which a heightened christocentricity (excluding all reference to theocentricity) can lead – and a sociologist can recognize the situation easily. The same slogan was always to be found: 'Outside Christ there is no salvation', and all the bridges were broken down (at least, let us remember, for some *avant-garde* theologies). In short, in every sphere of thought one could rediscover a kind of neo-catharism. People wanted to bask in pure faith in Christ, and in so doing they cut themselves off from the wisdom of the world. However, we shall return to this difficult subject a little later.

2. Christocentric principles of action

The analyses which I have just given are above all concerned with intellectual life. Of course, they also have an application in practical life. From the 1950s onwards, and more intensively from the 1960s, it was possible to see – among those who gave shape to religious life within Catholicism, both clergy and lay – a practical doctrine (some, symptomatically, spoke of a 'praxis') which was also denoted by the ambiguous term 'pastoral', and which covered both strictly apostolic acts and the various ways in which Catholicism was incorporated into social, cultural and political life. We therefore see the formation of a social christocentricity, a political christocentricity, and even a cultural christocentricity.

(a) A social christocentricity

According to this point of view, it is no longer a matter of defending some sort of 'social order' or even of creating the conditions for a happy relationship between social partners. Since all these social projections, which stemmed from theocentricity (as I showed earlier), had been renounced, the social realities were left to develop by themselves (it being tacitly accepted that they were necessarily evolving towards socialism). An attempt was, however, made to inject a certain degree of Christian spirit into the interplay of social forces. The approach was as follows: a position was taken up as near as possible to the centre of the social situation, and there, according to a formula in vogue, one 'proclaimed Jesus Christ', i.e., gave expression to the thoughts that Jesus Christ would have had, supposing he had been present at the event. The approach here was the same as that to which I have pointed in connection with morality in general. There was an attempt to inject the 'supernatural' in a pure state into a sociological context from which it was completely absent, in the expectation that a happy result would ensue. Experience shows that the results were generally deceptive. Most of the time, the message did not get through, which is not surprising, since the appropriate preparation for it had not been made; communication was not achieved. Sometimes the message got through: that is to say that the message, conceived along the lines of what was thought to be the spirit of Jesus of Nazareth, reached one or other of the social partners. The repercussion was represented by what was called a 'shift of awareness'. However, other difficulties arose: the action involved did not end up in any specific realization, any effective solution; and then people talked in terms of 'unreality'. The reason for this habitual failure was that no link with natural realities was set up; no account was taken of economic and social norms. There was a kind of 'angelism'. The instances of ventures of this kind are manifold; they can be found, for example, in the actions on J. La Pira as mayor of Florence; in the actions of certain worker-priests in the trade unions; in the intervention of certain mystical reformers in the Third World, and so on. The supernatural in a pure state could not make up for ignorance of economic laws, the organization of financial structures (often several centuries old, a fact which people tended to ignore), or the imperatives of planning. One can be inspired by the spirit of the Beatitudes – as long as one knows the consequences . . . of the modification of bank rate or a devaluation. At least that is what the impartial observer will be tempted to note from the perspective of social psychology.

Furthermore, we may observe that the problem can also be taken up from the other end, in the way in which people read the gospel to find in it the thought of Jesus Christ. Those who advocate a social christocentricity usually read the gospel texts literally. They cling to formulas which all too often they have detached from their context, without noting the way in which they are then likely to distort them. For example, they quote Christ's saying, 'Those who act by the sword will perish by the sword', and seek to make it into a formula which justifies the attitude of conscientious objectors, when, put in context, the arrest of Christ in Gethsemane, it has quite another meaning. Most of the time the mistake consists in not taking account of the circumstances of the period and the place in which these words were spoken. They were formulated, two thousand years ago, in a Near Eastern country with a rudimentary rural economy, and they were thought out by Semitic minds. It is very probable that they would never have been spoken in the context of our industrialized and urbanized Western society. The formula 'Sell your goods and give to the poor' can be justified in societies in which organic solidarity is dominant. It has to be transposed into societies with mechanical solidarity, where survival depends on systems of social security, on patterns of full-time education and social advancement. There is another particular feature which the social psychologist can note: the reaction which took place from the 1960s on over the very conception of historical progress and hence its influence on social life. The historicism in vogue in the Catholic church for several decades had been interpreted hitherto in a fashion which I would describe as cumulative: i.e., nurtured on the lessons of history, people seek to amass elements from them in order to obtain a progressive enrichment from features of this past. Thus the text of the mass was made up of the accumulation of contributions from successive centuries: one could find in it the remembrance of its theocentric origins, inspired by Judaism (acclamations like Alleluia, Hosanna, Amen, and the reference to the biblical texts of the Old Testament). A Greek element was added to this basis (Kyrie Eleison), and then a Latin one, comprising a large proportion of the texts; one could also discern Carolingian reminiscences. By the evocation of its holy founders, the church recalled its origins in Rome and then in the broader context of the Mediterranean (furthermore, this progressive enrichment could be enlarged on). Here we have a typical case of cumulative historicism; and it is this kind of historicism which, well managed, was able to give a substantial foundation to what people are accustomed to call the tradition. However, from the 1960s on we see the introduction of a kind of historicism (of Hegelian inspiration), and what one might call an 'evolutionary historicism'. There is still dependence on historicity, but instead of being seen in its enriching development (in Newman's sense of the word), it is seen in purely evolutionary terms, as a constantly renewed projection of novelty.

Those favouring this approach set themselves within the process, to experience its decay and constantly to await its revivals. They were on the lookout for the novelty that was going to appear (and which, of course, was sacralized, in accordance with the Hegelian perspective, as the 'ultimate' expression of conscience). Historicism thus experienced from the inside, and with its sudden revivals, led to a perpetual quest for novelty, a quest which often took anxious, not to say morbid, forms. People were haunted by novelty. This new type of historicism experienced an amazing boom in the Catholic church from the 1960s on. It implied an attitude of perpetual expectation. There was a constant expectation of novelty. Even more, there were attempts to promote it –

without regard for its possible harmful effects – by practising what was called 'permanent questioning'. The spell cast by such an attitude is not a concern for reform and thus for improvement; it is the fascination of innovation for its own sake. This kind of behaviour could, moreover, be subjected to psycho-analytical criticism: it was seen, beyond question, as the expression of a need to escape from the real (in short, a kind of schizophrenia). This type of evolutionary historicism was to develop considerably in the Catholic church between 1950 and 1970. This would be the age of innovation at any price: people lived for the myth of novelty. They virtually made a sacrament of the moment experienced in its 'newness'. Everywhere there was a search for 'God's today'.[12]

(b) A political christocentricity

The exclusive christocentricity which people endeavoured to adopt between 1950 and 1970 also had curious effects as far as politics was concerned. Granted, the church as always based its attitude to political power on the axiom put forward by Christ: 'Render to Caesar that which is Caesar's and to God that which is God's.' But down through history, in the time of triumphant theocentricity, it was nevertheless led to 'educate' Caesar or, more precisely, to teach him to live in conformity to a moral order which, if it does not relate to Christ (not everyone is a Christian, desirable though that would be), at least relates to God, to the 'God on whom all the empires depend' (Bossuet). The disappearance of theocentricity among the majority of active figures in recent times brings with it a complete change of attitude. People no longer seek to advocate a human wisdom, capable of directing the thought of princes and their mode of government: this has been renounced. Another attitude is adopted. Politics is left to its own order, and there is no preoccupation with techniques of government: people set out to 'proclaim Jesus Christ' to politicians, i.e. to put forward supernatural statements in an undiluted form, and then leave politicians the task of deriving whatever lessons they wish from them. This is sheer supernaturalism. The politicians are perhaps utterly disconcerted; but one also sees how they immediately point out the difficulties they have in introducing these dictates into their specific action. So they are tempted to regard these interventions as too 'angelic'. They do not need a supernatural conception of politics, but a natural one. Furthermore, one might imagine that this natural conception would be established in conformity to the supernatural order, that is to say, to the thought of Christ (though Christ did not give any direct teaching on political philosophy). This was the work attempted in the previous generation by, for example, Jacques Maritain. His perspective was theocentric and therefore natural, whereas in texts, like that on 'The Christian Attitude in Political Affairs', which have been put forward in more recent times, we find ourselves in a christological perspective. Hence the 'supernaturalism' which inspires them.

Where can this supernaturalism lead? It is difficult to say without going back. But one might guess that a city inspired by these principles, that is to say one which lived only by the 'dictates' of Christ, would end up by making itself a kind of 'christocracy' (a term which I have constructed on the lines of 'theocracy'). No one would practise any discipline: there would be a constant distrust of technical knowledge in all spheres (political, economic, social, legal, diplomatic, military, etc.). One would end up with a purely 'charismatic' society. I am not going to attempt to extrapolate here: I am content simply to observe the orientations.

(c) A new catharism

These are the features of a kind of catharism, that is to say, the ambition to create a world in which everything would be answerable to the demands of the gospel. Without doubt the disappearance of the distinction between the natural and the supernatural underlies this orientation. The natural is rejected, along with the theocentricity which supports it. Only the supernatural is retained, which clearly has christocentricity as its basis. There is a dream of a social and political supernaturalism . . . and even of an ecclesiastical supernaturalism. Perhaps I should explain this last point. This ecclesiastical supernaturalism would consist in favouring a religious life which would owe nothing to nature, and would nurture itself only on the supernatural (here I am thinking of the arguments put forward by certain theologians in the Catholic church during the 1960s). According to these conceptions, there seems to be a refusal to recognize – *de facto*, and even more *de jure* – the idea that a Christian must first of all be a human being, with all the natural demands which that presupposes. The notion of a 'Christian humanism' is decried and rejected. That is particularly evident in the new picture of the priest which people tend to have. The image of the cultivated, erudite priest, slightly apart from others, which had been handed down by former ages, is decried. The suggestion is that the priest should be uniquely the 'man of Jesus Christ'; it is therefore accepted that no account should be taken of his person, his culture and his 'humanities' (Bernanos, effusive in this direction, already said that 'a cultivated priest is in itself a scandal'). There is a concern for an outburst of grace in its pure state, as in virgin territory. The more a priest seems neglectful of his person, the more this is seen as a sign of the action of grace in him (this is the poor, harrassed priest of the *Diary of a Country Priest* faced with the robust Curé de Torcy, in Bernanos' book). Similarly, it is argued that in Christian life people must stop living in accordance with nature, and live in accordance with the supernatural. Thus, for example, any expression of sorrow at the departure of a loved one (though a universal sentiment) must be banished: people must sing Alleluia, the Magnificat. Any concern for nature is suspect. The same goes for the expressions of joy which accompany the essential rites of the life which the church has sanctified by providing them with sacramental signs (for example, birth, with baptism; initiation, with solemn communion; conjugal union, with the sacrament of marriage). These forms of popular rejoicing are denounced by the hyper-christocentric purists as alterations of the purity of the supernatural order. It is said that the very 'pure', supernatural significance which Christ gave to these rites must be restored. We end up in an inhuman austerity. We are on the way to a new catharism.

Many other features may be noticed. Thus the language which Christians, and particularly ecclesiastics, must use, is to lose all human distinction; it is even appropriate that it should be popular, to give the air of being more detached from nature, and therefore more supernatural. The same goes for clothing, which should not be a matter of concern; or places of abode, which must be deliberately (I was going to say 'conspicuously') on the verge of dereliction. Each of these forms of behaviour – and they all derive from a heightened christocentricity – is supposed to mark a firm distrust of the natural order, of such a kind that it is also supposed to be a better indication of total subservience to the supernatural order, in a life which is entirely lived out 'under the sole inspiration of Christ', without any 'pagan' reference to nature.

Be this as it may, we should note that about 1970, and in subsequent years, in various Catholic countries, a reaction has set in. Some of those who exercise influence in the church have tended to favour what is called 'popular Catholicism'. Here they represent an attempt to rehabilitate the natural order. Perhaps, however, the real significance of this development has not been noted. It is a shift on the part of certain theologians in favour of a return to theocentricity.[13] But I am doing no more than pointing to this reaction. We still need a study in greater depth to indicate the significance of the development for social psychology.

At the end of the day, in all the reactions which I have just described we must recognize a manifest return (however unexpected) to catharism. Here we find a dream of a pure Christianity, an unincarnated Christianity. So the term 'catharism', used in the etymological sense, seems quite justified. Here I have only drawn attention to a particular tendency. It is not for us to pass judgment on it.

3. Towards an exclusively christocentric spirituality

The themes developed in this way and the new directions taken gradually gave way to a new kind of spirituality, the main features of which emerged, from 1960 onwards, in large sectors of the church (of course, these were usually the most active sectors). Now that about fifteen years have passed, the observer can begin to see the main features. The doctrinal foundations (some would say 'ideological foundations', to keep in line with Marxist terminology) are an elaboration of radical christocentricity. In other words, any compromise with any kind of theocentricity is excluded. Faith is directed towards Christ and only towards Christ, who is regarded as a historical figure. Christ is believed in as a human guide, a saviour, an inspiration, who can be contrasted with the masters of thought championed by the partisans of other movements. The entirely new feature here is that we do not find any trace of reference to divine transcendence among many of these 'partisans' of Jesus Christ. The traditional words are still used, but people do not attach the same meaning to them. Thus faith becomes 'trust', the trust put in Jesus Christ as the guide of thought and life. Hope becomes the optimism that every human being must have anchored in his heart and which he must nurture, maintain and develop with Christ (the new hymns which then appeared often celebrated this 'hope' put in Christ to 'change the world' and make it 'happier and more brotherly', for example). Charity becomes solidarity, which people must establish among themselves at the invitation and the appeal of Jesus Christ. The words of these new hymns often call for the pursuit of the values asserted, following the Masonic societies, by the revolutionaries of 1789: liberty, equality and brotherhood. There is an appeal to Christ to guarantee and make fruitful these three human values by his example.

(a) The themes developed in preaching

In the so-called 'advanced' areas of the Catholic church, these are equally humanitarian. Thus in the name of Christ solidarity is required with poor and developing people; compassion for the various woes of the world (physical and moral suffering); vigilance in the struggles and fights that have to be carried on. In the strictly social order, sensitivity to inequalities is commended (no matter what they might be: just or unjust), inequality being an evil in itself: there is an invitation to universalism, beyond ethnic differences; poverty is sacralized for its particular value (while the fight goes on to remove it altogether). In the strictly political sphere an attempt is made to mobilize Christians for a fight for popular liberation (there are even proposals for a 'liberation theology', specially thought up to justify this kind of struggle). At other times, preaching takes the form of a eulogy on non-violence (with reference to certain political situations in the world), calling on certain of Christ's words which condemn violence (and tacitly ignoring those which, by contrast, are an invitation to violence: 'The kingdom of heaven belongs to the violent'). Thus the 'sayings' of Christ are interpreted in a secular sense.

I should also add that the traces of theocentricity which still remain are denounced in critical and often caustic terms. Thus certain phenomena – great architectural constructions, ceremonies, various rituals – intended from the theocentric perspective to 'hymn the glory of God' are denounced as expressions of 'triumphalism' (a term created to caricature them). By contrast, there is a preference for celebrations thought to be inspired in their simplicity by the renunciation which the Christ of Galilee seems to have practised (his moments of 'triumph' like the Epiphany, and later the Resurrection and Ascension, obviously cause difficulties!). Worship is called on to leave those places which still retain a sense of the glory of God. People are to leave the great traditional churches, and take refuge in modest abodes. Liturgy has to take on as sparse an appearance as possible (people no longer think of the Temple of God, the Temple of Jerusalem, but of the stable at Bethlehem or the workshop of Nazareth). Hymns have to lose all solemnity and become feeble laments. Everything has to reflect the humiliations of Christ. We shall see that this was a very free interpretation of the intentions of Christ, since in his worship he hymned the glory of God: he went to the Jerusalem temple and joined in its festivals. Besides, in his messianic life he never presented his humiliations and sufferings as an end, but as a means of achieving glorification. 'Was it not necessary for the Christ to suffer before entering into his glory?' But as here the reference to theocentricity has been completely eliminated, people henceforth feel led to consider the humiliations of Christ as ends in themselves; hence the preoccupation with misery and wretchedness which follows (by good social logic).

Another aspect of this development towards an exclusive christocentricity is a defence of the so-called 'community' spirit, which is to be practised in all circumstances, in both secular and religious life. The logical link between this appeal to 'community' spirit and the option for christocentricity is easy to bring out. I have already alluded to it above. The starting-point is the principle that the message of Christ is above all a message of human brotherhood (in the most human sense of the phrase). From that it is deduced that all men are brothers and must therefore live in an identical way: none may predominate. This gives rise to the idea that the community must govern itself, be autonomous. All activities must therefore be collective: people must think in common, decide in common, live and act in common. This way of acting, 'mystical' in inspiration, is not in conformity to human nature, which rather calls for personal responsibility; however, the procedure is maintained towards and against everything, even at the price of a harmful realism. The community spirit is lived out above all by so-called 'informal' groups which form for the practice of religious life, but it is also manifested in the liturgy and in sacramental life. There is a demand that all attitudes should be controlled by a concern for community spirit. The relative success of this tendency could also be explained by the fact that this need for community corresponds to the tendency towards collectivism which spread in civil society from 1930 onwards, in Western Europe in particular, and also as a result of concentration in cities.

(b) The evolution of rites of the mass

This is particularly interesting for the social psychologist to study. One feels, particularly among the 'most advanced elements' of the Catholic church, that the interpretation of the rites of the mass is evolving in an increasingly christocentric (and therefore in a decreasingly theocentric) direction. The mass is no longer the occasion of an encounter with God – a weekly meeting and, as far as the Sunday mass is concerned, a solemn meeting – but the occasion for Christians to come together and to reconstitute the Christian community. The rejection of theocentricity is represented by the progressive abandonment of rites indicating respect for the divine transcendence. Thus the sprinkling of blessed water (a rite which comes down to us from the Sumerians, and which represents the need for purification by water and 'by hyssop' in the face of the divine majesty) is abolished. The use of incense is reduced or suppressed, though this sign again comes down from the Sumerians, and by the rising smoke which it produces and the intoxicating smell which it gives out represents the need for adoration of the most high God. All forms of festivals are out: sumptuous vestments, lights, floral decoration, the richness of the sacred furniture, and so on, traditionally intended to give glory to God; they are replaced by simple and even coarse material, ordinary clothes, a rigorously utilitarian setting. The golden chalice, which in its way signified reverential faith and the real presence of the sacred, is replaced by a pewter goblet or even a piece of pottery. The end in view is always christocentric. It is a matter of living 'in community', in remembrance of Christ. In the commentaries which accompany these rites (and which are always profuse), there is constant talk of Christ, the human Christ, who lived in Galilee, who suffered and died. There is no longer talk of the glory of God.[14] In other words, a sympathetic atheist could easily join in the 'meeting' (it is no longer a ceremony). Of course, the essential feature of the meeting is a repetition of the rites of the eucharistic meal in which Jesus shared on Maundy Thursday. Bread and wine are offered; the words then pronounced by Christ are repeated; this bread and wine is shared. Then gestures of human brotherhood are exchanged. Someone, a priest (but it is thought that one day this could be a layman), presides over the meeting, because there is need of a coordinator of actions and gestures. He is expected to be the 'soul of the group', and not its director and chief. Here, as elsewhere, the priest is not regarded as the representative of God among the 'faithful': he is the *primus inter pares*. He has perhaps been told at his ordination *oportet sacerdotem preesse*, but according to these new interpretations he must forget this unfortunate formula and once again become one of the members of the community: if it happens that he is given a certain preeminence, this is as a function of his charismata, which have been noted by the community and freely recognized by it. It is the community which directs religious life at the mass, as elsewhere. The community spirit will even require him to say 'Let us go in the peace of Christ' and not 'Go in the peace of Christ' at the end of the mass: a small detail, but a significant one, since the latter, the imperative in the second person, indicates that he has the 'power' to call and dismiss the gathering. Finally, a last feature and one which goes for the performance of all these 'rites': the departure of the participants 'in silence' is avoided, since in silence the soul will tend to adopt an adoring orientation – in a personal form – which would be more in keeping with the spirit of theocentricity. A constant attempt is made to keep the community alert, *qua* community, by hymns, commentaries and actions, so that the participants are well integrated into the congregation and do not take up any autonomous spiritual life of their own.

(c) New attitudes from a practical and institutional point of view

The Catholic carried along by this current of thought, between 1960 and 1970, adopts new attitudes in comparison with his predecessors. It is clear, to begin with, that he no longer feels obliged to accord even a minimal place to the themes inspired by traditional theocentricity (which, it seems, he soon ends up by ignoring). His life-style is exclusively christocentric. For him, a Christian is someone who goes to school with Jesus Christ, as a Marxist with Marx or a Sartreian with Sartre. This is human involvement following a certain model. Imagining Christ from a purely human point of view, he sees in him a man who protests against the society of his time, who castigates blatant injustice, who prefers non-violence to violence. So he adapts his behaviour to this human model. He adopts a 'challenging' attitude. And he often goes a very long way in his zeal. He fights for justice. He is generous without counting the cost. He is non-violent on principle. Reproducing certain apparent attitudes of Christ in this way, he is led to have a predilection for those on the periphery (which allows him to accentuate his aggressiveness towards 'society', seen as an objective entity). He systematically takes the side of the poor (without verifying whether this poverty is deserved or undeserved, thanks to idleness or negligence). He is thus led to imagine the Catholic church as being uniquely the 'church of the poor' and, by extension, of all those who have not been able to integrate themselves into the social 'consensus': those on the fringe by virtue of their health (drug-addicts), morality (prostitution), or social life (delinquents). The social psychologist can even detect signs, among certain of the faithful, and in certain areas, of the rise of a certain 'fringe psychosis'. The abnormal becomes the privileged case (the psycho-analyst could go even further and see here the subtle manifestations of a certain sado-masochistic complex: there is greater pleasure in failure than in success). However, I must not press the point: here we come to the limit where the total rejection of the remnants of theocentricity (a sense of order or moderation . . .) leads to the adoption of a heightened christocentricity, which, if one looks closer, cannot be more than a bogus christocentricity, a vague humanism.

We can see similar developments in the institutional sphere (also in the same areas). With the rejection of theocentricity we have a rejection of all hierarchical sense. No one wants to hear any more talk of an authority which would maintain the believer in a state of alienation by the paternalism which it shows. Thus no one dares any longer to recognize the Pope as 'the common father of pastors and the faithful' (as the old catechism said). There is a concern to reduce his function to that of the co-ordinator of communities (without infallibility, without the power of administration, without the power of supreme judgment in questions of dogma and morality). There is a concern to restrict him to the symbolic role of the first of Christians, the Christian model, the 'servant of the servants of God'. There is a similar reaction to bishops. It is easy to denounce the triumphalist roles which they have been able to play, above all as 'primates' of important areas, roles in which they have been shaped by the mould of earlier functions performed by the ancient Roman imperial prefects. There has been a desire to strip them of these administrative and representative functions, so that they serve only to quicken faith in Christ. They are to be there only to 'announce Jesus Christ', and not to direct and administrate. Of course, as I have said, there is a problem over the identity of the bishop – from the point of view of the social psychologist. It is worth reflecting on this problem. Is the model to be sought in the moral magistrature exercised by the high priests in the Jerusalem temple; in the role of those responsible for the moral and political security of an area (like St Loup and St Germain of Auxerre; and like our contemporaries such as the Primate of Hungary, the Maronite Patriarch in Lebanon, or the Cardinal Primate of Poland, defender of the faith and of national Polish pride)? Many advanced Catholics sweep the board of all social and administrative functions which derive from theocentricity, and, accepting only exclusive christocentricity, reject these interpretations. They dream of bishops stripped of all social functions, living out their faith in Christ in an exemplary way within the Christian community. They dream of purely 'charismatic' figures.

The problem of identity arises even more acutely over the status of the priest. I have already mentioned this several times. In 'advanced' circles, people only envisaged exclusively christocentric norms here as well. They are concerned that the priest should be essentially the model Christian (he is readily assimilated to being the 'saint of the community'). His only task is to help to find the common spiritual inspiration, to bring together the efforts of spontaneous groups which are formed in his neighbourhood. Thus the priest is called to 'dilute' himself in the community: he is the 'salt of the earth', needed to enrich it; but like the salt, he will be led to 'melt' into the community to the point of disappearing.

The process I am analysing here, and which tends towards the 'dilution' of the priesthood, is indicated by a number of signs. These signs are in the sphere of social psychology (they do not challenge doctrinal or moral positions), but they are symptomatic. Among other things, one could cite the increasing recourse – from the 1970s on – to the liturgical rite of concelebration. Whereas for more than three millennia (since the priesthood of Melchizedek) a concern to exalt the transcendence of the priest has always led to a demand for one priest, at one altar, to offer a single sacrifice to the one God (just as there is only one celebrant on Maundy Thursday and one victim on Golgotha), we now see the spread of the practice of a sacerdotal pluralism at the altar: tens, sometimes hundreds of priests throng round the same altar to concelebrate the sacrifice (the need for an expression of 'community' spirit). We certainly cannot note any change in doctrine in connection with this practice. However, the sociologist will observe that the thousand-year-old image of the uniqueness and transcendence of the priest is inevitably altered in public opinion. This is a new evolution, which has to be added to other evolutions in the status of the priest under the influence of this christocentricity, which tends to become exclusive from the 1960s on. I shall not return to this problem, but simply state that these developments are completely in keeping with the internal logic of christocentricity.

Under this influence the status of the believers themselves also develops significantly. I have already spoken of this, since the evolution goes back to the 1950s. However, there is also a certain accentuation of the tendencies which emerged in this period, at least in so-called 'advanced' circles (to use the current description). In the exclusively christocentric perspective, the Christian is a man who models his life on the behaviour of Jesus Christ. This formula is one of the most classic, even though it refers only to the human side, the 'visible' part of the life of Christ (the other side, that which 'constantly sees the Father', is ignored). In this case, those who believe in Christ become those who work for a better world, as so many of the hymns which appeared after 1970 proclaimed. This phrase is not made more precise: is it a world which is better through grace, or better through nature? The ambiguity remains. So believers are the kind promoters of social clubs, unions, protest movements. Furthermore, as they meet together, believers are called upon to form a kind of 'spiritual republic'; they are often called 'the people of God'. However, this phrase remains obscure because of the ambiguities which surround the use of the particle 'of': are they a people who 'belong' to God (like the people of Israel in the Old Testament), in which case recourse to this formula would mark a return towards theocentricity? Or should we understand this 'of' in the sense of 'custodian of', in which case we would have a conviction, though quite vague, favouring faith in the existence of a God. (Is this faith received, or proclaimed? That remains obscure.) In that case, Christians could call themselves 'people of God' as others call themselves 'people of liberty'. This would not be appropriation: on the contrary, it would be immanent and subjective proclamation. Finally, one of the characteristics of these neo-Christians is that they put their trust more in direct action, to change the world, than in the mysterious virtues of prayer. Christians must be present in all the battlefields; they must be shoulder-to-shoulder with all the people who struggle, with all the populations who fight for their temporal and material 'liberation' (among the guerillas of Latin America, like Camillo Torres, and in trade union actions, like strikes, in Europe and America). This is the territory on which Christians must take their stand, in political and social action, and no longer lose themselves in *theoria* and in contemplation.

I shall bring this analysis in social psychology to a close by showing how this heightened and exclusive christocentricity, where Christ is considered essentially in his visible and human behaviour, must inevitably lead to many developments in all areas relating to the action of the Catholic church. It would take too long to list all the effects. Let me content myself with indicating some characteristic cases; for example, that of apologetic in general. The 'tactic' towards non-believers is to show the human excellence of Christ and the ideas which can be derived from his teaching. Christ is the most 'credible' of men, since he is the most 'revolutionary'. This theme is developed in all kinds of ways. There is talk of the 'revolutionary virtue' of the gospels. The development in connection with the catechism, that is to say the teaching of children, has also been very marked since 1960–1970. Here theocentricity is out almost completely, at least in the most 'advanced' methods (as in the famous *Dutch Catechism*). People talk only of Christ, and of Christ as a historical figure. The starting point for the approach is 'human wretchedness' (an obligatory starting point; if there is no wretchness, or only a little, it is presupposed, or at least stressed, since without it there would no longer be any starting point . . .). Then there is a demonstration that Christ is the only figure who can remedy this wretchedness; this is not, of course, a supernatural remedy, like grace, but a material, temporal remedy.

Christ alone can remedy human wretchedness. This approach is quite 'Pascalian' in style (Pascal developed the theme of 'the wretchedness of man without God'), except that we have now left the theocentric perspective for the christocentric perspective, and this christocentricity is given a purely human and material orientation. Finally, I should point out that a whole literature flourished from the 1960s on, aiming to show that one cannot live without having discovered Christ (i.e., the human Christ). The cinema has also developed this theme (for example, the films of Pasolini). We can also see the appearance of a great many songs on the theme of the imminent coming of Christ: 'Come Jesus', spread through pop music. People sing *Jesus Christ Superstar*. There is a vogue for gospel nights, and so on. Jesus has been finally elevated to the realm of human stars (and in his commercial success he is indeed top of the bill). This is where the diffusion of a 'myth' of Christ has ended up: a myth which started in the 1950s, was stressed in the 1960s and 1970s, and which proceeded directly from the adoption by some Catholic thought of a radical and exclusive christocentricity. Christ has been desacralized. Some films and songs are only symptoms and sociological epiphenomena, but for the social psychologist they are eminently significant. At the risk of shocking 'pious ears', that allows us to say that the evolution has continued – an evolution which is completely in conformity with the laws of social logic – from the first variations on Bérulle's christocentricity to the last variations of the pagan christocentricity of pop music and the image of *Jesus Christ Superstar*.[15] That is what I have established. It gives us food for thought.

4. The role of Vatican II

We know the profound influence which the Second Vatican Council exercised on the Catholic church. So we can ask in what sense this influence has made itself felt here, in connection with the problem with which we are concerned, that of the evolution from theocentricity towards christocentricity in large sectors of opinion in the Catholic church. Did it favour this evolution and even speed it up? Did it run counter to it, or at least try to slow it down? These are questions which we have a right to ask.

First of all, I shall discuss the official positions taken by the Council. Did it lean towards theocentricity or towards christocentricity? We have to reread the basic texts, that is to say the Constitutions, the various Documents and the Decrees.[16] The first Constitution that we find, the famous text *Lumen Gentium*, begins with an introduction which has quite a christocentric tone. We are asked first of all to look towards Christ, 'light of the nations'. Very soon, however, in the second section of this first chapter, we move towards doctrinal positions which are completely theocentric: the mission of Christ is closely connected with the will of the Father who is in heaven. Without this will of the Father, Christ would be only one human being among others. It is the Spirit of God which directs the whole adventure of redemption (sections 4 to 6). Then, once again, attention is directed towards the presence of Christ in human history: he has come to lead men to his Father; but it is then shown that this leading of men towards the Father is achieved by incorporating them into 'a mystical body', and that this body is none other than the body of Christ, which extends itself into the future of humanity. This mystical body is the visible church inaugurated on this earth, which is to exist to the end of time. The doctrinal positions having been thus taken up, the text spends a long time on the characteristics of the social body which is the church. It is here that we are told that the social body can be called 'people of God': (note that this study of the social body of the church is introduced as an afterthought: it was not foreseen in primitive times, hence its clearly 'modernistic' character). The people of God – and this must be acknowledged – is clearly described as coming from God, as belonging to him; there is no ambiguity in this respect. God is a reality transcendent over his people, and takes them in charge (Ch. II). We then see theocentric and christocentric considerations alternating in the text. Clearly those in authority in the church continue to maintain the bipolarity that we saw to be essential at the beginning. At the same time – and this is a new development – certain thrusts of christocentricity make themselves felt. Thus the people of God sees itself endowed with a certain capacity for inspiration and creation in religious matters (section 12); at the same time, it is made quite clear that in this capacity only the hierarchical church is judge. The last word remains with authority (a theocentric reaction).

When the time comes to discuss relations between this church, 'the people of God', and the other religious societies of the world (Jews, Moslems and so on), the positions adopted are markedly theocentric. The dangers inherent in an excessive christocentricity, which I have indicated, have been removed (section 16). The Council then goes on to pronounce on the internal organization of this church, 'the people of God'. We feel very clearly here that the positions to be adopted will be in reaction to those which had been adopted by Vatican I – in a haste excused by circumstances. The theme of papal infallibility (a very theocentric one) is 'counterbalanced' by that of the collegiality of bishops (Ch. III). However, if we look more closely, we shall see that nothing escapes the concern of the church to be a hierarchical society. The ultimate responsibility – in communion with the bishops – always returns to the authority of the Pope (section 22). As for the laity, here they receive an active place and mission in the church (sections 30–38). Then an appeal is addressed to all those who make up the 'people of God', with the laity, the religious (Ch. VI), the priests: all – taking the Virgin Mary as model – must seek sanctity in a church on the way to a final eschatology in which it will achieve its ultimate aim, the contemplation of God.

One might make three observations (as I indicated earlier) in connection with this text, which is regarded as one of the most important produced by the Council. First of all, it may be noted that here the church keeps to traditional doctrinal positions. Here we find once again the bipolarity which can be seen, sociologically speaking, from the first appearance of the doctrine of the church. The Christian is invited to relate all his behaviour to God and simultaneously to Christ. The text is a perfect echo of the positions of the primitive church. But can we now discern new tendencies? Yes, in one way; in the sense that we feel here a concern for a certain redistribution of balance, in contrast to earlier councils. I have already said that the last two councils, the Council of Trent and the First Vatican Council, echoing the spirit of their times tended to adopt a very theocentric style. The reference of all behaviour to God was especially marked (more than in the councils of previous centuries). Here, at Vatican II, there is a clear attempt to restore a more important place to reference to Christ, by way of reaction. In particular, the theme of collegiality (which, as is generally realized, counterbalances that of papal infallibility), is completely governed by christocentric considerations: references to Christ the priest, for example, can be found everywhere. So I would say that the tendency peculiar to *Lumen Gentium* is also a tendency towards the restoration of a degree of christocentricity. In fact it is a restoration of balance. However, from that point, some who are particularly sensitive to this reaction are taking advantage of it. This happens to such a degree (my third point) that many commentators note this reaction above all, and insistently underline it. This means that for public opinion, this text could have the effect of a plea for christocentricity; and it could be interpreted as constituting a kind of guarantee, a tacit approbation given to various enterprises, in favour of an exclusive christocentricity which was evident at that time. In fact, as we shall see, it was nothing of the sort. To sum up: the basic positions are more traditional (and in a sense more in conformity to the positions of the primitive church), than that of the Council of Trent or Vatican I; at all events, there is incontestably a certain tendency here towards a rehabilitation of christocentricity (in reaction against earlier theocentricity); all the 'interpretations' which are given of it must be regarded in the last resort as partisan.

We can make similar observations on the other conciliar texts. The text on ecumenism maintains the balance between christocentricity and theocentricity: perhaps it has a more christocentric resonance when it addresses Protestants, and a more theocentric one when it addresses the orthodox. The texts concerning bishops, priestly formation and Christian education also show the need felt by the Fathers to restore the balance of the doctrine of the church towards christocentricity. However, this is simply a restoration of balance; the thought of the Fathers never loses sight of the fact that the whole religious life of the church can only be understood as related to a God who transcends the world and is superior to historical events. The declaration on the relations of the church with the non-Christian religions evidently, as one would expect, stresses theocentricity, above all when it is addressed to Moslems. The Jews are reminded of their 'spiritual affinity' with Abraham; Christians and Jews live out the same faith in the God of Abraham. It is appropriately recalled here that it is good to think of Christ as a 'mediator', and that his mission can only be understood as essentially directed towards the adoration of God Most High.

The text on relations between the church and the modern world, better known under the title *Gaudium et Spes*,[17] deserves special attention. It has been seen as a text marking a break with the past and being open to ideas which had been widespread in the church for several decades, as we have had occasion to observe (in particular, the heightened reference to Christ, as man, the adoption of a degree of historicity, and so on). But precisely what does it say? One has to acknowledge that on first reading, it seems that we can in fact find the majority of the christocentric themes which we saw appearing between 1940 and 1960. Even in section 1 there is a reference to Christ, and this reference to Christ recurs throughout the text (there is very little reference to God, in contrast to the texts of earlier councils, and even earlier texts of the same Council). The mission of Christ is no longer to give glory to God, but 'to carry forward the work of Christ himself under the lead of the befriending Spirit' (section 3). The church is invited to scrutinize the 'signs of the times' (section 4): there is therefore confidence that history will 'indicate' them. The salvation of all humanity must be ordered around Christ. Very christocentric themes, emerging from the 1930s, find a warm welcome in this text: 'cult of man' (throughout the first chapter), 'community spirit', and so on. The theme that there is only one remedy against atheism, return to Christ, so dear to apologists of the nineteenth century and the beginning of the twentieth, is evoked explicitly. 'The church courteously invites atheists to examine the gospel of Christ with an open mind' (section 21). The God of the philosophers and wise men is unknown; there is no desire to know any other than the 'God of Jesus Christ', since he is known by history. Christocentricity is sometimes even deliberately invoked, as for example in section 22, where we read: 'The truth is that only in the mystery of the incarnate Word does the mystery of man take on light' (here we again find the formula with which I described this trend earlier: 'Without Christ, no salvation'). As for the community spirit, almost the whole of the second chapter (sections 23–32) is devoted to it. The third theme that we saw developing in the wake of christocentricity, that of action, is taken up all through the third chapter. Curiously, here action is considered in itself, detached from contemplation (in this text there is no reference to the traditional theory of the primacy of contemplation over action). Later on in the text the church is required to engage in dialogue with the world. Here, too, considerations revolve around the mission of Christ (Ch. IV). The theme of Christ the perfect man, inherited from Bérullianism, from the seventeenth century, is insistently taken up again. 'The Lord is the goal of human history, the focal point of the longings of history and of civilization', we find in section 45. The postulate of the 'meaning of history' is accepted, and is given a strictly christocentric interpretation. The text of the Apocalypse, 'I am the alpha and omega', which up to then was interpreted in an 'individualist' sense ('I come to render to each one according to his works') is invoked in a collectivist perspective. Christ will be the alpha and omega of the whole 'history' of the world. The chapters which follow have the aim of bringing solutions to the specific problems of the period (between 1962 and 1965).[18] The reference to christocentricity is certainly less explicit than in the chapters of the first part; however, an objective and careful reading of the solutions put forward reveals that they are inspired more by christocentric principles (which I identified earlier) than by those of theocentricity. There is more appeal to solidarity, to co-responsibility, to active participation, and to all the virtues arising – as we have seen – under the aegis of christocentricity than to wisdom and to the cardinal and theological virtues arising – as we have also seen – under the aegis of theocentricity. As for the decrees on the apostolate of the laity, religious freedom and the instruments of communication, I readily grant that they seem to be divided almost equally between theocentricity and christocentricity. Another text of some importance, in that it is presented as a dogmatic constitution, is that which relates to divine revelation. The positions taken up there are in full conformity with the tradition of the church. Revelation is regarded as being expressed jointly in scripture and tradition, in other words (according to the analytical language that I am using), theocentricity and christocentricity are held in balance.[19] The basic themes of theocentricity are even recalled there, since it is indicated in section 6 that access to God is first possible through reason. 'The sacred Synod affirms, "God, the beginning and end of all things, can be known with certainty from created reality by the light of human reason" (cf. Rom. 1.20).' And taking up the position of Vatican I, the Council sees in revelation the possibility of completing the effort of reason to obtain a 'solid certitude with no trace of error' concerning the knowledge of God. I would even go so far as to say that for the impartial observer the text of this Dogmatic Constitution on Revelation marks a clear return to theocentricity. We feel here that everything, everywhere, depends on God and only on God, including the mission of Christ. By contrast, in the last Decrees which I have to mention, the Decree on Missionary Activity and that on the Ministry and Life of priests (added *in extremis*), there is a marked return to christocentricity – without doubt because we find more topical and specific considerations in them. Missionary activity is presented in terms in which it had begun to be conceived of from the nineteenth century on, as the direct proclamation of Jesus Christ to pagan people, and not primarily as the awakening of faith in God. This problem of arousing faith in a transcendent God as a prelude to faith in Christ does not seem to be raised. The same spirit can be found in the Decree on the Ministry of Priests. The christocentric interpretation prevails. The priest is not presented as the man of God, set apart for his worship and to the radiance of his glory (the theocentric conception), but as the representative of Christ. 'By sacred ordination and by the mission they receive from their bishops, priests are promoted to the service of Christ, the Teacher, the Priest and the King' (section 1), though periodically the text recalls the other aspect of the mission of the priest (cf. section 2). Later on, however, the two interpretations are presented together. 'The purpose, therefore, which priests pursue by their ministry and life is the glory of God the Father as it is to be achieved in Christ. That glory consists in this: that men knowingly, freely, and gratefully accept what God has achieved perfectly through Christ, and manifest it in their whole lives' (section 2).[20]

To sum up, we gain a threefold impression from reading the

texts of the Council. Basically the dogmatic positions take up traditional viewpoints. An exception, however, has to be made for schema 13, which became the Pastoral Constitution (ambiguous title) *Gaudium et Spes*. In this last text, the tone of which seems to the impartial observer to stand out from the texts as a whole, the accent is clearly on christocentricity. Here we find echoes of all the positions maintained since Bérulle on the preeminence of Christ, conceived of as the only point of reference for faith. In particular, we find echoes here of the viewpoints put forward since the 1930s. This text is resolutely christocentric, whereas the others maintain the traditional equilibrium between the two interpretations. Secondly, one might say that we can feel the development of 'tendencies' towards christocentricity. Whereas the predominance of theocentricity is constant, as I have shown, in the texts of the two earlier councils, the Council of Trent and Vatican I, to the point that there is even a kind of imbalance in relation to the positions held by the early church, we feel that by contrast, the texts of Vatican II sought to restore the balance between the two interpretations. In this sense, these texts – in both their spirit and their accent – are nearer to the positions developed in the church during the first centuries. The spirit of the earliest church has been rediscovered. At the Council, a concern was repeatedly expressed to go back behind the Constantinian era. From the point of view which I have adopted, that of social psychology, one could say that the Council succeeded. It abandoned the pretensions of an exclusive theocentricity without, in reaction, abandoning itself to an equally exclusive christocentricity. Throughout the texts (with the exception of *Gaudium et Spes*, which tends towards christocentricity), the conditions have been created for some equilibrium between the two tendencies. However, since we know that this equilibrium is precarious, we have a right to ask – without going into doctrinal polemic, but from the simple point of view of social logic – whether it could be maintained over a long period. I shall try later (in Chapter IX) to assess the way in which coming centuries are likely to move.

It remains, finally, to indicate a third impression which arises from reading the texts. One feels – again in reaction to the predominant theocentricity that one can see in the texts of the two earlier councils – that there is a deliberate bias towards christocentricity. The Council is therefore led to introduce new viewpoints which have emerged from some of the ideas in circulation over the past half century. Those who hold these ideas will now have the impression that concessions have been made to them. They will therefore be led to cite the Council in support of their views. And this is the way in which currents of opinion have arisen which, after the Council, and above all from the 1970s, lean strongly in the direction of christocentricity, claiming to have the authority of the 'spirit of the Council'. They will say that they are 'the movement of the Council'. We shall look at them in the following chapters. Here I would simply point out that from the point of view of social psychology, we see a tangential social logic at work there: a derivation is produced which exploits a marginal current. In more simple terms, what we have is a free interpretation: a reaction with partial intent is exploited to give it an absolute value. In fact the developments towards the extreme forms of christocentricity which occurred subsequently – and which we shall now study – stem from currents of thought which have been under way for almost three centuries. They owe very little to the official texts which the Catholic church promulgated at Vatican II.

During the period 1960–1970, and particularly after the Council, we have the impression that two churches are being called on to live in the bosom of the one community traditionally called Catholicism: a church living in obedience to God and his commandments, and a church which lives in accord with the appeals of Christ and his invitation to the love of men. These two churches are to live together, come what may. However, before we take a closer look at this cohabitation, we must first take account of the latest developments in the move towards christocentricity which have come about over the last two decades.

VII

Extreme Forms of Christocentricity

A kind of logical fatalism among some thinkers takes the development we have been considering to its limit: to a form of christocentricity so exclusive that it does not seem to contain the least reference to a transcendent God. After the 1960s, we end up with the development of what might be called an atheistic Christianity. This radical movement develops in two stages. First of all, Christ is 'isolated' completely from all reference to a God; then, in a second stage, after the acceptance of the idea of the 'death of God', we are presented with a 'powerful and solitary' Christ who challenges humanity single-handed and saves it from its misery by the sole virtue of his human qualities.

1. The theme of the 'solitude of Christ'

Here the believer is invited to meditate on the image of a Christ who alone bears human torment and who, in a chilly solitude, seeks to take on himself all the weight of human misery in order to 'consume' it in himself, in a tragic holocaust. This theme could already be found in the religious thought of Kierkegaard. He sees Christ as a being who, in fearful solitude, lives out the drama of the moral misery of the world. From high on the cross Christ has seen the whole extent of this 'ocean' of misery, evil and crime; he has taken up this misery, being abandoned by all. He even feels himself abandoned by God: 'My God, my God, why have you forsaken me?' That is the supreme cry. And it is in the horror of this total forsakenness that the redemption of the world takes place. This theme of the total 'dereliction' of Christ is, moreover, an ancient theme, the first traces of which we find in the Protestant tradition, notably in Luther.[1] We find it again in a current of modern Protestant theology, which leads to Karl Barth. We can trace out its stages, and for that we must return first of all to Bonhoeffer.

The christology of Bonhoeffer, formulated in the 1930s, in fact marks an important stage in the evolution towards the 'Christianity without God' of the 1960s.[2] It is at the same time both a result and a starting point: it exercises a profound influence from the 1950s on, first on Protestant and then on Catholic thought. We must first of all realize that the theological thought of Bonhoeffer is in fact based on a philosophical foundation of Hegelian inspiration; his epistemology is Hegelian and his noeticism is Hegelian. His starting point in thinking is the idealist postulate, and he reasons according to dialectical schemes. He has accepted the idealist postulate, and has done so without qualification. For him, the very notion of God can appear only within the sphere of human consciousness (and there is no question of leaving it, since he shares in the initial act of faith of every idealist: 'What is beyond thought is unthinkable'). He speaks of the 'closed circle of the I' (in German he puts this in a compelling way: he speaks of the *nichtgegenständliches Ich*). Inevitably, the idea of God is an integral part of this sphere of the I. In this connection he draws on Fichte, for whom the idea of the Absolute is one of the productions of the human mind. This allows him to say that man has made God 'one of his creatures' (an old idea, which appears in atheist literature after Feuerbach). Bonhoeffer shared in this point of view from 1930 on. So there is no question of his referring to any kind of transcendent God; this pole of reference has entirely disappeared from his metaphysical horizon. But he continues to remain a Christian (Why? His reasons remain very obscure). He then finds himself led to develop a christology without a transcendent God. The metaphysical foundations on which he constructs this are also borrowed, to a great extent, from Heidegger. He adopts a picture of man (looking to that which would be provided by Christ) very close to that of Heidegger. Man is a being 'thrown into existence' (that is 'in-der-Welt-sein'), and in this condition, he cannot elevate himself to any kind of transcendence. As Bonhoeffer himself writes: 'Heidegger's man may not in the end bear any divine features.'[3] He then considers the condition of man 'without grace', and sees it as that of a completely solitary being, a being which has no refuge of any sort. Man is in a state of total dereliction. He feels abandoned by everyone and everything, and after so many centuries of trust in God he now feels 'abandoned by God'. If some inklings of a return to God are aroused in him, he has to drive away these deceitful temptations; he must thus be a 'deicide'. A clear-minded person must in fact 'be a deicide'.[4] However, despite everything, Bonhoeffer wants to be a Christian theologian: he has met Jesus Christ on his way. So he sees in Christ, too, man in a state of dereliction, with the difference that in this case the dereliction is total. It is this total dereliction which attracts the human mind, because it recognizes and finds itself there. And Bonhoeffer then gives himself over to the most intense act of faith that one could imagine. He gives himself to Christ as to the one who becomes 'superhuman' in dereliction. He has to adhere to Christ with all his soul and with all his strength; that is the great risk, the radical stake, the absolute leap in faith, which he must make with all his being. 'So it is only in faith in Christ that I know that I believe.'[5] He has to 'plunge' into Christ, immerse himself in faith in Christ. The believer has to go so far as to feel more in contact with Christ and his church than he feels in contact with the world. One has to substitute a 'being-in-the-church' for Heidegger's 'being-in-the-world'.[6] It is necessary to look for human 'salvation' by taking refuge in the community of the church.

Should we then expect that by the mediation of Christ and his church we shall rediscover the presence of God? No, replies Bonhoeffer. The reference to God is no longer necessary. This preoccupation must even disappear. We shall have to get used to the idea, says Bonhoeffer, that we can live out a Christianity without God. This Christianity will be all the stronger, all the more vigorous, when it no longer refers to this theme which has ceased to have any *raison d'être*, that of a transcendent deity. In its place, however, one could produce psychological substitutes which take on a more dynamic and more dynamizing force.

For instance, one could designate life, strength and action as substitutes for God. 'God wills to be known in life and not in death,' he writes, 'in health and strength, and not in suffering; in action, and not in sin.'[7] And, he adds, 'the reason for all this can be found in the revelation of God in Jesus Christ'. We have Jesus Christ; why look for God? And since the hypothesis of a transcendent God is rejected by modern thought, why insist on making it figure in the content of Christian faith? 'Man has learnt to deal with himself in all questions of importance without recourse to the "working hypothesis" called "God" . . . it is becoming evident that everything gets along without "God" – and, in fact, just as well as before . . . "God" is being pushed more and more out of life, losing more and more ground' (letter of 8 June 1944).[8]

Let us draw the conclusions which follow from these remarks. We are to construct a 'Christianity without God', to elaborate an atheistic theology. This is in fact the starting point for all forms of the theology of the death of God which subsequently appear, above all in the United States, as we shall see. However, Bonhoeffer also draws some conclusions of a practical kind. Let us divest theology of the last references to a God, a God who troubles man, who prevents him from expressing himself freely. Let us free man from the tutelage of God and make the Christian a being freed from all transcendence, and consequently from all reference to any kind of order, reflected in the practical life of faith in God. In short, Bonhoeffer calls on Christian awareness to make an agonizing revision of its conceptions: 'Christ does not call man to a new religion, but to a new life'.[9] The problem of God is 'out'; it is a problem which does not arise. The time has come for a Christianity without God.

This is the conclusion at which Bonhoeffer arrives. Having begun from the theme of the 'solitude' of man, he has moved on to that of the 'solitude' of Christ, to end up as a result with the complete disappearance of God. The influence of these analyses was considerable. A large number of theologians, both Protestant and Catholic, then argued in principle that 'God must be put in parentheses' and that it was now a matter of encountering a Christ 'divested' of God. Attention is henceforth to be concentrated on this person of a 'de-deified' Christ. From now on we see the blossoming of multiple atheistic christologies in which not only is God ignored (as was the case in the attempts that I have just mentioned) but he is deliberately 'chased out'; chased out as an intruder, a disturber, a kind of harmful 'fantasy', and an odious reducing agent. We must study them.

2. Some christologies without God

From the 1960s onwards, several christologies were in fact constructed which present Christ as a historical figure who played an important spiritual role, without it being necessary to explain the meaning of his mission by reference to some kind of divine transcendence (in fact, here we rediscover the ancient tradition of Renan, Harnack and other rationalists of the nineteenth century, but in a different philosophical context). For example, the christology of Bultmann could be located in the context of Heideggerian philosophy. He himself says that he found in Heidegger 'adequate conceptuality for the interpretation of the New Testament and the Christian faith'.[10] Now it is well known that Heidegger rejected any reference to a transcendent order. Supported by this metaphysic of the closed being, the *Seiendes*, the thought of Bultmann tends essentially to 'demythologize' the figure of Christ, to remove from him anything, however, small, which might suggest that his person could transcend the human order. For him, Christ is one who 'calls': he calls to risk, to involvement in senseless wagers. It is necessary to heed his call and 'leave everything to follow him'; and it is in this renunciation of all security, this 'leap into the unknown', that Christian faith consists. Here Bultmann arrives – in the letter, if not the spirit – at analogous positions to those of Luther and above all Kierkegaard. The Christian wagers all on a man, on his word, on his promises . . . without knowing where he is going. He 'throws himself on the water'.

Later, we can rediscover – and I do not think that it is forcing things to say this – similar positions in Tillich. He, too, thinks that it is necessary to have the support of a philosophical basis (in the wider sense). Now it is useful to begin from philosophical positions prevalent in our era. The historicism which he adopts leads him to regard as 'established' whatever has risen to consciousness most recently: it is fact which gives foundation to law. Because we think in a particular way in our time, then this is the way in which we must think. It is important to bow down before the law of numbers: here sociology takes the place of philosophy (and therefore of theology). Now what do we discover? We discover that our age claims to be atheistic: it is the era of the 'death of God'.[11] So it is from this 'atheistic culture' that we must begin; or at least, this atheistic culture must serve as the background to our speculation. In these conditions, how are we to consider Christ? It is clearly important first of all to have a 'reading' of his sayings and his actions with respect to our current way of thinking. So we must have 'an atheistic reading of the gospels', with the secret hope that we shall find there lessons for ourselves, by reason of the 'existential profoundity' which Christ has shown. Tillich sums up his thought well in this formula: 'Christ is no longer a being who has come from elsewhere, but the revelation of the new being towards which man tends at the heart of his human existence.' The mystery hidden in the heart of the human existence of this person of Christ must excite us. 'No one spoke like this man.' Every observer must be intrigued by his person. And we must subject all our life to the questioning of this Jesus of Nazareth. We must try to snatch his secret from him, to scrutinize the mystery that he conceals. All the questions raised by people of our day must therefore be put to Jesus. Only he, by virtue of the existential depth of his behaviour, seems able to reply to us. Thus a dialogue must begin between the culture of our time and Jesus Christ; and it is from this dialogue that revelation is born. For, Tillich explains, 'if revelation is closed . . . the process of revelation continues indefinitely, in each existence and in each culture'. Since the Holy Spirit is in fact history, we must listen to its appeals through whatever events may happen (these being regarded as necessary). So in these different christologies, whether of Bultmann or of Tillich, we can see christocentricity attaining its extreme forms: Christ is the unique source of truth to the exclusion of all others (above all, God), and he is, of course, Christ the man.

Subsequently, variants of the interpretations appear through other christologies. Thus Schoonenberg in Holland (going back both to Bultmann and to J. A. T. Robinson) regards Christ as the sole source of Christian faith, but he sees Christ as a simple 'model', offered to man's existential fervour. He regards Christ as, he says, 'a pro-existence of the man for others'. This is an incarnate appeal to a super-humanity; however, it is understood that this super-humanity is intrinsically immanent in human existence. That is why Schoonenberg says that he wants determinedly to 'reject the Chalcedonian model', to use his formula.[12] For him, too, it is necessary to subject the person of Christ to passionate scrutiny. For it is from Christ that all truth 'comes' in the strict sense. He is the one who creates them. Thus, in his creative power of truth, he goes so far as to create – God. The human person of Jesus 'confers his personality on the Word'. In other words, it is Christ who makes God exist. One only has to read the French title of Schoonenberg's main work to understand the drift of his argument: *Il est le Dieu des hommes*. (English has the more prosaic title, *The Christ*.) Christ lived the whole of his life so as to make men 'dream' of a God; he maintained the idea of a mythical God. If he died on the cross, it was to awaken the maddest dreams and the most pathetic fantasies in favour of a deity, perceived at the limits of the agonizing cries of a humanity sacrificing itself for love.

We find similar arguments in the writings of the Belgian theologian Schillebeeckx. For him, it is no longer a matter of looking for God behind the man Jesus. In his manner, and by his actions and gestures, the man Jesus is the presence of God in human reality. This humanity of Jesus – known and loved – must take the place of 'divinity' for us. After 1970, the Swiss theologian Hans Küng develops similar theories about the person of Christ with virtuosity. All his works set out to show that Christian faith must consist in adopting a new mode of being, and that we achieve this new mode by our identification, intellectual, spiritual and moral, with the historical person of Christ. According to his bold formula, it is a question of attaining to a *Christsein* (inadequately translated in the title of his famous work as *On Being a Christian*). This *Christsein* establishes a new identity in us. We are transformed 'in Christ'. Do we have to regard the references that Christ makes to a deity which is superior to him as openings towards a transcendence? 'Not at all,' says Hans Küng: these are formulas clothed in mythological form, which are intended to indicate nothing more nor less than the uniqueness, originality and insurpassable nature of the message which is expressed in Jesus (in this connection see *On Being a Christian*, Collins 1976, pp. 381–96). If the Council of Chalcedon proclaimed Jesus Christ 'truly God and truly man', the formula 'true God' is to be understood in a 'functional' sense, and not a metaphysical sense. We must consider Jesus Christ 'as if' he were a God. We must maintain a phenomenological attitude (the only attitude which is philosophically prudent). Finally, we can add to these references to Belgian and German theologians the name of Spanish theologians like J. I. Gonzalez Faus, who argues that Jesus is 'the absolute man';[13] J. Sobrino, for whom Jesus 'makes himself' Son of God;[14] X. Pizaka, for whom Jesus is 'a God for others'.[15]

In France, some theological thought has also approached these arguments, from 1970, but with some qualifications. Thus in works like his *Christologie*, and above all, *Jésus, homme libre*,[16] C. Duquoc does not hide his reserve towards the formulas of the Councils of Nicaea and Chalcedon. For him, Jesus must be considered as a man, acting with man's salvation in view. The author postulates a break with all forms of philosophical reflection and mistrust of all intellectual systematization, and also adopts a totally historicist conception of the use of reason. Another theologian, Henri Bourgeois, in his book with the significant title *Libérer Jésus*,[17] wants to liberate Jesus from all dogmatic interpretations. Jesus must be considered as a pure 'spiritual master' (rather like a guru), who does not have any clearly determined doctrinal preoccupation: 'Jesus does not seem to have wanted to found a religion' (op.cit., p.141). Finally, P. M. Beaude, in particular in his work *Jésus oublié. Les évangiles et nous*,[18] wants Jesus to be reintegrated completely into history. If we restore him rigorously to his historical context, and if we read the gospels literally, we shall discover that Jesus gave himself a constantly changing image. One could say that he did not want the admiring attention of his disciples to be too exclusively fixed on his person. 'Jesus wanted people to forget him,' so that they only remembered the spiritual message which he came to bring. Furthermore, it was the community of his disciples which in the first ages of the church was to construct the image of his person and idealize it. This manner of conceiving the 'Christian message' as emerging from the faith of the first generations of Christians, and not from Christ himself, has been shared by the majority of the commentators that I have just mentioned (this raises an exegetical problem, but that is outside the scope of this investigation into the development of christocentricity). At all events, the tendency, which is only accentuated in the theologians and commentators of the 1960s and 1970s, to derive the essentials of the Christian message from the witness and the sayings of Christ, to the exclusion of all other speculative and doctrinal considerations, is maintained. However, some want to go further and encourage radical atheism as a *conditio sine qua non* for faith in Christ. So we arrive at 'atheistic Christianity', the two principal expressions of which are the theologies of the death of God, inspired by Robinson and his disciples, with speculative concerns, and the theologies of liberation, inspired by Girardi and several other analysts, which have practical concerns in the social and political order.

3. Towards an atheistic christocentricity: the 'death of God' theologies

Here the disappearance of God is not only noted (and in a sense deplored), as was the case in the earlier christologies, above all that of Tillich, but it is accepted and regarded as a *fait accompli*. 'God is dead' is a conclusion of modern thought. Let us take note of it, and from now on try to construct a Christianity which will be without God, an atheistic Christianity. This is the predominant preoccupation of a number of theologians (if one can still use the term) of English and American origin, from an Anglican or Protestant background.[19] I mention them here because they exercise some influence on part of Catholic thought, above all after 1970.

(a) General themes: the adoption of dialectical schemes for theology

At the starting point of the elaboration of this 'theology of the death of God' we must put the adoption, by some theologians, of modes of thought characteristic of dialectical reasoning, and its application to theological thought.[20] This practice does not date from our era. Hegel himself had already written a Life of Jesus inspired by the applications of dialectical thought, and subsequently his conception of religion is constantly inspired by these patterns. So he sees the beginning of a dialectic within the Trinity between the Father (thesis), the Son (antithesis) and the Holy Spirit (synthesis). Another begins between the Trinitarian God (thesis), the created world (antithesis) and Christ, God incarnate (synthesis). Yet another is established between Christ (thesis), civil society (antithesis) and the church (synthesis), and so on. Here Hegel brings to bear all the resource of dialectic thought, that is to say, he considers each reality as involved in a continual process; and he considers this process as developing according to the laws of an internal opposition. This is what has led to the analyses I have just mentioned. This way of thinking had hitherto been regarded with suspicion by theologians, at least in the Catholic church. Certainly Christians had used it, on their own account, without a particular professional mandate from their church, above all in the Protestant world. As I have already indicated, Kierkegaard made use of it, and a number of German Protestant thinkers followed in his wake. One of the first theologians to resort to this type of logic, so-called 'dialectical logic' (which has nothing in common with classical logic, which is termed 'apophantic' logic, and is of Aristotelian inspiration), and to resort to it *qua* theologian was probably Karl Barth in his great work *Church Dogmatics* (volumes of which appeared in German in 1932, and from 1939 onwards). In Barth we rediscover views which are quite reminiscent of those of Kierkegaard. Certainly, he uses dialectical patterns in the very ordering of his thought; in particular, meditation on the content of the gospel (to which he constantly refers) develops in accordance with dialectical processes. But in reality the initial fact – as with Kierkegaard – is removed from the grasp of the dialectical schemes. The religious consciousness sets itself directly before the 'mystery' of the sacred; and it is on this mystery that it speculates. It goes without saying that in this case it is impossible that one can end up in atheism, in an atheistic Christianity. In fact, the theology of Karl Barth leads the Christian, rather, towards a very assured theocentricity. The Barthian Christian is above all a 'man of God'; a man who expects everything from God: faith and salvation. So let us leave this kind of theology on one side for the moment. What we must consider here are theologies which are formed radically and integrally in accordance with dialectical schemes, without reference to a transcendent faith in God.

In this case, the reaction takes the following form. The starting point is a historical fact (on the origin of which the theologian does not dwell), namely that there was a man who affirmed his faith in a superior being (the word 'supreme' is not used, because that would necessitate a departure from dialectical schemes, to take an option of an ontological kind). The starting point is the faith of Abraham and its content. This faith – as it occurs in the historicist context which the appeal to dialectical thought requires – must be considered as a 'moment' in the evolution of the religious conscience of humanity. It is an 'idea' which has arisen; and like all ideas it must give place, sooner or later, to another. Now according to the dialectical interpretation, this will establish itself by a process of opposition to the one that has gone before. The idea of a superior God will therefore be succeeded by the idea of an inferior God: this will be the idea of a God who humbles himself, in other words, of a God who becomes incarnate. Thus, following the idea of the Abrahamic God who shines through the Old Testament, there appears the idea of the God of humiliation who by contrast shines through the New Testament; hence the idea of the incarnate God, which is centred on Jesus Christ (the future synthesis will be the church). Let me make this clearer: for the religious consciousness to awaken to the idea of a Christ, God incarnate, it is absolutely necessary that – if this idea of Christ is to be attained fully – one accepts the idea of the complete disappearance of a superior God: so without reservation, it is necessary to accept the idea of the death of God. All this is very clear and, in addition, very logical (of course, in terms of dialectical logic . . .). In short, these analyses can be summed up in a compact phrase which can be found in the majority of theologies of the death of God: God must die for Christ to live. There is no incarnation without 'the death of God'. All the 'theologies of the death of God' are based on this pattern. We shall see later that it is the same with the so-called 'liberation theologies' (that is to say, essays in 'Christian Marxism'). These are the general principles common to all the 'death of God theologies'. But it is interesting to rediscover them in the particular formulations in which each one is expressed.[21]

(b) Some applications

The most famous representative of this kind of theology is, without doubt, the Anglican bishop John Robinson. He developed his ideas in his work *Honest to God.*[22] The dialectical inspiration is obvious. The God of Abraham, Robinson explains, dies in Jesus of Nazareth; and this death is accomplished on Golgotha when Jesus experiences the total dereliction (of which I have already spoken) expressed in his cry, 'My God, why have you forsaken me?' It is at this moment that Jesus – in his own consciousness – had felt to the point of anguish the most searing, the most total disappearance of God that he could imagine. For Jesus, God was dead, and he suffered a cruel bereavement (he himself did not die then, because he survived in the consciousness of his faithful; he only died much later – little by little – to give place to the church). However, let us keep our attention on Christ. All by himself (above him the 'sky is desperately empty'), he was the first to see, with the utmost intensity, the death of God. And it is *by himself* that he has to confront the mass of humanity, to bring them 'the message of salvation'. Christ, from henceforth living in the heart of his faithful, will therefore be for them 'the word' which resounds across time. It falls to him to recall men to their profound authenticity, that is to say, to their true humanity. That is why he is the living model of humanity: *Ecce homo*. And his true name, by which he should appropriately be designated, is no longer 'Son of God' (a title which in fact he never fully claimed), but 'Son of Man'. The Son of Man is there amongst you; and the Son of Man constantly returns to remind men of their dignity. Certainly he brings a 'light' of a superior order to their minds, and one could say in one sense that he comes to 'reveal' divinity to men. But this is no longer the 'God of Abraham'; it is now the 'God of Jesus Christ', that is to say, an idea of God which Jesus Christ bears within him, and which from henceforth takes the form of a lowly God, a God to be found in the intimacy of the heart and the conscience, a God which everyone carries within himself, in the most intimate of his dreams. Modern man is asked to recognize him 'honestly', as the title of Bishop Robinson's book suggests; it is a matter of recognizing a 'God without God', as the French translation was called. So it is fitting for all the disciples of Jesus Christ to have some 'idea' of an 'atheistic Christianity'. It is a matter of lucidity and honesty, so Robinson tells us. That is his major thesis. We can find it again in all those who maintain a theology of the death of God, who follow Robinson's views more or less closely. We find it again, for example, in the Spanish theologian J. I. Gonzalez Faus, who sees in Jesus the 'absolute man' in whom humanity achieves a truly 'divine' level. The God of Jesus Christ is the highest 'idea' that Jesus ever conceived; it is the idea which inspired him; it is the ideal which he dreamed of handing on to men. We also find echoes of these analyses in two authors from the Spanish Catholic world whom I have already mentioned, J. Sobrino and X. Pikaza.[23] In these two different cases there is resolute talk of an atheistic Christianity. In other words, the reference to God has completely disappeared: better still, the idea of God must be rigorously banished. Here theocentricity has completely vanished, and by reaction christocentricity is triumphant: it even attains its extreme forms, those beyond which it is not possible to go. However, the writers I have just mentioned are generally Protestants. We must now observe the impact of dialectical thought on the theologians of the Catholic world. And here 'atheistic Christianity' will undergo developments above all in the social order.

4. Another atheistic christocentricity: liberation theologies

We might note that speculative forms of atheistic Christianity are relatively rare in the Catholic church, or at least in the sociological sphere covered by the Catholic church. I may properly recall here the attempt at an atheistic 're-reading' of the gospel proposed by Fernando Belo in his *A Materialist Reading of the Gospel of Mark.*[24] As the title indicates, this is an attempt to try to understand the gospel from the materialist position (which, as one might imagine, is here the historical materialism of Karl Marx). Belo's attempt is more on the exegetical than the doctrinal level. We might also recall portrayals of Christ in films, beginning from a purely materialist view of the gospels.[25] The only traces of atheistic Christianity that one can find in the environment of the Catholic Church are those which I indicated earlier, and which appear in the wake of either Bonhoeffer or Robinson. Their originality is quite limited.

By contrast, in the Catholic church we find practical forms of atheistic Christianity which might be designated 'liberation theologies'. These have truly arisen from within Catholicism. They do not take a speculative form: they are presented as the expression of social preoccupations and as destined possibly to inspire revolutionary action. Some of these theologies are the fruit of personal analyses; others have taken the form of collective movements of thought. Among the first, one might mention the work by Joseph Comblin, *Théologie de la révolution.*[26] The author seeks to portray Christ as a revolutionary in respect of the institutions of his time, and therefore to present Christianity as a revolutionary movement. A similar tendency – but perhaps pushed still further – can be found in the collection *A la recherche d'une théologie de la violence* (Towards a Theology of Violence), which appeared in 1968,[27] in which the authors (in particular P. Blanquart) seek to show that despite certain appearances, Christ calls men more to violence than to gentleness, in the face of the injustices which can be found in any established society.

The most important effort of thought is of a collective kind. It has been made by a group of theologians who from the 1960s on tried to set in motion a coherent doctrine aimed at reconciling Marxism and Christianity, which is generally known as liberation theology. Here christocentricity is turning into a socio-political project. Christianity is built up into a doctrine of action, capable of giving form to a new society. The starting point adopted is the analysis made by Marxists of the social situation which has arisen in the twentieth century. Industrial society has given place to a confrontation between two classes of people, the exploiters and the exploited. For the latter, it is a matter of becoming aware of the major wrong which is done to them and then remedying it, ending up by forming a classless society, where the proletariat will take over the management of society. The theologians of this school adopt this analysis: they consider it to be correct. However, to remedy the state of things which I have described, they propose to resort to the resources offered by Christianity rather than those of Marxist materialism. They want to arrive at an analogous result, a classless society, but under the sign of Christ. The elaboration of this doctrine has been above all the work of J. Girardi.[28] It has been taken up and amplified by certain theologians to be found at Louvain, in Belgium, and also in Latin America. The essentials of the debate which has begun clearly focus on this new theme. Marxism has raised a certain number of problems; is Christianity as capable of bringing effective solutions as Marxist materialism? To answer this question, it must be shown that Christ first of all fully understood that humanity was on the way to a future situation of 'class struggle' (and thus, in the first place, that he had been aware of the existence of such things as 'classes', and that the only way out of this conflict would be a merciless struggle). It is then necessary to show – and this is the major object of this theology of liberation – that Christianity can feed this struggle, until the total disappearance of all the exploiters and the formation of the classless society. To that end, an appeal is made to certain texts in the gospels which point in this direction: parables, like that of the Prodigal Son, read in a new way; invectives against the rich, against the 'class' of the Pharisees; an appeal to generalized egalitarianism, and so on. Then Christianity is portrayed as a doctrine of social struggle. The militant Christian is presented as a militant revolutionary, who fights unceasingly, if necessary with weapons in his hand (in Latin America there is praise for the example of Camilo Torres, a priest killed in a revolutionary guerilla war). In short, there is a tendency to show that Christianity (the 'salt' of the earth, the 'leaven' in the dough) has as much revolutionary merit as Marxism, if not more. Here, then, the conversion of Christianity into a social movement is complete. In traditional Catholic countries, in particular in Latin America, for example, Christianity comes to play the role which elsewhere is assigned to Marxism. Jesus becomes the new Karl Marx. Here, of course, the evolution towards christocentricity, an evolution which I have been analysing since the beginning of this study, has arrived at its most radical form. It is scarcely possible to go any further.

5. Christianity as humanism

Before concluding, I must finally point out that without arriving at the extreme positions which I have just mentioned, in certain areas of Catholic thought some people nevertheless go so far as to cease regarding Catholicism, the spiritual movement to which they belong sociologically, as a religion (and therefore as an institution with a transcendent focus). They see it as a kind of humanism. For these Catholics, to adopt the Christian faith is to adopt a certain life-style, a kind of humanism. Its characteristics certainly derive from the gospel; but in the way in which one could derive humanism from reading Epictetus' *Manual* or Montaigne's *Essays*. This humanism is based on certain values which are, in fact, defended by Jesus Christ in the gospels and which anyone can discern simply by reading them, whether or not they are believers. Thus, among the values particularly stressed one can see: solidarity among mankind, compassion for the weakest, a sense of justice, an appeal to authenticity, confidence in the future, and so on. These are values a human being can live by; better still, a society can be inspired by them to give rhythm to its inner and outer life. In this way attempts are made to construct a 'Christian humanism', made up of purely human attitudes, which could even give birth, if not to a religion, then to a civilization. This civilization would have the advantage, among others, of being accessible to all mankind by reason of the universalism which inspired it.

It must be recognized that this tendency is quite widespread in the present-day Catholic world. The social psychologist may have some difficulty in discerning it, because it is still very much embedded in the remains of an attitude which outwardly still seems to be religious. The chief characteristics to note are as follows. The last vestiges of theocentric faith are renounced; there is no longer talk of sin or of the necessity of salvation or of penance or even of the beyond; the themes of grace and providence are abandoned. Only 'social' themes are taken into consideration. A Christian is someone who engages in social struggle, who seeks to bring remedies to material wretchedness (there is no longer any thought of moral wretchedness or moral faults).

'Religious' practice is reduced to the holding of meetings where social ardour and revolutionary fervour are shared. The rite of the eucharist is regarded as a fraternal agape, where the practice of eating bread and drinking wine plays the role of a symbol of mutual love. The sacraments are regarded as 'celebrations' in which a purely symbolic meaning is attached to the actions performed. So-called 'pastoral' activity is directed only to those who are fully alive and hold the key to the future (on earth): the young, the active, the combatants. Attention is directed away from the old, the sick, those in anguish (since they will lose their place in the living community). Buildings which were traditionally held in reverence as places consecrated to the worship of God are regarded as simple meeting-places for the Christian 'people'. Thus it is accepted that one can join in any group activities one likes (which sometimes turn into wild revelry, as several years ago in the cathedral at Rheims). Pop concerts are given, and protesters and contesters of all kinds are welcome. In their personal life, the Catholics who have arrived at this kind of purely temporal christocentricity no longer feel the need for prayer and contemplation. They devote all their energies to the visible world alone, i.e. to social and humanitarian action. The communities which they form scarcely differ from societies for mutual help or humanitarian mutual aid (in the style of Henri Dunant's Red Cross) which have flourished all over the world, above all in the nineteenth century. The major preoccupation is social justice, and the future of a better world, temporally speaking. The ultimate horizon remains the 'earthly city'. If things continue to evolve in accordance with this logic, after fifty or a hundred years, Christianity will end up by being reduced to a humanitarian movement, analogous to Stoicism, Epicureanism or some form of solidarity, and the churches will turn into social clubs. Christianity, this religion which turned the world upside down by the passionate appeal of its belief in divine transcendence, will turn into a vague humanitarian movement which will get lost in the sands and will end up 'dying, like all the civilizations'.

These are the observations that might be made by a social psychologist concerned to give an objective account of the developments which affect a given social movement. In the case of Catholicism (at least in its Western form of expression), these developments have been far-reaching, and we can understand the present-day confusion among its believers. To continue my comments: we saw the outline of a movement in the seventeenth century which tended to displace the centre of gravity of the inner life of Catholicism. Whereas for more than a thousand years faith and thought had been ordered around the pole of faith in God, subordinating everything, including faith in Christ, to him, Catholicism now saw the appearance in its midst of a movement which tended little by little to favour a second point of reference – in terms of social psychology – in contrast to this pole. Subsequently the second focus simply increased in intensity. And the more it increased, the more we see the reduction of the sphere which derived from the first pole. Everywhere theocentricity gave way to christocentricity. And as we have just seen, at the end of the twentieth century, at least in certain areas of Catholicism, this christocentricity has come to occupy the whole field, to the point of even having excluded all reference to theocentricity. So it is that we end up in a Christianity without God, an atheistic Christianity. This development is astonishing, but it is perfectly logical for the social psychologist. Before making comments on possible future developments, it may be useful to outline certain recent reactions which seem to be taking place, within Catholicism, against the excesses of christocentricity, reactions which we can see emerging over recent years.

VIII

Tangible Reactions to the Excesses of Christocentricity

In watching the progressive expansion of christocentricity over three centuries in the Catholic church, an expansion which reached the extreme forms I have just described, it would be wrong for us to suppose that the whole church followed this movement. We are seeing, rather, what it is useful to call the leading edge of the church, its 'advanced theologians'. However, they are not the whole church. In the course of the twentieth century, reactions also emerge – which are all quite respectable, even if they come from the 'silent majority'; they follow two directions. Resistance to the excesses of christocentricity is expressed in the name of a christocentricity which is better understood (above all, in less historicist terms), whereas others champion the cause of a theocentricity which, despite the attacks made on it for the last three centuries, has still survived, renewing and purifying itself. This is the twofold reaction that we must analyse and consider (still using the procedures of social psychology; that is to say, straightforward observation of the social body which is the Catholic church.)

1. Spiritual resistance

Whole areas of Catholicism have in fact escaped the expansion of christocentricity. We can note two types of reaction: passive resistance and active resistance.

(a) Passive resistance

These are the zones in Catholicism which, by the predominant intellectual structure, could not but escape the influence of the movement towards christocentricity. They can be defined both geographically and sociologically. The chief geographical areas are: North America, Africa (both French and English speaking) and some rare European zones. The Catholic church in North America largely escaped this movement. The reason is clear.

European christocentricity and, under its influence, South American christocentricity was carried on, as I have shown, by the expansion of dialectical thought. Now North American consciousness is basically rebellious. The pragmatism which moulds attitudes there means that it always remains profoundly realistic.[1] Every North American congenitally has an irreducible sense of the real: he is untouched by the charms of idealism (a basically European phenomenon, born, as Hegel said, in the 'twilight' of its long history). Along with the sense of the real, the North American has a sense of nature: so he has almost instinctively a sense of God (Rousseau's God, but recognized as being authentically transcendent). Consequently he has a sense of the sacred: he sees every 'clergyman' as a man of God.[2] He regards the churches and temples as havens of peace, where one is removed from the pressures of business and the soul can rediscover the presence of God (there is great fervour in the American churches). In North America, then, theocentricity retained all its original strength: from a sociological point of view there is continuity between the Temple in Jerusalem and St Patrick's Cathedral in New York or the Episcopalian cathedral in Washington. By contrast, one can see that this theocentricity disappears in the neighbouring Latin areas, as in the Province of Quebec in Canada where, from 1960 onwards, christocentric themes could be introduced quite easily (one could even see some references to the liberation theologies). It is the same in Mexico and, of course, in Latin America, of which I have spoken at length.

A similar resistance has been offered in Africa, where the Catholic church has taken root. The African churches have stubbornly resisted the excesses of christocentricity which I mentioned earlier. The reason is similar to that which can be found in North America. There, too, there has been resistance to any infiltration of dialectical thought. African thought is radically impermeable to this kind of thought, whether it takes a Hegelian or a Marxist form: within the universities we have countless proofs of this. The African is profoundly realistic – not as a result of pragmatism, like the American, but as the result of naturalism; there is an extreme sense of communion with nature and with the forces of nature. In this sense he has a naturally religous soul. He has an almost spontaneous sense of the divine mystery; he has an innate sense of divine transcendence. So he is theocentric by nature. Christocentricity – above all in the excessive forms which I have noted – had no chance of making an impact on African consciousness. In particular, contrary to what some people might expect – liberation theologies have found no echo in the African churches.

If we now adopt a sociological rather than a geographical perspective, we can make similar observations. Whole sectors of the Catholic population find themselves outside the reach of christocentric influence. We find such zones in areas which are marked by a Latin character. However, these are fragments of the population who have kept a sense of the real, of both a practical and a speculative realism which puts them beyond the influence of dialectical thought. Here it is a matter of populations with a rural background or poor populations (who need to stay in contact with the realities of nature and of life). These populations practise what is conventionally called 'popular Catholicism'. They have also been studied by sociologists.[3] It is clear that they remain very aloof, despite their geographical and even sociological proximity, from christocentric views, above all in their extreme form. This popular Catholicism shows an astonishing fidelity to theocentricity – despite the opposite influences which are experienced. In those populations where popular Catholicism is predominant (these are notable parts of the churches in the Latin countries of Europe and Latin America, and in Eastern countries where Catholicism was implanted, like Poland and Hungary), we rediscover all the characteristics of theocentricity which I described earlier, and which left so strong a mark on the Catholic populations in the Middle Ages and down to the seventeenth century. Among these, along with the sense of nature, we rediscover the sense of the sacred and the sense of God. This attitude is given tangible form in a concern to submit to God the principal elements of life: birth by baptism; entry into the life of society by solemn communion; conjugal union by the sacrament of marriage; and death by religious funeral rites. It should be noted that this popular Catholicism with a theocentric basis is violently attacked by the adherents of an advanced christocentricity: they denounce conventional customs, popular traditions, in the observance of these rites – the theocentric significance of which they do not recognize because they have opted for an exclusive christocentricity. They want to give such rites a new significance which will be purely christocentric: for them baptism is more an 'introduction' to Christ; solemn communion an 'adherence' to Jesus Christ; marriage a 'participation' in the life of Christ; funerals are a 'return' to Christ. It is very clear that here two social logics come into conflict: the logic of theocentricity and the logic of christocentricity. However, this conflict poses a danger for the Catholic church, that of a break between two churches, a mass church and an élite church. This latter, confined in a kind of spiritual ghetto, would find itself cut off from the great mass of believers, who keep to natural religion.

That is the danger which I have already analysed above, under the name of the new 'catharism'.

It is, in fact, strange to note, as all the recent surveys of public opinion have shown, that the mass of Catholics, even in Latin countries which have been affected by christocentricity, remain basically theocentric in their inner and personal life. In a country like France, for example, the personal prayer of believers, offered every day, is largely directed towards God the Father, and only in a small degree to Christ. The crude results of the survey, made in 1978, are as follows: God the Father, 53%; Christ, 20%.[4] The popular mind remains basically theocentric, even in countries where christocentricity has put down the deepest roots.

(b) Active resistance

For an attentive observer of this kind of phenomenon, this is an astonishing discovery. Christocentricity – by reason of the excessive forms which it has taken and which come up against the *sensus ecclesiae* among a large number of the faithful – meets with active resistance, and does so at the level of the very foundations on which it is based (which I analysed earlier), i.e. exclusive recourse to historicism and the claim to a doctrinal purity. Now a counter-attack has been made on these two points. In fact, as I have already recalled, the critique of the claims of history to establish itself as a scientific, and therefore normative, discipline has become a favourite theme in our time. Whereas in the nineteenth century history was seen as 'the science of the future, and even one day the only science which will rule over men's minds', as Marx said, it is now fashionable only to speak of historical relativity. People even go so far as to denounce 'totalitarian historicism'.[5] Professional historians no longer allow the possibility of a history which would be unique and which a historian could reconstitute 'as in a picture' (in the manner that Hegel, and after him Marx, dreamed of). 'There is no history of humanity, nor even a history of the West, but genetic, morphological, cultural and philological groupings, and so on, which are encountered only by historical research.'[6] We must even renounce the idea of a single history of human reason. It is the merit of Cassirer to have delivered us from this myth.[7] On the contrary, we must accustom ourselves to a kind of ahistoricism; we must learn phenomena not in their diachronic continuity, but in their achronic significance, as the leaders of structural analysis tell us (in particular Michel Foucault, for whom each age and each movement of thought within its epoch produces an *episteme*, an atemporal structure with its own particular meaning). All the 'meanings' which history bears, we are told, in fact amount to structures the significance of which is to be sought in the anthropological sphere, that is to say, in individual consciousness. So here it is a matter of involving all the resources of both human ethology and psychoanalysis (above all Jungian psychoanalysis), and, of course, of all structural comparativism.[8] From now on we have to begin history from a structural anthropology. The object of this is the description of all the 'derivatives' which the avatars of geographical, climatic, demographic or technological situations have imposed on the human mind. Consequently we cannot expect any wisdom from history; there is no philosophy of history, nor even a theology of history, since the problem of the meaning of history no longer arises. As a result of this, then, the generalized christocentricity that we have seen developing in the course of the last two centuries loses one of its principal supports. It is useless to ask history, and in particular the history of Judaeo-Christianity, to give us lessons in wisdom; it is useless to expect a lesson in faith from a historicized presentation of the Christian message; it is useless to expect a lesson in spiritual life from a meditation on the historical Christ, who cannot even provide teachings of a social and political kind, since all historicity is disqualified. To contemplate the historical Christ is to give way to mirages. Contemporary historical criticism can even feel competent to show us that in this contemplation we are only projecting the fantasies of our unconscious as men of the twentieth century. We should no longer yield to the mirages of historicity; that seems to be the advice which contemporary historical criticism is lavishing on us. Catholic theologians – who have been so imbued with historicism over the last fifty years – cannot long remain deaf to these warnings which come to them from secular science. So they must tone down the heightened christocentricity which they have professed. Further, we shall see that these works of contemporary historical criticism even make a positive contribution to the renaissance of a degree of theocentricity.

Another form of active resistance to christocentricity can be found in the vexations which all impartial observers have experienced faced with the setbacks – quantitative, at any rate – which have been felt in sectors of the Catholic church where christocentricity has been particularly cultivated. Thus it has been possible to note a decline in the number of churchgoers, a decrease in religious vocations, and so on. Social psychologists can in fact establish a strange statistical correlation between the two phenomena: the development of christocentricity and the diminution of religious practice. The correlation certainly remains on a purely statistical and therefore quantitative level (and religious attitudes are essentially of a qualitative kind, and in themselves do not lend support to quantitative conclusions). Nevertheless, it is possible to note some curious coincidences. Some people have drawn the conclusion that only a return to rigorous theocentricity could reverse the situation. Comparative studies in particular have been made of an age which presents striking analogies to our own from a religious point of view, namely the beginning of the seventeenth century. Then it was the theocentric reaction – embodied in the renaissance of the Carmelite order and the Carthusian monasteries, as we have seen – which set in motion the religious renaissance of the seventeenth century, and not Bérullian christocentricity, still less Jesuit humanism, which on the contrary introduced the germs of the later harmful evolution towards secular humanism.[9]

Another reaction to christocentricity can be discerned in Catholic circles concerned with 'mission', that is to say, with the presentation of the faith to non-believers: missionaries in the traditional sense of the word, and intellectuals involved in the problem of relations with Jews, Moslems and even atheists. Their hostile reactions are quite perceptible. Neither one nor the other can present Catholicism uniquely as the religion of Jesus Christ; they cannot, in the way of things, say that they come to announce Jesus Christ. With Jews, in particular, the first reaction runs the risk of being *a priori* hostile: God is first and foremost. Catholics and Jews must first show themselves faithful to the 'God of Abraham'. Here it is indispensable to defend a strictly theocentric position. To defend christocentricity under one of its current forms (above all its exclusive form) would at the least be an enormous *faux-pas*. It is the same with the Moslems (though with some qualifications). Here, too, fidelity to the God of Abraham is the common denominator. Faith in Christ must be the object of a delicate and above all very progressive approach. This is the attitude of all 'missionaries' working in Islamic countries; it is imperative for them *a priori* to adopt a theocentric attitude. They come to Moslems first of all to rediscover together faith in God (or Allah), and it is only on a second approach that they can try to spread faith in Jesus Christ. In the majority of cases, direct proclamation of the gospel has ended in failure (this is obvious in Islamic Africa).[10] The three great religions which arose out of the faith of Abraham are all monotheistic religions: they must acknowledge the preeminence of faith in God over all other faith (and Catholics should to some degree allow their faith in Christ to be left in the background). These are the observations that any contemporary researcher can make. Only theocentricity can allow dialogue between the three monotheistic religions. Christocentricity (whether inspired by Bérulle, the themes of Catholic Action, Bonhoeffer or the liberation theologies) can only lead to misunderstanding and even to insult. In all these cases the development of the Catholic church in this direction reduces it to growing isolation over against other religious movements of the world.[11] Here as elsewhere we can see clearly how christocentricity leads to a kind of 'purism', of 'neocatharism', which can only imprison the Catholic church in mental frameworks and social structures which cut it off from the rest of the world. This is what a large number of acute observers have noted, and this explains the first reactions in favour of a return to theocentricity.

2. Towards a renaissance of theocentricity

The conditions for a degree of renaissance for theocentricity seem to have been achieved in recent years, and in the short term this should turn into a reaction in its favour on the part of the Catholic intelligentsia. The secular sciences are in process of opening up the way in this respect. However, some theological thought is already hindering it. These two reactions are worth studying.

(a) The secular sciences

This movement can be noted at different points on the cultural horizon. Both the experimental and the humane sciences, above all since 1970, have had a remarkable propensity to refer the structures which they discover in their field of experience to a Superior Term which is more or less identified. Some of them readily describe this as Logos and regard it as a superior form of thought, the effects of which make themselves felt on the world. Physicists even allow themselves the luxury of thinking that the rationality which they observe could well 'open out on eternity', in the words of the French physicist Olivier Costa de Beauregard. In the United States, the great researchers at Princeton, Pasadena and centres of nuclear physics, in their moments of leisure and reflection say that they are obliged to accept that all this rationality of the world which they spend their time decoding can only be explained if it is derived from a superior Rationality. After almost two centuries of positivism, which negated all metaphysics and all theology, they are the first to dare publicly to affirm that their science leads them to a faith in a Logos, who orders the worlds. They have even attempted to develop a kind of theology oriented on this Logos. In this connection it is important to read the passionate volume devoted to them by the French philosopher

Raymond Ruyer, entitled *La Gnose de Princeton*.[12] Will not the most advanced physical science become theocentric again in its own way? Besides, developments might also be the same in biology. Teilhard already introduced a certain sense of the divine there: the whole of evolution is directed towards an Omega-point which opens up access to transcendence. But most recent biological research – more specifically, some molecular biology – has been able to go beyond the analyses of Jacques Monod in particular, and return (especially following F. Jacob) to a consideration of certain forms of teleonomy which – with all due reservations – could meet up in a way with the views shared by the researchers of Princeton on the pre-eminence of a Logos. Without forcing things, it must be recognized that in agreeing to combine all the structural data of the universe around a Logos, scientific thought is contributing to the restoration of the conditions of a degree of theocentricity, at least in the end. In any case, we can see the removal of one of the reasons which could be put forward at the beginning of the nineteenth century (with Lacordaire, for example) favouring the option of christocentricity: since the most advanced thought is turning away from God, let us proclaim Jesus Christ directly. This argument disappears, since science, far from calling itself atheist, has been arguing for more than two decades in favour of a certain deism (in default of theism). At all events, science refuses to take a negative position (which is in any case difficult to hold) and to proclaim explicit atheism. As a result of this the field remains open for metaphysical and subsequently theological speculation. Science is no longer attacking belief in God in any way. Philosophers and theologians have a chance to 'justify' this faith.

When we turn to the humane sciences, we get the same impression. A development has taken place in methods, and indeed in syntheses, which at the least allows the recognition of the possibility of transcendence. I have already discussed the evolution in historical method. Having rejected claims to historicism, contemporary specialists would willingly stop at the study of psychological factors in history, which would be utterly contingent. For example, they accept the determinative role played by myth in historical evolution. In this connection I might refer to the works of the 'school of myth criticism'.[13] The adoption of schemes of myth criticism can only lead to the recognition of the pre-eminence, in terms of human consciousness, of a rationality superior to the world (here beyond question one might talk of a Logos). That emerges from two different perspectives. First of all, a recognition of the role of these myths returns to accepting the determinative influence of spiritual factors in history; from there it is only one step further to the acceptance of a reference to a superior rationality in the explanation of certain events. The other humane sciences – sociology and psychology – may not argue directly in favour of a reference to transcendence, but at the moment their methodological status is such that nothing they indicate can be opposed to the development of metaphysical or theological thought leading to faith in God. To conclude this rapid analysis, I should point out that in one way the ground has been cleared: the present situation is more favourable to faith in God than it has been for a long time. All the horizons are open. There may therefore be a resurgence of theocentricity, in view of its particular virtues. There is nothing to prevent it from flourishing, as there was in the nineteenth century. Consequently there is no obligation for the Catholic to find salvation for his faith solely in recourse to Christ. Times have changed. Faith in God can return.

(b) Catholic thought

While, as I have said, one leading edge of the Catholic church is moving in the direction of an increasingly pronounced christocentricity, it should also be recognized that at the same moment a kind of revival seems to be taking place in an area of Catholic thought which is as respectable as the other, that of theocentricity. Reactions here take different forms. First of all, those in authority in the church intervened periodically between 1950 and 1970, at least to correct the excesses. On the other hand, distinguished theologians undertook studies aimed at restoring, in one way or another, conditions for a more theocentric faith, beginning with a more 'supernatural' and therefore less humanist interpretation of the gospels. Finally, lay thinkers have intervened in the discussion; and these are not just unbelievers who express their point of view, or at least their astonishment. In fact the 'official' church could not fail to intervene at first. It did so in a concern, not to combat an interpretation, but rather to restore equilibrium, at least provisionally. The influence of the Council – and we saw earlier how concerned it was to maintain precisely this equilibrium – did not play the role that might have been expected from it, sociologically speaking. The representatives of christocentricity in fact constantly sought to draw the Council in the direction of their theories.

As they could not decently argue from the letter of the texts, which told against them, they invoked the 'spirit of the Council'. It was 'in the spirit of the Council' that they tried to gain support for the most historicist theses, theses which favoured a break with all forms of transcendence. By placing themselves 'in the sphere of the Council', they claimed to justify all the innovations in the direction of immanentist historicism (even liberation theologies claimed to be 'in the sphere of the Council'). As a result, the official reactions of the authorities of the church at this period did not so much produce 'extensions' to the thought of the Council as correctives to the more or less fallacious interpretations that could have been given to them. This was the case with the interventions of Pope Paul VI after 1965. Such an interpretation can be given to the text of the encyclical *Mysterium fidei* (of September 1965), and more definitely to the publication of a Profession of Faith by the same Paul VI in June 1968. This recalls the traditional texts, i.e. the earlier creeds, the Apostles' Creed, the Nicene Creed and the Athanasian Creed, developing them and providing them with explanations. Here the equilibrium between theocentricity and christocentricity (which characterizes the texts that I analysed earlier) is fully safeguarded. The basic position taken by the church in the first centuries can be found in its integrity in the Profession of Faith of Paul VI (sometimes improperly called the *Creed* of Paul VI). This is not concerned to intervene in polemic. It does not denounce anything, and it does not criticize anyone. It simply seeks to reiterate the content of the traditional faith of the church. So we shall not be surprised to find again here the 'bipolarity' which I spoke of earlier. The Christian must put his or her faith, with equal fervour, both in a God who transcends the world, the creator 'of things visible and invisible', and in a Christ, the terrestrial incarnation of this God and saviour of men. The ardour of faith must be equal and rigorously shared. That is the very clear impression which emerges from a reading of this doctrinal declaration, as the objective observer will notice. But above all, it is a declaration of principle. The observer will not find that any position has been adopted in connection with themes discussed in Catholic opinion, above all over the last fifty years, as I have described them. Here we can only take note of the permanence of a doctrinal position which has been held for almost twenty centuries. But if the Magisterium serenely maintains principles, theologians allow themselves to take up more explicit, and sometimes more polemical positions.

In fact, theologians favouring christocentricity, including its excesses, will oppose other theologians who strive to defend positions favouring theocentricity, or at least capable of restoring equilibrium between the two positions. The observer – noting, as a social psychologist, the reactions which have occurred within the great social body which is the Catholic church – will be struck by the fact that since 1960, and more particularly since 1965, the theological works devoted to the question of the content of faith are more markedly theocentric than christocentric. That is the case with books by theologians like Hans Urs von Balthasar, Karl Rahner, and J. Ratzinger. To these names one could add those of Pannenberg and Kasper, who more recently have also contributed towards maintaining the rigorously supernatural character of the content of faith. Their common concern – carried on through very large works (like those of Hans Urs von Balthasar and Karl Rahner) – is to keep at a distance from very immanentist theologies like those of Bonhoeffer, Tillich and Hans Küng, and to affirm – in these very different ways – the transcendent character of the content of the faith. In this way, in their sphere, which is that of the study of revelation, they are working towards a restoration of the sense of a transcendent God and of the 'metahistorical' character of the mission of Christ. Part of their strength as witnesses lies in the fact that, since they are almost all German by background, they are at the very sources of the forms of thought which led to historicism. (As I have shown, this historicism encouraged the excesses of an exclusive christocentricity and led from there to atheistic Christanity.) Sociologically speaking, their positions therefore have a certain influence in the Catholic church. This obliges us to note that – at least at the time of writing (1980) – the theologians of the church thus form two great schools with divergent positions: one continues to develop christocentric themes, while the other is rediscovering the determinative importance of theocentric themes. However, I will limit myself here to making this simple observation, without going into comparative studies which would take us a long way off the beaten track.

To these theological works, aimed at a kind of restoration of theocentricity, can be added spiritual movements which are going in the same direction. In this connection we may note the influence of movements like the charismatic renewal, which puts the accent on faith in God and his contemplative demands; or the 'Schools of Faith', created by Père Loew, a Swiss, which have since spread all over the world. I might also add the evident public interest in the contemplative life led by the monks in the great Catholic monasteries like Monte Cassino, Ligugé, Solesmes, and so on. Since about 1970, we can certainly see a renaissance of the need for contemplative life among the Catholic population in different parts of the world.

To theological and spiritual work can also be added that of writers, secular writers, literary figures, philosophers, who have given their personal 'witness'. In fact observers cannot but be struck by the sudden flood of books whose authors proclaim their faith in God, in the transcendent God (whereas in the previous period it was faith in Christ that was proclaimed). Let me mention, at random, some titles taken from French literature over recent years: A. Frossard, *God Exists, I've Met Him* (*Dieu existe, je l'ai rencontré*, 1969); D. Decoin, *It's God* (*Il fait Dieu*, 1975); P. Chaunu and G. Suffert, *God's Corpse is Still Stirring* (*Le cadavre de Dieu bouge encore*, 1975); M. Clavel, *God is God* (*Dieu est Dieu*, 1976). The great inquiry by C. Chabanis into the belief of our most representative contemporaries bore on the question *Does God Exist?* (*Dieu existe-t-il?*, 1973–1978). Numerous replies show both negative and positive attitudes to God. It is striking to note that, generally speaking, there is no reference to Christ. The collection of testimonies published by Editions Grasset under the title *What I believe* (*Ce que je crois*) gives numerous reactions to faith in God: we find only a few references to Christ. Clearly, after the very christocentric phase of 1930–1960, when people were above all making up their minds on the question that Christ himself posed, 'Who do you think that I am?' (and which brought us the detailed answers of Claudel, Bernanos, and even of Gide, Papini and so on), we have come to another phase when the positions adopted go straight to the essential point and take a more metaphysical and theological form, i.e. a reply to the great question which everyone asks. Is there any meaning in the world? Is it enough by itself? Must it not depend on a superior being, a God? Whatever the responses, the preoccupations are at a level which one might call, in the broadest sense, theocentric. That is the present position.

Strangely enough, the aesthetes and the men of culture have the same reaction, at least when they are investigating certain disconcerting 'developments' in the thought of the Catholic church, or at least among some of its representatives. Thus the surrender to historicity which some theologians seem to demonstrate scandalizes the mediaevalists, accustomed as they are to seeing Christ always represented as above time, as 'master of time', the Chronocrator on the tympanum of cathedrals or in the narthex. It is also pointed out – an aesthetic point of view which meets up with that of the philosopher and the theologian – that the break with theocentricity and the option for an exclusive christocentricity involves a break with the whole world of Greek and Latin culture. The Middle Ages, which turned up its nose at all historicity, did not have any trouble in associating, in a way transcending cultures, Christ with Orpheus or Hermes; the Jewish prophets with the priests of Apollo and the Sibyls (*teste David cum Sibylla*).[14] Now I have already indicated the damaging religious consequences of the option for christocentricity: here the Catholic church cuts itself off from non-Christian religious groups. Here we can see that it also cuts itself off from humanist culture. I showed earlier, in fact, that by reason of its intellectual structures, its realism and its sense of 'eternity', humanist culture quite naturally led towards theocentricity (whereas christocentricity requires a degree of historicism, which is at the opposite pole from classical humanism: Bossuet is theocentric, but Lacordaire is christocentric).

Strangely enough, these reactions from aesthetes and humanists have found an extension in protests coming from unbelievers or agnostics reacting against certain recent developments in the church, in the very name of culture. Thus one can understand a Maurice Druon protesting vehemently against the abandonment by the Catholic church of cultural factors of universal value, in the name of a christocentricity with an anti-cultural bent: the abandonment of the splendours of the Roman liturgy, of distinguishing marks for clergy,[15] and so on. Malraux also expresses his astonishment and his disgust at such cultural dereliction. Reacting as an ethnologist, and faced with a development of rites in a religious society, C. Lévi-Strauss, too, has not hidden his disgust (though he feels quite alien to this society). 'I want to tell you that what has happened in the church since the last Council troubles me. It seems to me that, viewed from the outside, religious faith (or its practice) is being empoverished or divested of a large number of its values which affect human sensibilities.'[16] It is certain that the developments in the direction of cultural impoverishment to which certain extreme christocentric theses have led can only disconcert a humanist, a cultivated man. I analysed earlier the conditions in which this break between Catholicism and culture took place, in this second half of the twentieth century. The reactions of educated men and those who study civilizations should not therefore astonish us. In the last resort they are to be included in the collection of positive reactions against christocentricity which I have been noting.

These last remarks bring me to the end of my analysis. We can make an assessment – from the sociological point of view adopted here – of the situation in which the Catholic church now finds itself. Having attained its extreme forms towards the 1970s (in particular with theologies of the death of God and liberation theologies), the christocentric movement is now beginning to come up against antagonistic reactions. We are beginning to find changes in certain theologians (as I have indicated; however, I have not passed judgment on them, always maintaining the attitude of an observer). On the other hand, new conditions have been created for theocentric thought by science and contemporary philosophy; and protests have begun in the name of culture and humanism. We may stop our enquiry there. Our aim has been achieved: we have surveyed the facts and drawn up a balance sheet. We have looked at the evolution of the society which is the Catholic church, and more particularly at the state of latent conflict which always underlies the inner life of this society, the conflict between two 'social logics', the logic of theocentricity and the logic of christocentricity, again from the viewpoint of social psychology. This analysis has arrived at the conclusion that after a long period of supremacy, theocentricity was countered by a resurgence of christocentricity from the seventeenth century on: then this christocentricity, after a slow development, arrived at its maximal form in the twentieth century, in the 1960s and 1970s. Finally, we saw some advance signs of a possible renaissance of theocentricity in the near future. I could have stopped at this 'archaeological' reconstruction (using the word in its structural sense) of this portion of the history of the Catholic church. But having arrived at this point, I am tempted to make some forecasts about the future; a temptation to which I shall yield in the last chapter.

IX

Prospects: The Chances of a Return to Bipolarity

My concern has been to undertake an inquiry, from the perspective of social psychology, into the present situation of the Catholic church. I must now make some comments on available future options. That will mean abandoning an objective approach. However, the method which I have adopted and practised does not prevent me from making forecasts based on the facts that I have assembled – provided that they are made with the necessary rigour. By a series of extrapolations we can try to guess at the future, the future of the Catholic church.

First of all I must put the problem clearly. The comments I have made have been sociological. The Catholic church is a society the characteristic of which is bipolarity. From its beginnings, as a religious society it has found itself in this somewhat uncomfortable position. I drew attention to that in the first chapter. The nature of the bipolarity is that the inner life of the church is governed by two logics: one which orders the life of believers around faith in God (like the mother society, Judaism, from which it was born); the other which orders it around faith in Christ, a historical figure. These two logics are juxtaposed in the Christian church, as I have shown, and believers have tried as best they can to accommodate themselves to this psycho-social bipolarity. They have divided their ardour – one might say, in equal parts – between their faith in God and their faith in Christ: rites, pietistic practices, morality, and apostolic activites are distributed on the one hand around faith in God and on the other around faith in Christ. Or, to use the terminology which ultimately wins the day: all in all, theocentricity and christocentricity find a balance. Subsequently we have seen disturbances of this equilibrium. A first break was to the advantage of theocentricity: from the age of Constantine, in about the fourth century, to the seventeenth century. Then, after a new and quite brief spell (the space of about a century, the seventeenth), when for the moment the balance was restored, we see a new disturbance of equilibrium. This time it is in favour of christocentricity, and the disturbance leads to a kind of reduction to a single christocentric pole in the twentieth century (with atheistic Christianity). That is the situation. The question which must occur to the reader is obvious: what will happen next? Will the church attempt a restoration of balance between the two currents of thought which are congenital, theocentricity and christocentricity, by a defensive reflex of the kind that we can establish in all social bodies? That is the question that we might raise. But what kind of answer can we give to such a question? It can only be a reply in the form of a presumption, presented by the sociological perspective in which we find ourselves.

One can try to guess the direction that Catholic thought will take, and that is relatively possible in its case, because we know in what conditions this society – which is in any case of a very 'special' kind – has been founded and willed. Its founder, Christ Jesus, willed to make it a social body (mystical body) which is called on to develop in accordance with the continuity peculiar to all organic development: he continually uses organic metaphors to describe this future development, like a growing vine, a grain of mustard which sprouts and gives birth to a tree, a living body of which he is the head and all the faithful are members, and so on. If the metaphors used are of an organic kind, we should not envisage a mechanical break in this development: the continuity of the initial project should remain through all the changes. The same 'organization' (in the etymological sense of the word) should be perpetuated. That is apparently the interpretation called for.

In these conditions, then, we should accept that whatever the inconvenience caused by our intellectual need to simplify and unify, an initial bipolarity is inherent in the Catholic church. Born a bipolar church, the Catholic church must remain one. Any enterprise aimed at a reduction to logical unity, whether for the benefit of theocentricity or for the benefit of christocentricity, seems bound to encounter 'organic' resistance from all the social body. Let us go a little further (engaging in a spot of 'theological fiction'). Suppose that theocentricity definitively won the day, and worship of Christ was gradually reduced to nothing: in that case, the Catholic church would rejoin the monotheistic religions. Would it rejoin a Judaism which had become universal? Perhaps. Such a hypothesis is at least plausible (Spinoza dreamed of a similar development in the seventeenth century). Would it rejoin an Islam which had also become universal? That is not impossible to imagine (many Christian Islamic scholars, from the Middle Ages to our own day, have dreamed of this). At all events, in each of these instances Christianity would have lost its own identity, and that, sociologically speaking (and *a fortiori* doctrinally speaking) would be quite unthinkable.

Suppose now that, by contrast, christocentricity gained the upper hand and Catholicism in its entirety took up the positions of the death of God theology or liberation theology, what would be left of Catholicism? In the end, nothing. Over two or three centuries Catholicism would join the great dead religions of the past in the memory of mankind: in turn it would be wrapped in the 'purple shroud in which the dead gods sleep' (Renan). Alternatively, in the archaeological commemoration made by historians it would join those great humanitarian movements, like Stoicism, Mithraism and humanitarianism (in the style of H. Dunant or Romain Rolland) which for a while sustained the hopes of humanity. Its particular identity would disappear, by a kind of osmosis, into universal humanism. Its name would survive only in 'the legend of the centuries'. Thus it would seem evident to the impartial observer that, if Christianity wants to survive (and its founder gave it 'promises of eternal life'), it (and Catholicism in particular) must remain integrally faithful to the bipolarity on which it has been based from the beginning. Each time it departs from this it alters its identity.[1] Thus the point of view of the sociologist here is that Catholicism is and must remain a bipolar religion. The believer must divide his ardour in equal parts between faith in God and faith in Christ. All the texts of the creed repeat this. This is the constant position of those in authority in the church down the ages, whatever may have been the positions put forward by the theologians or the activists in this church.

Given this, we can try to make some forecasts about the future of the church. My attitude will be as follows. We have discovered certain facts. In principle, Christianity postulates the practice of bipolarity between faith in God and faith in Christ. However, after a long period when there was a predominance of the theocentric pole, more recently (over the past two centuries) we can see a counter-balancing effect in favour of christocentricity, going to the extreme positions of an atheistic christocentricity. In these conditions, it would appear that by instinct the church will favour every reaction within it that will re-establish a degree of equilibrium; consequently we can foresee that, with the help of the current climate, the church will again incline towards theocentricity. Conditions outside the church seem to predispose it in this direction, as we have seen (both science and philosophy favour it). The church itself will certainly take note. I firmly believe that. So it is to discovering the advance signs of this future resurrection of theocentricity within the church that I want to devote the last pages of this study.

1. The rediscovery of the sense of God

The evolution towards this rediscovery can easily be seen by the sociologist. In fact we can see a general need to get down to essentials in all areas of opinion. In the countries of the First World, that of advanced industrial societies, materialism is diminishing, because a kind of saturation point is being reached in regard to the technical progress that has been accomplished. People may go into ecstasies for a while over cars which can travel at great speed, over electric cookers or refrigerators which make housekeeping better, over the extension of telecommunications which increase the possibility of conversations, and so on, but this ecstatic admiration never lasts more than a generation. The following generation takes these various techniques for granted and, as we can already see in America, runs away from technological materialism and begins to devote its attention to other objects. For example, we can now feel that interest is being directed towards the quality of life, and also towards a nature which is regarded as the source of innocent happiness. We may wager that this rediscovery will be in turn followed by others, and so on. Now among these rediscoveries there is a permanent object to which man always returns, because it is always present to him: man himself and his disquiet. What is the goal of life? What is the meaning of the universe? In the last resort, to what do we relate the whole mystery of the world? The passion for science has had its day; the passion for technology has had its day also; it will be the same with the passion for nature. These are 'themes which wear out', to paraphrase Bergson, whereas the great question about man and the great questions man asks are 'themes which never wear out'. Humanity always returns to them, in almost cyclical fashion.

That is certainly the situation in the First World. In the Second World, that which is covered by Marxism, the situation is also developing steadily, as is well known. There is a rupture between the political structures which have been in place for more than fifty years, and an élite who can no longer support them. In fact Marxism is in process of losing two of its basic structural supports, history and science. History has undergone the development that I have described; it is scarcely possible now to accept the idea of a global, totalitarian history. The professional historians have rejected the idea of historical determinism; in that case, how can one talk of a materialism which history would justify, a historical materialism, when history no longer vindicates anything? As for science, it has never really been able to integrate itself into the patterns of dialectical interpretation, though they are a constitutive part of the doctrine of dialectical materialism. That is why scientists (mathematicians, physicists and astronomers) escape from Marxist régimes. It is the same with artists (writers, like Solzhenitsyn, or film-makers) who cannot tolerate the constraints of praxis, another constituent of Marxism. The way is thus suddenly open in these countries of the Second World for metaphysical reflection and religious meditation. We can see that a renaissance of one or other of these preoccupations is now under way in these countries. As for the countries of the Third World, those in process of development, they have not been touched either by the scientism or the technological approach of the First World or by the influence of Marxist materialism; they remain open to metaphysical speculation (this is the position of Léopold Senghor and Aimé Césaire). Furthermore, I have remarked above that this Third World kept aloof from movements favourable to the excesses of some (atheistic) christocentricity. It has kept intact the necessary elements for a revival of theocentricity. General conditions in the present-day world are thus relatively favourable to a return to metaphysical reflection; and I think that it is possible to forecast, by sociological extrapolation, a return to a sense of God.

However, it is not enough just to have the necessary conditions; there must also be active causes. We have already seen these causes in the development now to be found in the sciences and some philosophy. I commented that the great masters of contemporary physics welcome the idea of a universal Logos (I recalled *La Gnose de Princeton*, which R. Ruyer has echoed in his famous book). This recognition of a Logos marks a crucial stage in favour of an intellectual development towards a return to the sense of God. Granted, here we are still in the ambience of a degree of pantheism. But all the same, this is a radical departure from the atheistic positivism of the nineteenth century. The way is open to deism, and perhaps to theism.

Now it is clearly once again up to philosophical thought to exploit these scientific discoveries, in the name of the old agreement which has always existed between philosophy and science. We can see this agreement from the Ionians onwards, and even more after Aristotle (there is no serious philosophy which is not based on the science of its time). Since scientists – and that means scientists from all disciplines: physicists and astrophysicians, astronomers and biologists – have come to recognize that their efforts in research consist in trying to decode a coded message inscribed in advance in the world which they are exploring, the philosopher must intervene to ask the nature of this message. How is it constituted, and whence does it come? It is possible to forecast that future philosophy will be built up on the amazing foundations that the most advanced science of our age can produce? Is it presumptuous to think that a new theodicy is on the way? Certainly it will have nothing in common with what has gone before. It will no longer be founded, like that of Aristotle or St Thomas, on empirical science: it will no longer be founded, like that of Descartes and the post-Cartesians, on mechanistic science. It will be based on quantum and relativistic science. The effort involved will be considerable, but the paths have already been marked out by the scientists themselves in the reference that they make to a Logos of the world. We shall then move a long way from the absurdist atheism of a Sartrean kind, which has made the scientists smile (because the absurdist hypothesis cannot but repel those who are now so imbued with the radical significance of phenomena). We shall also move a long way from Marxist atheism, which in fact scientific thought has never really accepted (despite the efforts of Joliot-Curie in France and Lyssenko, for example, in Russia). An entirely new theology will be born, which will be to quantum science what, for example, the theodicy of Leibniz was to Newtonian science. This will not be so much an extrapolation obtained from science (which would only end up with a hybrid result, neither scientific nor philosophical). It is more a matter of an intense philosophical meditation, starting from a purely scientific datum.

For the philosopher will recall that his own domain is that of being (whereas the domain of the sciences is appearances, phenomena). Now meditation on being – so far as we can judge from our observations in social psychology – is again becoming possible and even highly probable. The reasons which suggest this are as follows. After a generation, the most advanced Western thought seems to have rediscovered the sense of being, beyond all phenomenological reduction. Kantianism has been 'by-passed' (the study by Heidegger of Kant and the problem of metaphysics is symptomatic in this respect). One senses through all the dominant philosophies of this century – though under very different forms (which come from the existential meditations of Heidegger, Gabriel Marcel, Jaspers, Blondel, Dewey and Whitehead, not to mention Russell and Huxley) – an authentic sense of metaphysical being.[2] Furthermore, the sense of the rationality of the given is also reappearing in force, above all through analyses inspired by structuralism. So one can suppose that an encounter might take place between the rediscovered sense of *being* and the recourse which is constantly being made to the *significance* of things. One could then forecast – this is only the presumption of a social psychologist observing the development of a certain logic of ideas (rather like Cournot, with so much skill)[3] – an imminent renaissance of metaphysics. This metaphysics will certainly give rise to an ontology. 'New philosophers' seem ready to elaborate this ontology. Now at the end of this ontology or, if one prefers it, this neo-ontology, it is impossible to escape taking the analysis as far as the ultimate meaning of things; this is the point at which a theodicy – or a neo-theodicy – will appear. That is what can be discerned of the future, with a great degree of probability, by a prudent forecast. And it is by this perspective on the future that the church should orient itself.

The church must not fail to arrive at this meeting place, if it is to maintain a presence in the world as it is. Certainly, the church can fail to arrive, for as social psychologists have often pointed out, social bodies of a spiritual kind (religions, schools of art, moral systems) are by nature hostile to innovation. They are 'misoneists', as Gabriel Tarde put it. They prefer to remain faithful to themselves, aware that they have a moral magistrature. So it would be regrettable if the church, for example, remained buttressed on historicism, when that is in process of being broken up under the repeated assaults of structuralisms; if it remained imbued with the 'community spirit' when the future is with 'differentialism', and so on. If it can faithfully arrive at the meeting-place promised to it by tomorrow's culture, the Catholic church could be led to rediscover eternalism beyond temporalism, transcendence beyond immanentism, rationality beyond all the irrationalisms. Its capacity for clarity – always belated, but never absent in the long run – allows it to anticipate that.

What will then be the doctrinal prospect which opens up for the church? We might suppose that this could well be that of a new 'scholasticism'. In fact, once its thinkers have rediscovered the rational meaning of God (having rejected the unfortunate distinction, established by Pascal, between the God of the philosophers and the God of Jesus Christ), they could again elaborate a conception of God which, in conformity to the demands of science, enriched by philosophical meditation and nourished by the noetic contributions of revelation, could shine out in the realm of universal human thought. Monotheism would enjoy a new splendour, and the great religions would beyond question recognize their profound affinity (whereas they diverged so much during the time of christocentricity). The church itself would experience a great era of spiritual enrichment. One could well say that this restoration of the foundations of theocentricity could give place to 'a new scholasticism'. In fact present-day thought (and doubtless the thought of the future) will require that any doctrinal presentation, of whatever kind, should be made with the most extreme rigour and absolute coherence, qualities demanded from now on by the exercise of structuralist thought. A future requirement will be that the presentation of all bodies of doctrine should be made from base axioms on which the structure of the knowledge under consideration is founded, and that the way in which they are developed rationally should be in accordance with the demands of deductive thought. All the doctrinal expositions of the future will be presented, like modern mathematics, from base axioms, and according to hypothetical deductive patterns. This is the only way of working in the days of computers and computer science. The presentation of philosophical doctrines already tends to be made in this kind of structuralist manner (for example, Cartesianism is expounded 'in accordance with the order of reason', as M. Guéroult would say). It is the same with linguistics, literary criticism and so on.[4] Thus we may assume that, under the guidance of this concern for intellectual rigour, there will be an attempt (which has every chance of being successful) of presenting theodicy in accordance with the most rigorous methods, which have more chance of meeting criticism. That is what makes me say – by analogy – that the church's future thought about God will take the form of a new scholasticism. It will have the rigour and coherence of the old scholasticism (which, we should not forget, held sway for six centuries). However, the content of the new scholasticism will clearly be quite different from that of the old. The starting point will be an ontology developed on the foundations of quantum science; on that will be established a network of noetic structures which will escape Kantian criticism and even Husserlian criticism. However, I do not have to make forecasts about the future of philosophy here. I shall limit myself to saying that it is probable that we shall have a period of great metaphysical rigour, when theodicy regains a reputation which is universally acknowledged, by scientists, metaphysicians and therefore even by theologians.

The appearance of this universalist theodicy will determine the possibility of a renewed contemplation of this Supreme Being, God again recognized as the privileged 'pole' of all religious life. One can even suppose that a new ardour will develop towards him. The contemplative life, accredited by scientific thought, founded on reason by philosophy, and purified by the indispensable reductions of psychoanalysis, could attain degrees of intensity hitherto unknown. Rich in intellectual and spiritual promise, it would present itself to all noble and open minds as the ultimate goal of their aspirations.

This sovereign contemplation of God will then give rise 'architectonically' to all the intellectual and social structures from which a new humanism would naturally take shape. In other words, a new theocentricity could once again come into being – analogous to that which I described earlier (in Chapter III), but enriched with contributions from modern thought. New social and legal structures will develop, aimed at creating the cadres of a new form of theocentric society (more probably based on a flexible, rather than a rigid, order). In short, there will be a new humanism. But this is not the place to outline its features. I must keep more closely to my plan. So I shall go on to consider what will happen, according to the forecast which I am attempting, in connection with the other pole inherent in Christianity, and which always underlies Catholicism: namely, christocentricity.

2. Towards a renewed christocentricity

The foreseeable strengthening of the theocentric 'pole' in the church will necessarily lead to modifications in ways of representing the other, christocentric pole. One can foresee the development of a new christology, this time more influenced by theocentricity; from that will develop a new theology of the incarnation, rethought in terms of theocentricity, and perhaps also a new conception of spiritual life, 'life with Christ'. To provide foundations for this new christocentricity, it will be necessary to take up the problem where it arose, that is to say, in the seventeenth century. Was it appropriate for Bérulle and the French school of spirituality to try to make Christ into a second pole of faith, against the theocentricity at that time defended by the Carmelite and Carthusian schools? This exact status of Christ the man in relation to God must certainly be rethought clearly. The Councils (Nicaea, Chalcedon) have marked out the doctrinal lines. It is now a question of marking out the lines of spiritual behaviour. Without question we shall have to revise our ideas. Because this is a study in social psychology, I have had to analyse orientations and determine logics, not formulate doctrines. It is in this connection that I must point out that the problem arose with Bérulle and his disciples, and we know how, in accordance with the rules of an inexorable logic, it has ended up in the modern consequences which I have described. The first cause for this 'lack of equilibrium' from which the Catholic church has suffered over the last centuries can be found in Bérulle and his followers. So it is Bérulle's positions which need to be criticized. Perhaps, in particular, it would be appropriate to reconsider the objections which some people made to Bérulle's arguments during his lifetime. Criticism coming from the Carmelite and Carthusian schools was perhaps better founded than was supposed. These schools must certainly form the starting point for our analysis. At least, that is what we seem to be led to suppose. Perhaps we shall see a renewed flowering of the features of Carmelite or Carthusian christology which could orientate, or rather reorientate, the life of the church in quite a different direction, and spare it from the misadventures which have followed. That is all the serious comment that one can make on the problem – again from the standpoint of social psychology which I have adopted. Each individual, whether a theologian or simply 'spiritual' – should try to work out what a Carmelite christology could be (it does in fact exist in a hidden fashion; it would be enough to extract it from the works of St John of the Cross, St Teresa of Avila and their successors); it would be the same with a Carthusian christology. One can see that in either case Christ would not play the same role in the economy of Christianity. He would no longer, perhaps, play the role of the second pole with so much importance (ending up by becoming the only pole, as we have seen). He would, moreover, doubtless be regarded as a 'reflection' of God the Father, the communication of God the Father, the 'mediator' of his presence. Starting from the doctrine of the first centuries, and without falling into the exclusive theocentricity of the Middle Ages, one could doubtless see the reestablishment of conditions for a spiritual bipolarity which, difficult though it might be to live out, is nevertheless the foundation on which Christianity, and Catholicism in particular, is based. Again, theocentricity and christocentricity would be in equilibrium: and the church would resume its secular advance. That is all one can appropriately say here. We do not have to take the analysis further.

This would certainly give rise to a new theology of the incarnation. Those constructed during the past three centuries, and above all during the last century, have certainly been too exclusively christocentric. Christ has been seen too much 'in himself', as a human personality too distinct, too remote from the divine transcendence. Granted, the Councils of the first centuries defined perfectly, in the terms of their time, the way in which relations between God and Christ were to be considered. These facts must be conserved with a jealous care, because they represent a burning faith which emerged out of an existential experience lived out by a handful of men and their immediate disciples. But it goes without saying that these notions of substance, nature and person, while keeping their original meaning, have undergone considerable semantic enrichments in the course of twenty centuries, and that while keeping their intended orientation, we can present them in a completely new way. In fact, dozens of specialists are engaged in this task at the moment (on the invitation of Vatican II). However, what must be made clearer here is that the theology of the incarnation which is formulated must take account of the foreseeable renaissance of theocentricity, of which I have spoken at length. So the starting point must be an elevated sense of the divine transcendence, if we are to provide a secure reconstruction of this theology of the incarnation (without falling back into docetism, or some variants of Arianism). Whatever difficulties may arise, in the future the church certainly needs a renewed theology of the incarnation, conceived from the starting point of theocentricity. As one journalist said, it is a matter of 'rewriting the creed'. Paul VI used this phrase: his audience was restrained. The reason is that the terms used were very traditional, and they were no longer understood by present-day thought. Paradoxically, we would say that it is to Heidegger, Marcel and Whitehead – supposing that these were steeped in the thought of the Fathers of the church – that we would return for a formulation of this new theology of the incarnation. This 'unfindable' author would also have to make use of the valuable discoveries of psychoanalysis, hermeneutics, and so on. The task could not fail to be difficult, but it will soon be an indispensable one for the Catholic church, if it wants both to remain faithful to itself and to regain the attention of a modern audience.

From there we shall also have to find a way towards a better definition of the church as it continues the work of Christ. Granted, Vatican II has provided directives, in particular on important texts like *Lumen Gentium* and above all *Gaudium et Spes*. However, many debates have taken place since these texts were produced, and certain formulations must already be reviewed, above all in connection with the place of the church in modern society – which is changing so much. It is a question of the church inserting itself into society, not identifying itself with society. So positions must regularly be revised (roughly speaking, every ten years). It is periodically necessary to remake a 'map' of the situation and give it to the church in the world, with a specifically theocentric orientation; such a map certainly needs to be remade at present. Compromises must be denounced, attitudes defined, options taken, tactics (in the best sense of the term) determined. I point out these needs as an observer. We do not have to respond to them here.

Finally, we must also rethink a christocentric spirituality, in terms of the rediscovery of theocentricity which will soon take place. A new form of 'life with Christ' will have to be envisaged. Certainly anyone could rightly consider the assimilation of his or her own life to that of Christ as a way of approaching the divine life. However, the 'states' of Christ will no longer be considered in and for themselves, as was required by Bérulle and those who represented christocentric spirituality in the seventeenth century. They will be seen more as 'intermediary' (or more precisely 'intermediate') states between men and God. For it is God who is to be sought for himself and in himself – and not Christ. A spirituality of very pure contemplation of God could be reborn, one that would be practicable even in everyday life (the *Introduction to a Devout Life* needs to be rewritten), and this contemplation will, of course, take a more intense form in the liturgical celebrations held in the churches. We can foresee that these will rediscover their role of 'holy places', which they had from the beginning, and they will again be made places of prayer and refreshment, more intensely than ever. The church will be the house of God, and no longer that of the Christian people. We may also suppose that the liturgy will rediscover incantatory forms; but it will be clothed in expressions which it is difficult for us to divine, since each century has its own way of celebrating the sacred.

One characteristic sign to follow – and I have already pointed out how much the social psychologist could make it an 'organic witness' to evolutions – is the role which will be assigned to the altar in churches and chapels. We can foresee that it will again be surrounded with mystery: people will not go back to grilles round the choir, characteristic of an age captivated by wrought iron; there will be new materials and new techniques. There are so many ways of veiling mystery from human eyes; could one perhaps use luminous effects (laser beams)? It is also probable that the altar will no longer be turned towards the congregation: it will no longer be 'towards the people', but 'towards God', and it will be conceived of in accordance with the appropriate techniques. Liturgical rites will again be surrounded with mystery. Silence will regain its place. Finally, the priest himself, again becoming essentially the man of God (and no longer the man of Christ), will no longer be trivialized. Regarded as a sacral figure, he will behave in a way which makes him recognizable to all, as a visible sign of the presence of God among men. In short, ecclesiastical life will again order itself around the sacred.

This redistribution of balance in favour of theocentricity will also bring about notable changes in the practice of the Christian life. Faith, hope and charity will again become the pivots of the spiritual life; they may even have acquired new force. Faith will be directed firstly to God ('God must be served first') and secondly to Christ, regarded as the revelation of God, mediator between God and men. Hope will be directed entirely towards waiting for an encounter with God, to what the ancient authors called 'the beatific vision'; certainly the formula will be changed, but the content will be rediscovered and even enlivened. As for charity, it will rediscover its fundamental finality: it will above all be 'love of God', and the love of the neighbour will be sought and practised only as a way of achieving love of God. The second commandment will again be modelled on the first. People will love their neighbours for the love of God and not for themselves. Thus everywhere theocentricity will come to provide a harmonious counterbalance to christocentricity.[5]

3. Towards a new bipolarity: God and Christ

Let me end by saying again that, according to the forecast that we might reasonably make (by extrapolations starting from facts provided by social psychology, and the beginnings of the reactions we can see under our own eyes), it seems almost certain that the period to come will offer the church every chance of restoring within itself the standards of theocentricity, modernized, but as imperative as that which has held sway for so many centuries. However, we can equally foresee that the drive towards christocentricity, which has become increasingly evident for more than three centuries, will nevertheless remain a positive contribution. It cannot be otherwise. That is why I would be inclined to think that the Catholic church is moving towards a period of equilibrium – again, required by the Councils – between theocentricity and christocentricity. The formulations in which the equilibrium is expressed will certainly be new, but a correct division will again be respected. More than ever the Christian, and in particular the Catholic, will love God and Christ with the same love. This is what prompts me to speak of a new bipolarity.

A new, or at least renewed, style of life will appear in the life of the church. I have left this open at the moment. A new era is beginning, a new era of rejuvenation. However – and this should be noted – everything that I have just said must be conditional. All of this will happen only if the sense of God is reborn in minds and in hearts. Now I think that I have shown adequately that that does not depend either on the church or on Christians. It depends on those researchers who at this moment again find themselves faced with this problem. If scientists and philosophers pursue the course on which they seem to be engaged, if after more than a century of darkness and obscure negations they rediscover the sense of a certain superior Rationality; if those who reflect and think then move from there to a degree of transcendence, and if the church authorities can recognize the interest of this work and these researches and can turn them to spiritual advantage, then a new era could open for theocentricity, and the restoration of equilibrium which I have just mentioned will come about. But there will be a need for much vigilance and intellectual courage.

Where will this vigilance and intellectual courage come from? We cannot answer with certainty, but we might think of a vigilant papacy, open to the development of current ideas, and above all totally free towards a recent past. And I might be allowed to say that Roman Catholics have great hopes in this respect. The development will also come from the intellectuals who belong to the church. Versed in the great areas of science and culture (in particular the history of the world), they will be concerned to reflect on theological problems and will not be afraid to take up positions on these problems. The renewal may even come from the theologians themselves, provided that they do not remain imprisoned in frameworks from the past (historicism, in particular), and are not afraid to elaborate strong and autonomous thought which does not jib at claiming the title of an intellectual discipline (since after all, of all the gifts that human beings have at their disposal, intelligence 'sees the furthest'). If in addition spiritual figures feel disposed – and without doubt it is here that the church can have the greatest hope – to live out in a pure state the demands of the most elevated mystical contemplation, then the church may be allowed to cherish all these hopes. It will emerge from its present crisis, and soon the hyper-christocentric adventures of this twentieth century will just seem like a bad dream. Finding equilibrium in the faith, and devoting equal love to God and Christ, it will have rediscovered the very conditions for its innermost life which were willed for it by its founder. It will rediscover the splendour of a new youth.

Postlude

A Word to Believers

The book which you have just read is addressed to both believers and unbelievers. It has set out to give as objective a survey as possible of the Catholic church, following the methods of social psychology. It shows what happens to a church when it develops tendencies within itself relevant to different social logics, including the appearance of a tendency towards excessive christocentricity, which soon becomes exclusive.

Believers, who of course want their church to come out of its present crisis as soon as possible, rightly think that they might resort to prayer to hasten the coming of days of peace. In this postlude I suggest that they might like to make their own this splendid prayer which was composed at the beginning of this century by a humble Carmelite mystic, Sister Elizabeth of the Trinity (who died at the Carmelite convent in Dijon in 1906). In the petitions which ascend to God through this prayer they will recognize all the aspirations that a clear-sighted soul, thirsty for truth, and concerned for the interior life of the church, can experience, faced with the difficulties of which the preceding analysis is merely an echo. It is in the sublime exaltation described here, towards the Holy Trinity, that the soul can find the source of all the inspiration capable of renewing the inner life of the church.

Prayer to the Holy Trinity

O my God, Trinity whom I adore, help me to forget myself entirely, to establish myself in you, motionless and at peace, as if my soul were already in eternity. May nothing trouble my peace or make me depart from you, who do not change, but may every minute take me deeper into the depths of your mystery!

Give peace to my soul; make it your heaven, your beloved dwelling and the place of your repose. May I never leave you there alone; may I be there with all my being, awakened in my faith, adoring, utterly given to your creative action.

O my beloved Christ, crucified by love, I would be a bride for your heart; I would cover you with glory, I would love you – even to death. But I feel my powerlessness and I ask you to reclothe me with yourself, to identify my soul with all the movements of your soul, to submerge me, to carry me away, to substitute yourself for me, so that my life is simply the radiance of your life. Come to me as worshipper, redeemer and saviour.

O eternal word, word of my God, I would spend all my life listening to you, I would have myself taught so that I could learn all from you. Then through all the nights, the emptinesses, the times of helplessness, I would keep you always and live under your great light. O my beloved star, charm me so that I may never depart from your radiance.

O consuming fire, spirit of love, come upon me so that a form of incarnation of the Word can come about in my heart; may I be for him an excess of humanity in which he can renew all his mystery.

And you, O Father, lean towards your poor little creature, cover her with your shadow, see her as the well-beloved in whom you have put all your pleasure.

To my 'Three', my All, my Blessedness, infinite Solitude, the Immensity in which I lose myself, I deliver myself as a prey. Bury yourselves in me that I may bury myself in you, awaiting the contemplation in your light of the depths of your greatness.

21 November 1904

May this prayer inspire the thought and heart of those who are learning to work for the future of tomorrow's church, a church all radiant with the love of God . . . by the mediation of Christ.

Notes

Chapter I Christianity, a Religion with Two Polarities

1. Some classic texts on the methods of social psychology are: Roger Daval et al, *Traité de psychologie sociale*, two vols, Presses Universitaires de France 1963, 1964. Also Otto Klineberg, *Social Psychology*, Holt, Rinehart & Winston, rev. ed. 1962; Jean Maisonneuve, *Psychologie sociale*, Presses Universitaires de France 1951; and above all, Jean Stoetzel, *La psychologie sociale*, Flammarion, Paris 1963. I should point out to the reader that in this work I have constantly been influenced by the remarks made by the initiator of social psychology, Gabriel Tarde. In particular, see the study which I have made of him, *Gabriel Tarde et la philosophie de l'Histoire*, Vrin, Paris 1970; also the more popular account of his methods, together with a selection of the most significant texts, published in 1973; G. Tarde, *Ecrits de psychologie sociale*, choisis et presentés par A.-M. Rocheblave-Spenle et J. Milet, Editions Privat, Toulouse.

In particular, it seems to me that G. Tarde has established that social life is made up of interactions between psychological currents which, stimulated by imitation, end up by forming a criss-cross of networks which build up eventually to form a whole social 'fabric'. Social life is made up of inter-psychological relations. The laws which govern these interrelations are well-known. G. Tarde demonstrates their essential principles in his great work *La Logique sociale*. A condensed form of the argument can be found in the more popular work mentioned above. I shall regularly make use of the analytical techniques mapped out there in this study of the present situation in the Catholic church.

2. It should not therefore be supposed that here I am making a critical analysis of the philosophical and theological positions which were adopted at this time (I shall doubtless do that elsewhere). What I am concerned with is a study in social psychology. A man, a people, shared in this faith: what could have been the results of this belief on their attitudes? I am concerned to ascertain a particular position; I shall then analyse it 'scientifically' as far as I can.

3. Here I would refer the reader to the actual text of the Bible, in particular Genesis 1, and then chs. 12–15, which report the calling of Abraham, and its sequel. There are plenty of analytical studies of the calling of Abraham. Here I am relying above all on the work of C. L. Woolley, *Ur of the Chaldees*, Bern 1929, which presents all the historical documents on the calling of Abraham: also the more general, but schol-

arly, work of Père M.-J. Lagrange, *Le Judaïsme avant Jésus-Christ*, 1931. For a comparative study I would refer to the collection *Peuples et Civilisations*, ed. Halphen and Sagnac, and, of course, the specialized works of André Parrot.

4. Gen. 12.1.

5. The biblical notion of 'glory' represents the outburst of the fullness of being. It is 'this fullness manifested, known and communicated in its splendour' (D. Lallement). It is manifested to the people of Israel by a 'column of fire' which bears the name of the *Shekinah*. There are numerous manifestations of the 'glory of God' in the history of Israel. See Ex. 40.32–36; 34.5–7; 3.14. It also fills the tent of the covenant (Ex. 40.32–36), and later the temple of Solomon (I Kings 8.10f.; Ezek. 10.18; 11.22f.; 43.4f.). The reference to the glory of God also appears in prayers. Moses entreats God, 'Pray let me see your glory' (Ex. 33.18); and the Psalmist says: 'You will receive me in glory' (Ps. 72). 'Be exalted, O God, above the heavens. On earth, your glory' (Ps. 56).

6. To understand the force of this 'polarization' of all the conscious faculties around God (both personal and social conscience), read some of the great texts, like the famous prayers which are scattered through the Old Testament: the prayer of Moses, the prayer of Esther, and even more perhaps the prayer of Nehemiah (Neh. 9.6–34).

It should be noted that this reference to a supreme being is also manifested, in a mystical form, in the traditions adjacent to the Jewish community. A. Parrot has shown that 'men of God' show themselves at Mari from the eighteenth century BC. In Ugarit, between the nineteenth and seventeenth centuries BC, the gods are distributed in a pantheon. However, they are dominated in turn by a supreme God, called El. Of him, too, it is said that he is Father of men, creator of creatures, blessed and merciful. He dwells 'at the ends of the earth', which is a way of saying that he transcends the world (cf. the documentation on Ugarit in the Louvre). So religious faith in a supreme being manifests itself very markedly in these regions of the Near East from the eighteenth century BC. This faith dominates the behaviour of the privileged people who hold it in the millennia which follow.

7. Here I am referring to the famous text of Book Lambda of Aristotle's *Metaphysics*, which I regard as the climax of the effort of Greek thought and also of all antiquity.

8. Let me recall the famous text in which St Paul evokes for the Athenians the possibility for all men to elevate themselves at least to the 'God of the philosophers': 'And he made from one every nation of men to live on all the face of the earth, having determined allotted periods and the boundaries of their habitation, that they should seek God, in the hope that they might feel after him and find him. Yet he is not far from each one of us, for "In him we live and move and have our being"; as even some of your poets have said, "For we are indeed his offspring" ' (Acts 17.26–28). It is also worth noting here that the Catholic church came to give official recognition to the possibility that human reason can

find the 'true God' unaided. In this respect I would refer to the often-quoted text of Vatican I, *De Revelatione*, Can. 1 (Denzinger, no.1806).

9. Christ's affirmations of his divinity are extremely numerous. See all the textbooks on apologetics; they outdo each other in citing them. Here I mention only some particularly significant references: Matt. 11.27; Luke 10.22; John 16.14f.; 14.26; 15.26; 16.7.

10. Here too, there are a great many possible references. I mention only the chief of them: John 2.1–11; Matt. 8.27; Mark 4.41; Luke 8.25; Matt. 14.13–23; Mark 6.35–44; Luke 9.12–17; John 6.1–14; Matt. 15.32–39.

11. It was at Antioch that this term Christians was used for the first time to denote those who thenceforth detached themselves from the believers in the Jewish community to put their faith in Jesus Christ as well as in God. This will have happened round about 40–43, during the preaching of Paul and Barnabas (cf. Acts 11.26). In the *Dictionnaire d'Archéologie*, Henri Leclerc states: 'The word *christianus* must have proved popular and have been immediately taken up into current usage, to such an extent that from 64 the common people made ready use of it' ('Chrétien').

12. Of course, here I can do no more than give a very general account of the tendencies which emerge. I am simply concerning myself with presenting the elements of the debate which prove indispensable for understanding the analyses which follow, concerning tensions between faith in God and faith in Christ in the primitive church.

13. I have only taken account of the notorious 'heresies' which were contested as such by the church authorities. However, the regular appearance of others at the time clearly shows the intellectual difficulties encountered by those faced with the problem of practising the 'double faith'. In fact all the fathers of the church, both Greek and Latin, will come up against this problem. By way of a simple indication I might mention here the very strange position taken up, for example, by St Gregory of Nazianzen about the mission of Christ, and his 'strange silences', or at least his laconic way of dealing with the Holy Spirit. According to him, Jesus did not completely reveal the doctrine of the Holy Spirit to his disciples, so that they were not utterly dazzled all at once: the Old Testament had revealed the Father clearly and the Son in an obscure way; the New Testament brought a clear revelation of the Son, but not of the Holy Spirit. This very 'personal' interpretation is amazing; however, one could find dozens of others even among the most assured writers. Intellectual embarrassment is evident everywhere.

14. Numerous echoes of the perplexity experienced by the first educated Christians can be found in the work of P. de Labriolle, *Histoire de la Littérature latine chrétienne*, Editions Belles-Lettres 1947, passim.

15. On this question of Peter's faith see G. Thils, *L'enseignement de Pierre*, Editions Lecoffre 1943.

16. Op. cit., p.23.

17. Ibid.

18. Ibid.

19. Ibid.

20. Op. cit., pp.24, 27ff.

21. Here one could certainly cite almost all the epistles. The most striking passages on the subject are certainly to be found in the Letter to the Ephesians. 'It is in this Son, in his blood, that we find redemption, the remission of our sins . . .' (1.7); thus it is a question of 'inaugurating all things in Christ' (1.10): 'we have been created in Jesus Christ' (2.10). 'Christ dwells in our hearts by faith' (3.17). We are invited to come to 'the unity of faith and the knowledge of the Son of God, to the state of the complete man, to the stature of the maturity of Christ' (4.13). One could go on quoting texts like this indefinitely: they all invite us to live 'with' Christ.

For more information, see the well-known work by P. Prat, *La théologie de saint Paul*, Editions Beauchesne, or more recently the work by F. Amiot, *L'enseignement de Saint Paul*, Editions Desclée, new edition 1968, especially, pp.25, 27f., 92f.

22. For St John's beliefs about Christ see in particular the works by P. Durand in the collection *Verbum Salutis*, Editions Beauchesne. I have been particularly influenced here by the views of P. Huby. See his work *Le discours de Jésus après la Cène*, Editions Beauchesne; in this volume I would particularly commend the final study entitled 'La connaissance de foi dans Saint Jean' (The Knowledge of Faith in St John), pp.125–8.

23. Note that the conclusion of the text of the Canon of the Mass appropriately combines these three currents in a single formula: 'By him, in him and with him . . . all honour and glory'.

24. For a general introduction to the Gnostics see Serge Hutin, *Les Gnostiques*, Collection 'Que sais-je?', Presses Universitaires de France 1970. As well as a general analysis, this also contains an excellent bibliography. The most celebrated of the Gnostics are: Simon the Magician; Nicolas, founder of the sect of Nicolaitans; Cerinthus, who taught at Ephesus; Basilides, who taught at Alexandria; Bardesanes, at Edessa. The most famous is, of course, Marcion, who founded a well-known sect, the Marcionites, in the region of Pontus.

25. I am only taking up the question of heresies again here because I am concerned to show how the Christian conscience reacts to the challenge posed by the practice of the double faith which is required of it. So this is not a complete exposition but an analytical study. Let me also recall that in this volume my preoccupation is solely one of social psychology: I am trying to study social behaviour, not doctrines.

26. Anyone visiting Coptic churches, for example in Egypt, will be struck by the fact that Christ is always represented as an 'apparition': his silhouette always has a nimbus of light. The Christ is treated like Our Lady of Lourdes in a pictorial representation.

27. All the details of the development of the primitive liturgy can be found in Dom Cabrol, *Le livre de la prière antique*, Librairie H. Oudin 1913, an excellent volume despite its age.

28. Echoes of the inner tension experienced by St Augustine can be found in Alfaric's study *L'évolution intellectuelle de saint Augustin*; other

even clearer echoes can be found in the excellent study by J. Finaert, *L'évolution littéraire de saint Augustin*, Editions des Belles Lettres 1939.

Chapter II Theocentric and Christocentric Belief

1. On this question see Joseph Moreau, *Le Dieu des philosophes*, Vrin 1969.

2. This is the precise origin of the difficulties which Galileo encountered. The personal study which I have made of this period has shown me that the chief charge made against Galileo (which is reported to us by his correspondent Canon de Tarde in an unpublished document) is that his hypothesis postulates the stability of the sun; and that as a result, he is forced to question the possibility that Joshua could have stopped it in its course. This was to put sacred scripture in doubt; it was to shake the Bible and revelation: it was a blasphemy.

3. The best possible analysis of this evolution can be found in ch. III of Bergson, *The Two Sources of Morality and Religion*, Macmillan 1935. The author shows us how a complete reversal of morality came about: to use his terminology, there was a transition from 'closed morality' to 'open morality'.

4. In this connection one can reread all the psalms, and in particular the so-called penitential psalms (above all the Miserere). Everywhere man recognizes himself to be in a 'state of perdition'.

5. For connections between Christian behaviour and psychoanalysis, see the works of Françoise Dolto on the gospels, and more particularly the analyses given in Pierre Solignac, *La Névrose chrétienne*, Éditions de Trévise 1976.

6. One cannot help thinking of the analyses which Freud was able to make of 'oceanic consciousness', regarded as a substitute for the sense of the sacred, when one re-reads certain pages of Mme Guyon, not to mention Fénelon.

7. For the necessary documentation on these points I would refer the reader to the excellent *Vocabulaire de Psychanalyse*, edited by J. Laplanche and J.-B. Pontalis, Presses Universitaires de France.

8. All the necessary information on this question of the two types of authority can be found in Gabriel Tarde, *L'opinion et la foule*, 1901. See also the famous book by Gustave Le Bon, *La psychologie des Foules*. To make the analyses of G. Tarde more accessible, I have summed them up in my *Gabriel Tarde et la philosophie de l'Histoire*, Vrin 1970, ch. V, 257–65.

9. Note how buildings are still oriented on Jerusalem.

10. One could comment that the very life of Jesus nevertheless has 'triumphalist' features. A little after his birth he was hailed by the visit of the magi, with exceptional pomp (the gifts of frankincense, gold and myrrh); he experienced the glory of the Transfiguration, the triumph of Palm Sunday, the victory of the Resurrection; the exaltation of Ascension Day. These aspects of the life of Christ have been taken up by the Eastern tradition (the commemoration of the Epiphany has long eclipsed that of

the Nativity, which is not regarded as being very important). In the Western tradition, it will soon be 'in good taste' to pause on the periods of humiliation and suffering (with a curious preoccupation with the gloomier side: the crucifixion makes more impact than the resurrection). This is a piece of psychological and social behaviour worth noting, because it is a good indication of the dominant psychologies of each of these cultures: the optimistic East and the pessimistic (Latin) West.

11. See C. G. Jung, *Psychology and Religion*, Routledge 1958, esp. pp.247–96, 'The Psychology of the Mass'.

12. In fact, in the case of the altar, it is not two ideas which are in competition but three: the idea of the sacred stone, that of the tomb of the martyrs and that of the table of the paschal meal (which becomes the eucharist). From the beginning, those who built altars tried to bring together these three ideas: the altar stone contains the relics of martyrs and serves as a resting place for the vessels needed (chalice and paten). The first idea is obviously of theocentric origin; the last two are christocentric. Thus in the last resort two logics come face to face here . . . in three ideas.

13. The novelist Bernanos has given a good picture of these two 'types' of priesthood in his novel *The Diary of a Country Priest*. He contrasts the Curé de Torcy, a man full of dignity and constantly concerned to manifest the greatness of God, with the 'little priest', humiliated, harrowed by physical and moral problems, the failure. These are two types of priesthood which are presented with equal attraction, and which strangely exist side by side in the Catholic tradition.

It should be noted in passing that we do not find such pointed social psychological contradictions in the other Christian traditions. The Orthodox priest is a specifically theocentric figure: he is a man who serves to present the majesty of God. The Protestant pastor – whose mission is in any case quite different from that of the Catholic priest – is also the witness to the glory of God; moreover, he often plays a moral role; and in this respect he shares in the respectability of the sovereign judge. The question obviously does not arise in connection with the representatives of non-Christian religions: the rabbi is the 'man of God', in fear and respect; in Islam, the imam, the marabout, the ayatollah are men of God in the service of his glory and his justice.

Chapter III The Theocentric Tradition

1. See Robert M. Grant, *The Early Christian Doctrine of God,* Univ. Press of Virginia, Charlottesville 1966, p.48: 'According to the Jewish expectations of God's reign, God was going to effect a new creation in the last days; and the apostle Paul frequently refers to this new creation as having come into existence for Christians.'

2. One whole part of the Christian church of the first centuries continued for a long time to think that the ultimate aim of the coming of Christ on earth was not so much the exaltation of the incarnate Word in his own person as the preparation for the coming of the Holy Spirit which

happened at Pentecost. The culmination of the whole venture of the Incarnation was the coming of the Holy Spirit. On this question it is worth reading P. Emmanuel-Pataq Siman, *L'expérience de l'Esprit par l'Eglise d'après la tradition syrienne d'Antioche*, Beauchesne 1971.

3. In particular, recent work has shed light on the resistance of James and above all of Barnabas. In this connection see the thesis submitted to the Sorbonne in 1975 by Luigi Cirillo on the Gospel of Barnabas (from manuscripts of the sixteenth century kept at the National Library of Vienna, in Venetian dialect).

In this connection great importance has been attached to the text known as the Gospel of Barnabas. This text is said to have been produced by Jewish Christians at the end of the first century. Considerable hesitation can be detected in it over the orientation that Paul gave to the Christian mission. Expressions are even violent. The author denounces the excesses committed in the 'divinization' of Christ by certain zealous Christians, 'among them,' the author says, 'Paul himself, and I do not speak without sadness'. The canonicity of this Gospel of Barnabas is a matter for discussion, but we must recognize that at all events it has been established historically that there were tensions between the apostles as to the exact mission which was to be accorded to Christ. The tendency towards christocentricity which can be discovered in Paul was certainly challenged in the name of the theocentricity of Jewish inspiration.

4. Dom Cabrol, from whom I have taken the substance of my analysis, remarks that he in turn relies on the learned studies of Bickell. 'It is Bickell's achievement to have shown, with his profound knowledge of Christian antiquity and Jewish ritual, that the Christian mass was grafted on to this Passover ritual, and that we can find the outlines of this ceremony in the primitive mass' (Dom Cabrol, op. cit., p.77). He refers to Bickell, *Messe und Pascha*, Mainz 1872 (ET: *The Lord's Supper and the Passover Ritual*, T. & T. Clark 1891), and to earlier works by Sepp and Probst.

5. Dom Cabrol gives a good analysis of this transfer of the intentional meaning of the mass, op. cit., pp.79f. He does not disguise the fact that the influence of Paul must have played a considerable part in this transfer (p.79). He also points to the 'mealtime' excesses which took place: the mass was turned into a 'Socratic banquet'.

6. However, as we shall see, christocentric interpretations of the mass return in force at the beginning of the twentieth century.

7. Cited by Dom Cabrol, op. cit., p.86.

8. Ibid., p.91.

9. In this connection, Dom Cabrol notes: 'It was the bishop who had the responsibility for these readings. The choice of these books was an important matter, and discernment was needed. The books of the Bible were not in a volume approved by all the church, as they are today. The majority of them formed separate volumes; heretics and forgers sought to introduce apocryphal books' (p.102). It will be recalled, for example, that the *Shepherd of Hermas* was part of the 'canonical' texts down to the fourth century.

10. Quoted by Dom Cabrol, op. cit., p.153.

11. The festival of Pentecost changed its meaning only slowly, and after prolonged ambiguity. The commemoration of the exodus from Egypt was replaced by that of the resurrection of Christ, which almost coincided; it was the same for Pentecost, when the harvest festival was adapted to that of the coming of the Holy Spirit.

12. Dom Cabrol, op. cit., p.311.

13. Henri Marrou, *Saint Augustin et l'augustinisme*, Editions du Seuil 1955, p.43.

14. On this question see the basic works by Étienne Gilson, in particular *The Spirit of Mediaeval Philosophy*, Sheed & Ward 1936 and *The Philosophy of St Thomas Aquinas*, Heffer 1924.

15. In this connection it will be useful to consult *L'Histoire spirituelle de la France*, Beauchesne 1964. For all Christian countries see the *Dictionnaire de Spiritualité*.

16. One could qualify this hypothetical christocentricity of St Francis further. If his love is directed to Christ in his humanity, it must not be forgotten that the Christ who appeared to him and who marked him with his stigmata is a superhuman Christ: in fact, as St Francis said, he took on the form of a 'crucified seraphim'.

17. Vladimir Lossky, *The Mystical Theology of the Eastern Church*, James Clarke 1957.

18. J.-C. Marcade, *L'icône comme miroir*, 1976, p.133.

19. J.-C. Marcade, op. cit., p.137. For the sacred significance of the icon see Leonide Ouspensky, *Essai sur la théologie de l'icône dans l'Eglise orthodoxe*, Paris 1960, or Michel Evdokimov, *L'art sacré*, Paris 1953. Let me quote two particularly significant texts from Ouspensky: 'The person represented is the bearer of divine grace; the icon must indicate his sanctity to us' (op. cit., p.196); 'The icon is a revelation of eternity in time' (p.197). Note the profoundly theocentric resonance of these two texts.

20. In the end of the day, it is as a result of the failure of this attempt to revive theocentricity by the expedient of mysticism that the seventeenth century will fall back on christocentricity for its lifeline, as we shall soon see.

21. For a deeper study of the themes dear to the Rhenish and Flemish schools of spirituality see the numerous works by Mme Ancelet-Hustache, especially those on Meister Eckhart.

22. Christ is considered by these Renaissance figures as a kind of super-Apollo, super-Hermes. In this connection see the sculpture of Michelangelo, the painting of Botticelli, and so on. One could, however, ask to what extent these works of art are still religious!

23. Louis Cognet, *La spiritualité française au XVIIe siècle*, Editions la Colombe 1949, p.35.

24. Pascal already dreamed of arguing that one could know God only through Jesus Christ, as this text bears witness: 'Except in Jesus Christ, we do not know the meaning of our life or our death, or God or oursel-

ves', *Pensées*, no. 602, Harvill Press 1962, p.287 (translated from the Lafuma edition, Paris 1954).

Chapter IV The Renaissance of Christocentricity

1. The chief sources to which I shall refer for the study of the French school of spirituality are as follows: Henri Brémond, *Histoire littéraire du sentiment religieux en France*, Vol. III, Bloud et Gay 1921; Jean Gautier PSS, *L'Esprit de l'Ecole française de spiritualité*, Bloud et Gay 1936; P. G. Rotureau, *Le Cardinal de Bérulle*, Pages Catholiques, Albin Michel 1947; Louis Cognet, *Etude sur la spiritualité française au XVIIe siècle*, Revue Catholique 4, La Colombe 1949; J. Dagens, *Bérulle et les origines de la Restauration catholique (1575–1611)*, Paris 1952; Paul Cochois, *Bérulle et l'Ecole Française*, Les maîtres spirituels, Editions du Seuil 1963; Jean Orcibal, *Le Cardinal de Bérulle. Evolution d'une spiritualité*, Editions du Cerf 1965. I would also commend the article 'France', *Dictionnaire de Spiritualité* V, cols. 785–1004, and the volume *Histoire spirituelle de la France*, Beauchesne 1964, which takes up the essential elements of the *Dictionnaire* article.

2. Dare one recall that experiments were unfortunately tried with sacramental matter? A correspondent of Descartes recalls that there had been an attempt to observe fragments of the consecrated host in a microscope (a completely new invention of science), to compare them with fragments of the ordinary host. Of course the experiment did not produce any result, to the great disappointment of the investigators.

3. His biographers tell us that on his way to Paris the young Descartes had attended a conference given at the Nunciature by the Sieur de Chandoux on 'some questions of physics'. He spoke at the end of this conference, and demonstrated with such panache his interest in a 'new method' for demonstrating the truth, which he had just tried out, that Cardinal de Bérulle, present at the conference, intervened publicly to impress on him his duty to put his 'genius' at the service of the Christian faith. We are told that this confirmed Descartes in his design to reform knowledge.

4. Clearly the account of the philosophical debate which I have given here is very schematic. This is not the place for debating it in depth. One could go on to refer to the basic works on these questions by Gilson, H. Gouhier, M. Guéroult, G. Rodis-Lewis, and perhaps more specially those of P. Lenoble, who through his thesis on Mersenne has given a good description of the crisis in philosophical (and scientific) ideas at this period. I regard these investigations as definitive, and can only make an assessment in connection with the problem which concerns us here.

5. A good study of the person of Mme Acarie (1566–1618) has been made by Père Bruno de Jesus-Marie OCD, *La belle Acarie*, 1943, a book which aroused as much passionate discussion as did M. Acarie in her lifetime.

6. L. Cognet, op. cit., p.38.

7. Cited by Cognet, op. cit., p.39.

8. Ibid., p.43.
9. Ibid., passim.
10. Cognet, op. cit., p.53.
11. Ibid., p.54.
12. This is the opinion of Paul Cochois, op. cit., p.22. It is also that of J. Dagens.
13. P. Cochois, op. cit., p.22.
14. This was the more personal opinion of L. Cognet, op. cit., p.55.
15. J. Orcibal, op. cit., p.129.
16. L. Cognet, op. cit., p.54.
17. Quoted by P. Cochois, op. cit., p.23.
18. L. Cognet, op. cit., p.63.
19. G. Rotureau, op. cit., p.41.
20. Ibid., p.41.
21. Ibid., p.57.
22. J. Orcibal, op. cit., p.80. One consequence of this modification in the hierarchy of being would be to allow Mary to be declared 'queen of the angels', which was not possible in earlier interpretations. Her creaturely dignity, sharing in that which her Son had received here, allowed her to ascend in the hierarchy 'above the angels'. For his part, Malebranche wrote about the relations between the angels and Christ: 'The angels did not wait after Jesus Christ, because Jesus Christ is before them. He is the first-born of all creatures: *primogenitus omnis creaturae*. He was born only two thousand years ago in Bethlehem, but he was sacrificed six thousand years ago: *agnus occisus est ab origine mundi*' (*Entretiens métaphysiques* XIV, Edition Cuvillier, Vrin, II, p.183). This text raises many problems: if Jesus Christ existed since creation (amusingly put at 'six thousand years ago'), in what could the incarnation have consisted? Besides, if the existence of Jesus Christ coincides with the whole history of the world, we should not be surprised that at a later date, by a perfectly logical development, people came to 'sacralize' history itself. The positions taken by Bérulle, and with him by Malebranche, are therefore full of significance; all modern historicism is there in nucleus.
23. P. Cochois, op. cit., p.64.
24. For this question see J. Orcibal, op. cit., p.61.
25. Ibid.
26. Ibid.
27. These themes are developed above all in his great three-volume work, *De la Recherche de la Vérité*, Vrin 1965. One might also refer to the study by H. Gouhier, *La philosophie de Malebranche et son expérience religieuse*, Vrin 1948, in particular the chapter devoted to Malebranche's Augustinianism. One might also refer to Malebranche, *Les Méditations chrétiennes*, where he is not afraid to involve Christ even in research into philosophical and scientific truth.
28. All details on this subject will be found in particular in the work by J. Gautier, op. cit. Abbé Brémond confirms that M. Olier was one of the best diffusers of the ideas of Bérulle. 'The particular charm of M.

Olier', he writes, 'has been not so much to popularize Bérullianism, as to present it with such limpidity, such richness of imagination and such fervour, that this metaphysics, which seems somewhat difficult, becomes accessible and seductive to the average reader' (quoted by J. Gautier, op. cit., 29).

29. J. Orcibal, op. cit., p.12.

30. P. Cochois, op. cit., p.166.

31. L. Cognet, op. cit., p.76.

32. Ibid., p.90.

33. L. Cognet, op. cit., p.51.

34. For the attitude of Port Royal, see *Histoire spirituelle de France*, Beauchesne, pp.257f.

35. One might read with amused curiosity the work by Dumontet, *Le désir de voir l'hostie et les origines de la dévotion au Saint-Sacrement*, Paris 1926. It contains picturesque details on the ridiculous forms that devotion to the Blessed Sacrament could then take; racing to be present at the recently created rite of the elevation of the host and the chalice after the consecration.

Chapter V The Growing Predominance of Christocentricity

1. A symbol of this 'equilibrium' could be found, for example, in the choir of the church of St Merri in Paris (decorated at the end of the eighteenth century). There one can see a 'glory' of enormous size dominating the whole choir with its curved rays: it is intended to hymn the 'glory of God'; this is the typical expression of theocentricity. However, on it has been superimposed a crucifix of no less a size which covers a large area of it and is the expression of christocentricity. For the secular visitor, it gives the impression of a gripping contrast. One could certainly cite numerous examples of this kind.

2. For this question of the relationship between the church and the movement of ideas in the nineteenth century (and in particular the growth of atheism), see: C. Pouthas, *L'Eglise catholique au XIXe siècle*; Dansette, *Histoire religieuse de la France contemporaine*, two vols, Paris 1948; A. Latreille and his collaborators, *Histoire du catholicisme en France*, vol. III. For the development of the currents of spirituality see by preference the works of P. Pourrat, F. Cayré and, of course, H. Brémond (the volume of his *Histoire littéraire du sentiment religieux* on the nineteenth century).

3. All the same, there could have been people who held the theories of Epicurus or Lucretius. There were none of these in the regions where Christ lived. One would very much like to know what his reaction would have been to doctrinal atheism. We are reduced to conjectures.

4. J.-P. Sartre has shown well that Cartesian voluntarism contains the germ of absurdity. On this subject see the very relevant analysis which he puts forward on this question in *Situation* I, Gallimard 1947, pp.314f.

5. As P. Dubarle comments, no one will be deceived by this 'mutation' proposed by Hegel. 'The religious spirit has not accepted the Hegelian

Aufhebung of its religion and its theology in philosophy', P. Dubarle and André Doz, *Logique et dialectique*, Larousse 1972, p.104. With the authors, I would refer for a deeper study of this question of the relationships between Hegelian theses on religion and Christian thought to Karl Barth, *Protestant Theology in the Nineteenth Century,* ET SCM Press 1972, ch. 10 on Hegel. In connection with Hegel's view of God, see also the study by Henri Niel, *Les preuves de l'existence de Dieu*, Aubier 1947. I have taken the following text, which seems particularly significant, from Hegel himself. 'The fact that man knows God is a shared knowledge, that is to say that man only knows God in so far as God knows himself in man. This knowledge is awareness that God has of himself, but also knowledge that man has of God, and is none other than the spirit of God himself' (op. cit., p.162). It is clear that there is no place for a transcendent conception of God in Hegel. For this important question see the collection of essays *Manifestation et Révélation*, Collection Philosophie, Beauchesne 1976. See in particular the important study by P. Dubarle, where it is demonstrated that Hegel only made Christianity the absolute religion by divinizing man.

6. It goes without saying that here I am on the verge of making a sociological statement: I am affirming that public opinion (at least the opinion of cultivated circles) reacted in this way to Blondelism, then to neo-Thomism, to Bergsonism, to Teilhardism and so on. I am not making an absolute pronouncement on the validity of these reactions. There would be a good deal to say on this question: these reactions were often unfair because they were too superficial.

7. We should be careful not to forget that some studies are concerned with atheism considered in its strictly rational form. I am thinking in particular of the works of P. de Lubac. See above all his book *Le Drame de l'humanisme athée*. The method followed here is related to that of Pascal: man cannot live without God. Humanism which wants to be atheistic is a useless humanism. The starting point is man's needs: God is necessary for man to live properly; so it is 'proper' that God should exist.

8. Here I am only mentioning the different attempts at 'reductions' of christology shall make a detailed study in due course.

9. A good deal has been written about what is called 'situation ethics'. The ground on which it stands is clearly very slippery: we know since Pascal's polemics of the seventeenth century (see *Les Provinciales*) that it is very risky to look for compromises with the world. The Roman authorities intervened several times in this area from 1950 onwards to correct the interpretations put forward by certain Catholic moralists about, in particular, the ethics of marriage, the problems of sexual ethics, and so on.

10. See, for example, the amazing success in this period of the reissue of works by the great Carmelite authors, St Teresa of Avila and St John of the Cross.

11. One work would soon enjoy considerable success (about 1943), that of Abbés Godin and Daniel, *France, pays de mission?* This success,

which spread further, giving rise to similar works in other countries than France, is very symptomatic of feelings at the time.

12. Here I am only recalling some facts of general philosophy. One can find developments in this connection in J. Maritain, *Neuf leçons sur les notions premières de la philosophie morale*.

Chapter VI The Triumph of Christocentricity

1. The theory of the 'sacralization' of history receives some support from certain representatives of Orthodoxy. Thus the Russian theologian Bulgakoff does not hesitate to write: 'History is not an empty corridor which must be passed through in some way in order to escape from this world to that of the beyond; it proceeds from the work of Christ in his Incarnation; it is Apocalypse, tending towards the eschatological consummation; it is theanthropic work on earth' (*Du verbe incarné*, p.373). This last thesis reappears very often in Soloviev as well. In short, the incarnation is achieved not only with the humanity of Jesus of Nazareth, but by him with all humanity. All men participate in the Incarnation. All men are bearers of divinity: we end up in historical immanentism (of a visibly pantheistic kind).

2. However, some themes tending in this direction made a timid appearance in the encyclical which Pius XII had devoted to the church as mystical body; later this bold idea would advance as far as the text of the mass: in one of the prefaces (no. 4) recommended by the Roman authorities, from 1975, Christ is hailed as 'Lord of history'. However, these allusions are very discreet. In general, the Roman authorities always show obvious reticence to anything that could lead to historicism.

3. Some Catholics – who commonly go under the name of 'integralists' – denounce these developments as giving rise to the appearance of a new church (marred by modernism), which in their view bears no relation to the traditional church. I have tried here to analyse developments in social psychology. I shall not take part in strictly doctrinal debate.

4. If I wanted to describe this development from the point of view of social psychology, which I have constantly adopted, I should say that the Catholic institution is engaged in an operation of striking a new balance between its two poles: here it is tending towards its christocentric pole.

5. Blondel himself puts forward this theory in his great work *L'Action* (1893). For him, there is what he calls 'a Christian philosophy' which, like any respectable philosophy, must respond to everything. On this question see especially Part V, Chapter II. We shall find this theme developed still further (though less involved in metaphysics) in his work *La philosophie et l'Esprit chrétien*. For Laberthonnière one might refer to his *Essais de philosophie religieuse* (1903), or perhaps with more profit to synthetic studies of his thought which have been made by M.-M. D'Hendecourt in his *Essai sur la philosophie du P. Laberthonnière*, Paris 1947; and more recently the excellent presentation of his theories made by an African philosopher, A. Ngindu, in his work *Le problème de la connaissance religieuse d'après Lucien Laberthonnière*, Edition Uni-

versitaire de Kinshasa 1978. The theme of the possibility of a 'Christian philosophy' is particularly well developed here.

6. This interpretation may be the background to the intention of the organizers of a televised debate between the theologian J. Daniélou and the Marxist philosopher R. Garaudy. We see the opposition of a theology to a philosophy: the two protagonists were not on the same wavelength. They had little chance of making contact. However, it was supposed that a theology (based on faith and revelation) could engage in dialogue with a philosophy based only on reason. No contact was possible.

7. François Varillon, *L'Humilité de Dieu*, Editions du Centurion 1974. See another book by the same author with a particularly significant title: *La souffrance de Dieu*, Editions du Centurion 1975.

8. I mentioned this 'situation ethics' at an earlier stage. I am returning to it here only to give a better indication of attitudes in relation to those which have been mentioned, and in particular to show the nature of the break which has come about with so-called 'traditional' morality, based on the sense of moral wisdom.

9. At a later stage I shall point out the promising consequences for the future of the church that can be drawn from this disappearance of methodological conflict between science and faith. See Chapter VIII below.

10. Raymond Ruyer, *La Gnose de Princeton. Des savants à la recherche d'une religion*, Fayard 1974. We shall see later the benefit that a profound reflection on the themes developed here could bring to the church if it seized its opportunity. See Chapter IX below.

11. Further details of this question can be found, for example, in the works of P. Roqueplo.

12. The analysis which I have made of these two possible aspects of the use of history is clearly very summary. I cannot develop it further here. However, a more extended reflection might give us the key to coping with the difficulties which the Catholic church is encountering at present (getting to grips with 'temporality').

13. On this question see the investigations made by Père Pannet and his team on this 'popular Catholicism'. In the religious reactions of people who have not been initiated into the speculations of modern theologians it is possible to find attitudes which in the framework of this study we have been led to describe as 'theocentric'; they seem to me to be dictated by the naturally religious sense which man has when confronted with the realities which surround him, and which bring him before a God, Lord of men and worlds, rather than towards a Christ who can be known only by history (since these 'good people' are ignorant of history, or at least mistrust it).

14. When I had occasion to take part in a 'mass' (if one can call it that) in the so-called 'progressive' style, I was able to note that the priest pronounced the name of Christ one hundred and thirty times, and did not mention the name of God at all. Do I need to add that in each one of these allusions the Christ was seen from a human perspective, under a social and humanitarian aspect?

15. All the observations that I have just referred to can only be made

in certain regions of the Catholic church: in particular in Western Europe (France, Belgium and Holland, etc.), and in some areas of Latin America (including the fragment of 'Latinity' made up by the province of Quebec, in Canada). It goes without saying that the whole of the Catholic church did not experience this evolution. However, as it is customary to consider these regions as representatives of an 'advanced Catholicism' (which claims to be particularly lucid and aware), I have been led to concentrate my principal observations on this zone of the Catholic world.

16. See *The Documents of Vatican II*, with notes and comments by Catholic, Protestant and Orthodox authorities, edited by Walter M. Abbott, SJ, Geoffrey Chapman 1967.

17. Although this text was regarded by many commentators as the most important of the Council (as we shall see, this interpretation was perhaps tendentious), I should indicate that it was not included in the initial programme of Vatican II (see *The Documents of Vatican II*, pp.183ff.). The critical observer could use this fact to explain the very 'particular' character of this text in relation to the other texts of the Council. The initiative towards producing it came from exterior 'pressures' which could have been brought to bear during the three years the Council lasted. Furthermore, it was produced very rapidly, and the vote was passed at the very last session. See all the commentaries on this question.

18. The observations were made between 1962 and 1965. We can already measure their relativity (and the relativity of any judgment made on the pretence of being 'the meaning of history'). Here humanity is presented as being called to unbridled rejoicing, to unthinking profligacy. There is no suspicion that only fifteen years later there would be talk of lack of sources of energy, slow growth and unemployment (the word 'unemployment' does not even appear in the text). No historical forecasts are possible in either politics or economics.

19. The editing of this text was very difficult. Seen first of all as a 'basic introduction' to all the texts of the Council, after countless rejections it was only adopted (after five previous versions) at the last session in 1965. These difficulties are the reflections of tensions which arose between the two tendencies that I have here denoted as theocentricity and christocentricity. Where is the ultimate source of revelation to be found: in the word of God or in the word of Christ? After three years of discussions, the Council ended up with a kind of balance between the two interpretations. See *The Documents of Vatican II*, pp.183ff.

20. Any objective observer will be struck by the disparate character of this text. The two tendencies which I analyse here and which, as I have already said, come together and clash above all in the problem of the status of the priest, here play their particular parts. The two conceptions of the priest, theocentric and christocentric, are here more or less harmoniously in competition.

Chapter VII Extreme Forms of Christocentricity

1. One can already find reflections on this theme in the thought of Luther in Bossuet, *Premier avertissement aux Protestants*.

2. Bonhoeffer began writing in the 1930s. He is therefore clearly under the influence of Hegel, of the religious sociology of Ernst Troeltsch, and of Karl Barth. His chief work, *Act and Being*, dates from 1930. His courageous stand against Nazism made him a kind of spiritual prophet for Catholics from 1955–1960 onwards. I found a good account of his thought in an article by Cornelio Fabro, *La Table ronde*, December 1967.

3. Quoted by C. Fabro, op. cit., p.36.

4. Here the positions of Bonhoeffer represent an ultimate point which lies beyond all the other theologians of his time. This is a point of view even more radical than that of the 'dialectical theology' of Barth, Tillich and Bultmann, who did not completely break off all connections with philosophy, as C. Fabro, op. cit., p.38, points out.

5. Ibid., p.38.

6. Ibid., p.39.

7. Ibid., p.42. Here Bonhoeffer meets up again with the old biogeneticism of Goethe: life is the sole reality.

8. Ibid.

9. Quoted by C. Fabro, ibid., p.43.

10. See his first work, *The Theology of the New Testament*, ET SCM Press 1952–55, and above all his chief work, *Jesus Christ and Mythology*, SCM Press 1958.

11. He takes this *de facto* declaration as a *de jure* one. On this subject see his basic work *Systematic Theology*, 1951–64, and a popularized expression of his ideas in *The Courage to Be*, 1952. For a good general account of his thought see G. H. Tavard, *Paul Tillich and the Christian Message*, Burns and Oates 1962.

12. These quotations are taken from the interesting study made of the various christologies which I am surveying here, published in the *Cahiers* of the association *Lumen Gentium*; see the very well documented study by Père Jean Galot, SJ, fasc. 35.

13. J. I. Gonzalez Faus, *La Humanidad nueva, Essayo de cristologia*, Madrid 1974.

14. J. Sobrino, *Christianity at the Crossroads*, SCM Press 1978.

15. X. Pizaka, *Los origenes de Jésus*, Salamanca 1976.

16. C. Duquoc, *Christologie*, I and II, Editions du Cerf 1968–1972, and *Jesus, homme libre*, Cerf 1973.

17. Henri Bourgeois, *Libérer Jésus, christologies actuelles*, Editions du Centurion, Paris 1977.

18. P. M. Beaude, *Jésus oublié. Les évangiles et nous*, Editions du Cerf, Paris 1977. It is also worth consulting the collection devoted to the various possible forms of christology entitled *Dossier Jésus. Recherches nouvelles*, by G. Bessière, J.-P. Jossua, A. Lion, M. Pinchon, A. Rousseau, etc., Editions du Chalet 1977.

19. The chief sources here are: John A. T. Robinson, *Honest to God*,

SCM Press and Westminster Press, Philadelphia 1963; G. Vahanian, *The Death of God*, Braziller, New York 1961; P. van Buren, *The Secular Meaning of the Gospel*, SCM Press and Macmillan, New York 1963; Harvey Cox, *The Secular City*, SCM Press and Macmillan, New York 1965.

20. For non-specialists, let me recall some essential facts about the practice of dialectical thought. According to traditional philosophy, after Socrates, Plato and Aristotle it is accepted that the observer who sets out to reflect on the world considers himself *distinct* from this world. He adopts the attitude of *theoria*: he seeks to know in order to gain knowledge of the object which presents itself to him. He adopts a 'contemplative' attitude in the broadest sense of the word. From a certain period onwards – which we might locate somewhere between Kant and Hegel – people began to think that this attitude is vain and otiose. The observer has not to remain detached from the object which he is considering; on the contrary, he must never forget that he himself is part of the reality which he wants to observe. So knowledge is no longer contemplation, detached from things; it is as it were a dialogue entered into with things, a dialogue in which the knower and the known enter into a reciprocal relationship. This reciprocal relationship takes the name of a 'dialectical' relationship. The introduction of this interpretation of knowledge evidently marks a revolution of considerable noetic significance. The reference to contemplative *theoria* no longer makes any sense. The notion of objective truth disappears. Even the conception of an objective science no longer has any bearing. Since all knowledge is a 'dialogue' between the knower and the known, it follows that this dialogue is no more than a 'historical moment' in the evolution of culture (or of conscience). The insertion of thought into the historic continuum postulated by the dialectical interpretation thus eliminates *a priori* all possibility of reference to a hypothetical reality transcending history. This becomes no more than a chimaeric hypothesis.

Now if we apply this interpretation to theological science, we can see that of necessity we include its very content within the sphere of historicity. The God of Abraham can only be the God whom Abraham was able to think of: he belongs to the sphere of his knowledge.

Thus the whole problem is to establish what type of knowledge should be adopted at the beginning: contemplative *theoria* or dialectical *praxis*. Here it is a matter of the adoption of an epistemological attitude which is anterior to the exercise of all knowledge . . . starting with that of theological knowledge. However, I am only raising the question here – to help the reader understand; I have no ambition to develop the enormous aspects of this question. For that the reader must consult specialist works. To anyone who wants to make a start on the procedures of dialectical thought I would commend the excellent volume by Paul Foulquié, *La Dialectique*, Collection 'Que sais-je?', Presses Universitaires de France [7]1969. The work contains a careful bibliography which will help the reader develop knowledge of the subject.

21. The introduction I have tried to give here to the principles of

dialectical theology is clearly very summary. In accordance with the general spirit of this work I have given the necessary information for understanding the direction taken by the evolution of ideas within Christianity during this period, in terms of social psychology.

22. See above. I should point out that this work is fairly easy to read.

23. See above, p.196.

24. Fernando Belo, *A Materialist Reading of the Gospel of Mark*, Orbis Books, Maryknoll 1981. Study circles have been formed to pursue the analyses made by the author in this book.

25. See Pasolini's film on Jesus.

26. Joseph Comblin, *Théologie de la Révolution, Théorie*, Editions universitaires, Paris 1970.

27. Published by Editions du Cerf 1968.

28. Père Girardi put forward his ideas in numerous articles. He also expressed his thought in a more didactic way in very well-written works. An account and critical analysis can be found in P. Fessard, *Chrétiens marxistes et Théologie de la Libération*, Lethielleux 1978.

Chapter VIII Tangible Reactions to the Excesses of Christocentricity

1. A good deal might be said on this question of the limits of dialectical thought, which derives above all from Germany. I have been able to note that it comes up against difficulties with all forms of culture which have kept the traditional sense of knowledge, *theoria*, and with it a sense of the real, regarded as the object of *theoria*. That is the case in North America, but also in Africa and a large part of Asia. However, in Asia the sense of the real as an object of *theoria* is less developed (the Asiatic easily accepts the idea of a fusion between consciousness and nature), so that dialectic finds more favourable ground, as is evidenced by the relative ease with which the dialectical materialism of Marx, taken up by Mao-Tse Tung (and adapted to circumstances), could find a footing.

2. Anyone who has lived in North America will know the respect which public opinion attaches to the man of God, no matter to what religion he belongs (Catholic priest, Protestant pastor. Jewish rabbi, etc.). The American Congress (both the Senate and the House of Representatives) opens its sessions with a prayer, 'In God we trust'.

3. See the work of Père Pannet and his team and their enquiries into what he calls 'popular Catholicism'.

4. Survey carried out by the journal *Prier*, September 1978. The results are strange: God the Father, 53%; Jesus Christ, 20%; Mary, 14%; a saint, 4%; the Holy Spirit, 2%; no reply, 7%.

5. A formula used by the historian Gilbert Durand.

6. Gilbert Durand, *Publication de l'USSJJ*, 1974, p.66.

7. One might refer to each of the three volumes of his vast study *Philosophy of Symbolic Forms* (*Language*, 1929; *Mythical Thought*, 1925; *Phenomenology of Knowledge*, 1929). He can be seen as a precursor of the methods of structural analysis to which I shall refer later.

8. At this point I am making a brief reference to the most interesting aspects of the applications of structuralist methods to historical knowledge.

9. One might recall Pascal's cruel comment on this attitude of the Jesuits. 'The Jesuits have wanted to join God to the world and have only succeeding in incurring the mistrust of God and the world' (fr.810, *Mercure de France* 1976).

10. The halt called to the evangelization of the Moslem world as a result of christocentricity is notorious. It is not Christ who should be proclaimed first of all to the Moslems, but faith in God, albeit the 'God of love', whom as yet they do not know. This was the reaction of Père de Foucauld.

11. As for relations with the non-monotheistic religious world, it is now clear that priority must be given to proclaiming God, and not Jesus Christ. Father Matteo Ricci – who was a master in this respect – proposed to teach God to the Chinese, but not Christ. In this connection see his discussion of 'The true idea of God', in his *Catechism*. Sadly, he was reproved for this method, and that led to failure.

12. Raymond Ruyer, *La Gnose de Princeton. Des savants à la recherche d'une religion*, Fayard 1974.

13. Under this title one might group all the scholars who have been led, in history, to accord a determinative role to the action of myths. One might think of people like Lévi-Strauss, Mircéa Eliade, Georges Dumézil, J. Brun, Philippe Sellier, etc. Of course all these works support the strictly psycho-analytical analyses made a long time ago by Jung and the researches into the structures of civilizations by S. Lupasco and Roger Caillois.

14. The reader will doubtless be aware of the strange pages which Barrès has devoted to this question of the association of the theme of the Sibyl with Christian themes; cf. his writing on *La Sibylle d'Auxerre*.

15. In addition to the reactions of Maurice Druon, one might also mention those of Rémy Chauvin (cf. the whole work which he devotes to this question, *Le synode des fidèles*, Editions Vernoy 1979).

16. Interview given to *La Croix*, 24 January 1979.

Chapter IX Prospects: The Chances of a Return to Bipolarity

1. I would not argue that in itself this bipolarity is a factor of life. This theory was certainly put forward in the 1930s by some German theologians, in particular by A. Rademacher in his famous work *Religion und Leben*, Herder, Freiburg 1925. This idea of 'Polarität', dear to the German thought of this period, depends too much on the dialectical thought of Hegel; all internal opposition is the condition of the particular life of an organism. I persist in thinking that all opposition must be regarded as an 'abnormal' situation which, if possible, must be reduced in the interests of peace and harmony. For Christianity, the bipolarity which is congenital to it is a given fact which the sociologist must content himself with noting; however, if at the same time the sociologist is a philosopher, there is

nothing to prevent his thinking that the movement towards unity, arrived at beyond this bipolarity, is in conformity with human nature and the good order of things, and as a result he may be allowed to dream that the church will have a much greater unity around one of the poles which give it life, this pole being able to dominate the other without extinguishing it. Clearly, some could hope here that the theocentric pole would normally predominate over the christocentric pole. Furthermore, in its best moments the Catholic church has been able to give happy expression to this (those best moments being in the Middle Ages and the best years of the seventeenth century).

2. Here, of course, I can do no more than make a rapid survey of some tendencies. My comments are in the realm of sociology; I am noting a 'fact of society'. I have no intention of pronouncing on the legitimacy of the approaches described here. Perhaps later I shall write another book on these questions.

3. See A. Cournot, *Traité de l'enchaînement des idées fondamentales dans la science et dans l'histoire*, 1881.

4. Among the advanced works in these disciplines let me recall those of Chomsky, Bloomfield and Benveniste in linguistics; of Roland Barthes and his school in criticism. For a good approach to structuralist methodology see the excellent volume by J. Piaget, *Le structuralisme*, Presses Universitaires de France, Collection 'Que sais-je?', 1968.

5. It goes without saying that it would be a good thing to restore its true significance to apostolic action, to Catholic action. The need for this can be felt; in the 1980s, which we have now entered, there is awareness of the need to derive spiritual action from spiritual contemplation. There has in fact been a new edition, after years of misunderstanding, of the work which, as I pointed out, guided the course of the first Catholic Action, that of Pius XI: Dom Chautard, *L'Ame de tout apostolat*, Editions Saint-Paul 1979.

Index